CITIES OF GOD AND NATIONALISM
Mecca, Jerusalem, and Rome as Contested World Cities

KHALDOUN SAMMAN

Paradigm Publishers
Boulder • London

Paradigm Publishers is committed to preserving ancient forests and natural resources. We elected to print *Cities Of God And Nationalism* on 50% post consumer recycled paper, processed chlorine free. As a result, for this printing, we have saved:

2 Trees (40' tall and 6-8" diameter)
724 Gallons of Wastewater
291 Kilowatt Hours of Electricity
80 Pounds of Solid Waste
157 Pounds of Greenhouse Gases

Paradigm Publishers made this paper choice because our printer, Thomson-Shore, Inc., is a member of Green Press Initiative, a nonprofit program dedicated to supporting authors, publishers, and suppliers in their efforts to reduce their use of fiber obtained from endangered forests.

For more information, visit www.greenpressinitiative.org

Published in the United States by Paradigm Publishers, 3360 Mitchell Lane Suite E, Boulder, CO 80301 USA.

Paradigm Publishers is the trade name of Birkenkamp & Company, LLC, Dean Birkenkamp, President and Publisher.

Library of Congress Cataloging-in-Publication Data

Samman, Khaldoun.
  Cities of God and nationalism : Mecca, Jerusalem, and Rome as contested world cities / Khaldoun Samman.
    p. cm.
  Includes bibliographical references and index.
  ISBN-13: 978-1-59451-293-3 (hc : alk. paper)
  ISBN-10: 1-59451-293-0 (hc : alk. paper) 1. Nationalism—Religious aspects. 2. Ethnicity—Religious aspects. 3. Ethnic relations—Religious aspects. 4. Jerusalem—History. 5. Mecca (Saudi Arabia)—History. 6. Rome—History. 7. Judaism. 8. Christianity. 9. Islam. I. Title.
  BL65.N3S36 2006
  201'.72—dc22

                                                                2006015115

Printed and bound in the United States of America on acid free paper that meets the standards of the American National Standard for Permanence of Paper for Printed Library Materials.

11 10 09 08 07 1 2 3 4 5

To
my father Subhi
and my sister Manar

"This book is a tour de force in different fields of knowledge. It takes world-city and world-history literatures to a higher level of depth and understanding. Samman moves beyond the economic reductionist assumptions of these literatures. It is difficult to imagine a more pioneering, in-depth study of world cities."

—Ramón Grosfoguel, Professor, Department of Ethnic Studies,
University of California at Berkeley

"A remarkable and original discussion of three great sacred cities across time, and their transformation by nationalism in the modern world. It ends with an appeal to the renewal of the symbiotic existences they have known and may know once again. A necessary basis for rethinking the present and the future."

—Immanuel Wallerstein, Yale University

CONTENTS

ACKNOWLEDGMENTS

Throughout the many hours spent typing away on a computer, as this project that spans over two millennia grew in scope, I have clearly come to understand that this effort has largely been a communal enterprise. My deepest debt is to my editor Arie Kupferwasser, whose extensive understanding of the writing process has served immeasurably useful in bringing my words and ideas to full fruition. Over the course of our working together, he has generously read and reread numerous drafts of this manuscript, providing excellent suggestions and astute criticism. I cannot overemphasize the amount of time and level of care that he has provided, tirelessly absorbing and integrating an area of study that has been secondary to his own pursuits in a relatively short period of time. With an impressive capacity for comprehension and a keen sense of observation, he has continuously urged me to consider unforeseen angles and more interesting approaches than I had earlier imagined, providing crucial insights at critical moments. His detailed and valuable critiques of this book have been essential to its completion.

Arie is a highly innovative editor and writer, and he has been a great source of motivation for me. His talents further extend to his practice as a creative arts therapist, his work as a teacher, and his prolific output as an artist. I have immensely enjoyed working closely with him and look forward to a future collaboration.

I have been fortunate to have the continuous support of Immanuel Wallerstein throughout the writing of this book. His steady comments and advice which accompanied an early draft of this manuscript made its completion a wonderfully pleasant experience. Through my acquaintance with his many great intellectual achievements and his supportive personal presence, I acquired the skills to contemplate such a concept as the *longue durée* and I developed the courage to write a historical treatise that expands over two centuries and two continents.

The idea of writing about sacred world cities began to take concrete form several years ago, during conversations with Giovanni Arrighi and Ramon Grosfoguel, both, at the time, professors in the sociology department at Binghamton University. I am now very pleased to have taken their recommendations to heart. I am also grateful to Dale Tomich for his useful methodological and theoretical comments on an earlier version of this manuscript.

Also, the late Terence Hopkins inspired me in many ways to think imaginatively and encouraged me to continue my academic work at a time when I found it very difficult to remain connected to my efforts. Through his generous hospitality and my regular meetings with him at his home a couple years before I began this book, I found in Terence not only a wonderful source of support, but also a fine model for the essence of academic pursuit.

I also owe much to Paradigm Publishers and am especially grateful to Dean Birkenkamp for his energetic support of my ideas and writings. Paradigm Publishers is a new author's dream publishing house and they have provided me with much competent and timely assistance.

Although the list is too long to do justice to all those I'd like to mention, I'd like to give thanks to Mohammad Tamdgidi, Anna Beckwith, David Baronov, John Till, Sharon Schultz, Abye Assefa, and Trichur Ganesh for many years of serious and lively discussions that have no doubt informed some of the ideas found in this book. I'd like to give special thanks to my good friends Shoshana Lev, Krishnendu Ray, and Steven Sherman. These three wonderful people have been essential to both my intellectual and my self development. Shoshana has been especially important to me over the last fifteen years and has provided me on numerous occasions with insights into the troubling yet fascinating world of self-inquiry that I would surely have missed without the presence of her genuine wit.

I'd like to thank as well my colleagues at Macalester College, especially Terry Boychuk who read the manuscript in its entirety. He is a fine chair, carefully sheltering me from the normal demands of a college professor. He has taken on more than his fair share of departmental burdens in order for me to successfully complete this project. I'd also like to thank Mahnaz Kousha, David Blaney, Soek Fang Sim, Ferruh Yilmaz, Muhammad Bamyeh, Paula Cooey, Kathy Haddad, and Liza Burr for their generous support.

And I want finally to thank my entire family. My wonderful mother Shahira, my sister Mona, and my brothers Aiman and Mamoun have all sacrificed a great deal to make my education possible. To my wonderful nieces and nephews I also give thanks for bearing with me throughout these years. My four nieces Nesreen, Lucy, Lina, and Jessica have survived through difficult times over the years and now have become four intelligent and beautiful women. I dedicate this book to my late sister Manar and my late father Subhi, both of whose spirit, although they never saw the completion of this book, inspires every single word of it.

1

MODERNITY, RELIGION, AND VIOLENCE: SACRED CITIES AND THE ROOTS OF CONFLICT

It is simply not true that capitalism as a historical system has represented progress over the various previous historical systems that it destroyed or transformed. Even as I write this, I feel the tremour that accompanies the sense of blasphemy. I fear the wrath of the gods, for I have been moulded in the same ideological forge as all my compeers and have worshipped at the same shrines.

Immanuel Wallerstein, 1983

There is a Mr. Hyde inside each one of us. What we have to do is prevent the conditions occurring that will bring the monster forth.

Amin Maalouf, 1996

I
Liberating Sacred Cities from Religion or Modernity?

As of April 2006, the Israeli government continues its construction of a Separation Wall through Jerusalem on the grounds, according to Israeli officials, of halting terrorism. After some concern by Jerusalem residents over the practicality of the Wall, Ariel Sharon publicly stated, "You know who built the fence? Terror built the fence."[1] As Virginia Tilley observes, the Israeli government has characterized its struggle as

---

1. "Overnight, a Towering Divide Rises in Jerusalem," *New York Times*, January 12, 2004.

that of a "beleaguered Jewish people trying to build a homeland in a tiny country huddled on the Mediterranean while fending off irrational/Islamic Arab hostility."[2] Following suit, Haim Ramon, the Jerusalem cabinet minister, echoes the assertion that the purpose of building the Wall in Jerusalem has been "first and foremost to prevent [terrorism]."[3] Such national security claims of protecting Jews from fanatical Muslims have been regularly used in defense of Israeli policies intended to segregate and remove Palestinians from the Jewish state and particularly from Jerusalem.

The building of the Separation Wall, which Israeli officials prefer to call a security "fence," follows a continuous effort by elements of the Israeli government to de-Arabize Jerusalem. Indeed, accompanying this discourse of protecting Jews from Islamic religious terror, the very same cabinet minister cited above states unequivocally that, security issues aside, the barrier "also makes [Jerusalem] more Jewish. The safer and more Jewish Jerusalem will be, the more it can serve as a true capital of the state of Israel."[4] This is unlikely to change with the election victory of Ehud Olmert's Kadima Party in March 2006. As a matter of fact, immediately after his victory, Olmert announced that during his administration he will ensure Israel's "Jewish and democratic" character, and just like he did in his Likud days, he continues to use the nationalist language of ethnic purity as the basis of his platform.[5]

Since the 1967 occupation of Jerusalem, the Israeli government has pursued a demographic purge aimed at "Judaizing" the city by "de-Arabizing" it.[6] This effort begins with the demolition of the Maghrebi

---

2. Virginia Tilley, "The One-State Solution," *London Review of Books*, vol. 25, no. 21, Nov. 6 (2003).

3. "Israel Admits Wall Is Not Just about Security," *Palestine Monitor*, August 3, 2005: http://www.globalresearch.ca/PrintArticle.php?articleId=798.

4. Haim Ramon cited in "Israel Admits Wall Is Not Just about Security," *Palestine Monitor*, August 3, 2005: http://www.globalresearch.ca/PrintArticle.php? articleId=798.

5. Graham Usher, "Finished with Likud," *Al-Ahram*, March 30, 2006: http://weekly.ahram.org.eg/2006/788/fr3.htm.

6. According to Rhoda Kanaaneh, *Birthing the Nation*, Berkeley: University of California Press (2002:53), "The examples of Judaization plans are abundant. Information about a new planning map for Galilee (by the regional planning board) was leaked to the press in 1995. The goal of the new plan was explicitly stated as Judaization: to increase the number of Jews in the Galilee in relation to Arabs and 'to distribute them in such a way that they would disrupt any Palestinian geographical continuity.' The plan allocates considerably more land to Jews

Quarter of the Old City, which took place immediately after occupation, and arrives at a recently proposed demolition of the Arab neighborhood, Silwan, in East Jerusalem. In the first instance, 6,000 were made homeless in order to create a space for what is called the Wailing Wall Plaza, while in the case of Silwan, the construction of an Israeli archeological park has been suggested. From 1967 to the present, Israel has "revoked Palestinian residencies, demolished Palestinian homes, and stringently limited building permits given to Palestinians."[7]

These examples are not intended to single out Israel, for similar ethnic cleansing policies can be found elsewhere, to varied degrees of intensity. Rather, the current illustration is offered to introduce a discussion of how nationalism as an expression of modernity has affected the lives of people and communities connected to sacred cities. In this respect, two issues of concern emerge from the case in view. First is the usefulness of a discourse suggesting the immediate dangers of religious fanaticism, behind which nationalist officials advance national agendas, whether overtly or covertly. Second is the attempt to nationalize a city that has historically been a hybrid demographically, culturally, and religiously— to subordinate such a city to the will of one particular nationalist vision intended to effectively erase notions of difference occurring on sacred land that traditionally belongs to no one single group.

While many Israeli national elites choose to justify repressive policies through a political claim of defense from religious fanaticism, a parallel discourse can be found among contemporary academics that target religion as the root cause of many modern-day acts of politically motivated violence. Within the Western world of academia, a renewed interest has emerged among a sector of intellectuals who have called for the need to secularize societies, using examples of contemporary violence as proof that a religious worldview is opposed to modernity, progress, pluralism, tolerance, development, rationality, and science. While the current debate seems to revolve in response to violent outbursts and attacks attributed to fanatical religious fundamentalists, both in the Middle East and in the West, many authors are taking clear aim at the heart of religious identity, disregarding the extremity of fundamentalist interpretations and attributing an essentialist perspective in describing an inherent

---

than it does to Arabs as part of an attempt to ghettoize the Arabs" (*'Ittihad*, June 9, 1995, cited in Kanaaneh (2002:53).

7. "The Jerusalem Wall: Barrier to a Two State Solution," report from a Palestine Center briefing by Anwar Darkazally and Amjad Atallah: http://www.the jerusalemfund.org/images/fortherecord.php?ID=32.

religious bias toward conflict. This radical secularist point of view characterizes religious resurgence, especially of the Islamic variant, as negating a peaceful modernist project. As one such commentator has proposed, "September 11th was an attack on *modernity* by Islamic fascists,"[8] paradoxically implying, as fascism is an aspect of the modern political landscape, that such a movement as Al-Qaeda is *not* itself a modernist project. Thus, hugely lacking in this discussion is the examination of a much broader spectrum of the human imagination within which we may consider the possibility that current conflicts are systemic to the modern world and to the way we, as its inventors and participants, construct our identities as peoples, nations, and religions.

In order to illustrate the nature of this debate, the three sacred cities of Jerusalem, Mecca, and Rome will largely comprise the focus of this study. Central to it is the notion that current characterizations of religion as archaic, time-immemorial, and pre-modern, assuming a natural evolution toward the more advanced social construct of modernity, offer little by way of understanding the violence that occurs around major sacred spaces today, such as in the case of Jerusalem. The extreme logic at one end of the spectrum of this debate suggests "desacralizing sacred space" with an authoritarian project designed to produce secularized peoples the world over.[9] The perspective offered here presents the view that such ideas represent major and dangerous distortions of the problems we face today and suggests, by contrast, that contemporary conflicts are largely the creation of what many have perceived to be their antidote: a modern, secular concept of national spaces.

The integration of contemporary sacred spaces into the modern world has most often occurred with great difficulty and controversy. Rigid conceptions of national spaces and subsequent *recent* forcing of *nationalized* communities upon such sacred spaces have contributed to the modern dilemma of civilizational identities that span a transnational spatial scheme. In this sense, Jerusalem, Mecca, and Rome represent examples of how modernity, through the apparatus of nationalism and the nation-state, has redefined constructs of Self and Other in fundamental ways, with major implications for the way these cities are conceived by the inhabitants of the world who identify with them. Therefore, from the perspective of this study, the cataclysmic transformations produced by

---

8. Martin Woolf, *Financial Times,* September 4, 2002, emphasis added, cited in John Gray, *Al-Qaeda and What It Means to Be Modern*, New York and London: New Press (2003:20).

9. For an in-depth discussion, see section III of this chapter.

modernity are an essential component in understanding the contemporary plight of these three cities and resolution of such conflicts as those over Jerusalem requires an exiting of modernity and a re-imagining of the institutional basis upon which it is built.

Over the past two centuries, Rome, Mecca, and Jerusalem have been sites of nationalist activities that have attempted to appropriate these holy cities and incorporate them into territorialist projects. Such attempts have invariably been met with resistance and have become major issues on the international scene, creating political crises known as "the Question of Rome," "the Question of Mecca," and "the Question of Jerusalem." In each case, the right of the nationalist movement to appropriate the sacred city within its newly defined territorial boundaries has been hotly debated, at times spilling over into major clashes. As these three cities have long served as sacred centers of the Islamic and Christian empires of the Middle Ages, such status as they have been afforded continues to resist attempts to appropriate them by nationalist movements in the modern period. This is so primarily because the symbolic status these cities share expresses the universalistic religious and spiritual aspirations of *civilizational imagined communities,*[10] which comprises a far more complex and inclusive system than any nationalist imagination can produce, exceeding the spatial machinery of states on which they are located. Furthermore, the conflicts over these cities are tied to contradictory notions of community embodied by the concepts of *nation* on the one hand and of *civilization* on the other. In the case of Jerusalem, this tension is exacerbated by the fact that three different communities make sacred claims on the city.

A quick introductory sketch here may be useful in illustrating the process by which these three sacred centers became world cities. The Christian and Islamic imperial conquests of Jerusalem in the first and seventh century mark a significant turning point in the city's history. Prior to this period, Jerusalem's sacredness belonged to a religious community, the ancient Israelites, that was staunchly particularistic in its worldview and highly defensive against the universalistic pretensions of the surrounding ancient empires. It is only with the introduction of Christianity and Islam (in the first and seventh centuries, respectively),

---

10. The term "imagined communities" is not used by us in the same sense that Benedict Anderson intended it in his book, *Imagined Communities: Reflections on the Origin and Spread of Nationalism,* London: Verso Press (1995). He employs it in discussing a *nationalist* imagination. Our intention, on the other hand, is an exploration of *transnational or civilizational imaginations.*

through the medium of powerful world empires, that Jerusalem became a sacred *world* city. This is largely due to the fact that Islam and Christianity, while incorporating many elements of the Jewish religion, broke off decisively from their parent faith by creating a universalistic vision of the world. They created communities that, from inception, negated all of the particularistic aspects of Judaism and developed a new notion of community that was open to humankind as a whole.

Although Rome and Mecca differ historically from Jerusalem, they are important in that they also represent sacred centers that, in contrast to national identities, have engendered civilizational identities, *ummas* of a pan-Islamic type. Their histories extend far back into the pre-modern world and their developments are shaped by the rise and fall of empires. Both cities have experienced major structural transformations as a result of their empires having fractured into a multitude of nation-states, which has had a tremendous effect upon the way in which they have articulated systems of identity to their respective communities. Under the new system of states, Rome and Mecca have had to adapt to an age in which identity, space, and belief function differently from the premises on which they were first structurally developed. As a result, great tensions have emerged between nationalist aspirations and the universalistic, transnational characteristics of these two cities, resulting in "the questions of Rome and Mecca." Both the Italian nationalist movement and the Wahabi/Saudi movement have attempted to appropriate these universalistic cities and make them their own, only to encounter resistance.

Thus, the source of conflicts in these three sacred world cities is not simply the product of some grand narrative found in religion and the sacred, as many employing an essentialist, time-immemorial perspective have argued, but indeed lies in the projection of nationalist projects into urban sacred spaces whose sacred quality is imagined as belonging to no one political authority. The Italian nationalists' attempt to seize Rome and Vatican City in the mid-nineteenth century, the Wahabis'/Saudis' seizure of the Hijaz and the two holy cities of Mecca and Medina in the early part of the twentieth century, and, finally, the attempt of the Zionist movement to make Jerusalem "the eternal capital of the Jews" today are all of this type. These sacred cities are mental structures that, according to Fernand Braudel, "get in the way of history," a lesson that all the nationalists in these three states have learned and, in the case of Israel/Palestine, are still learning.[11] Limitations that arise from a narrow nationalist and sanitized imagination fail to encompass sacred grounds that envision the world and beyond on a far grander scale and with much greater profundity. In the words of Ali Shariati, a famous Shiite Muslim intellectual from Iran, "Mecca belongs to nobody. It is free from the reign of rulers and oppressors; therefore, no one controls it. Allah is the owner of Mecca while the people are its residents."[12]

Capturing these cities for nationalist purposes is thus a tricky business, which is why "the questions of Rome, Mecca, and Jerusalem" spring up at the very moment when nationalist movements close in on their gates. It is because Rome, Mecca, and Jerusalem are sacred world cities that they are free from most nationalist control. They tend to slip from the strong arms of the state, and no matter how many resources the latter invests in such cities, they continue to remain culturally and spatially independent.

In this sense, sacred world cities, functioning as mythographies,[13] operate beyond the boundaries of a nation-state, enabling the construction of an imaginary community that stretches over a wide area of the world. They mobilize the imagination of individuals by directing attention away from a localized, immediate experience and placing it into another context of existence that comprises the activities and feelings of a larger world community. The sacred site itself captures the imaginations of people and lures them away from a more localized identity toward a much larger transnational one. As Victor Turner and Edith Turner state, they impose "the direct, immediate, and total confrontations of human

---

11. Fernand Braudel, "History and the Social Sciences: The *Longue Durée*," in his *On History*, Chicago: University of Chicago Press (1982:31).

12. Ali Shariati, *Hajj,* Houston, Texas: FILINC: Book Distribution Center (1980:22).

13. Arjun Appadurai, in his *Modernity at Large: Cultural Dimensions of Globalization*, Minneapolis: University of Minnesota Press (1997:8), uses the term "mythographies" to examine a notion of transnationalism, in contrast with the "myth and ritual of the classic sort," which he equates with nationalism. Using this backdrop, he posits the existence of a "transnational public sphere," characterizing the significance of global media. In his view, mythographies "create solidarities of worship and charisma regionally," providing a "community of sentiment" in which collective groups feel and imagine things together. Largely building upon Benedict Anderson's concepts, Appadurai keenly demonstrates how every form from print capitalism to other types of mass media produces an imaginary community that thinks itself into existence.

identities which tends to make those experiencing it think of mankind as a homogeneous, unstructured, and free community."[14]

Following this line of reasoning, sacred cities have, from inception, played a fundamental role in integrating their empires into unified social and political entities. The remarkable expansion of Islam into the Far East and Africa and the success with which Christianity converted the Roman Empire are in no small measure due to the manner by which they absorbed the multiple local cults and directed them toward an imagined center of the world. These cities have introduced the possibility of transcending locality, of bonding together large numbers of men and women who would otherwise have no apparatus through which to imagine having any relations with one another. They are spaces that are highly conducive to the creation of imagined communities upon which their respective empires came to depend. Hence, of pivotal importance to any inquiry concerning these centers is an examination of how the fracturing of their respective empires into multitudes of nation-states has affected their symbolic status.

Thus far, it seems as though these cities have evolved, continuing to function as universal centers, albeit within a context of multiple competing nationalist identities. Given the fact that they draw social energy away from local, tribal, or national affiliations, luring, for example, Muslims and Christians away from nationalist schema while refocusing them through a civilizational lens, they are in essence competing with modernity's most powerful organizing institution: the state.

Nowhere is this more apparent than with the constant flow of pilgrims attracted to sacred centers. The journeys of these pilgrims, as Victor Turner explains in his series of books and articles on this theme, are rich, evocative experiences, and the centrality of the sites they visit acts as a magnetic field, drawing pilgrims from remote and "otherwise unrelated localities."[15] The implication of this experience is a profound one where, as Anderson argues:

> The strange physical juxtaposition of Malays, Persians, Indians, Berbers and Turks in Mecca is something incomprehensible without an idea of their community in some form. The Berber encountering the Malay before the Ka'aba must, as it were, ask himself: "Why is this

14. See Victor Turner and Edith Turner, *Image and Pilgrimage in Christian Culture*, New York: Columbia University Press (1978).
15. Benedict Anderson, *Imagined Communities* (1995:53-54).

man doing what I am doing, uttering the same words that
I am uttering, even though we can not talk to one an-
other?" There is only one answer, once one has learnt it:
"Because *we*...are Muslims."[16]

Many pilgrims visiting such places as Mecca, Rome, or Jerusalem
emphasize upon their return home that they have experienced something
much more meaningful than a trip to a local or national place. Their experiences embody what Victor Turner identifies as an anti-structural consciousness. The plight of an individual pilgrim taking leave of his or her
local and national habitus to enter a new type of experience produces, to
varying degrees, a new sort of identity antithetical to the older, national
experience.[17] The fact that these sacred cities exist for the pilgrim at the
"center of the world" has a radical effect, individual by individual, upon
a community dispersed the world over. It impels a new and refined vision of an imagined community that moves away from a national identity
and toward a civilizational one.

Two recent *hajjis*[18] best express this change in consciousness: Malcolm X and Ali Shariati. They come from two different parts of the
world, one from Iran and the other from the United States. Both write
elaborately about such a change of consciousness:

Malcolm X:

There were tens of thousands of pilgrims, from all over
the world. They were of all colors, from blue-eyed
blondes to black-skinned Africans. But we were all participating in the same ritual, displaying a spirit of unity
and brotherhood that my experiences in America had led
me to believe never could exist between the white and
the non-white....You may be shocked by these words
coming from me. But on this pilgrimage, what I've seen,
and experienced, has forced me to *re-arrange* much of

---

16. Benedict Anderson (1995:54) examines this theme, but fails to appreciate
the implications that pilgrimage has for negating the nationalist past that many
pilgrims experience as a result of this journey.

17. Victor Turner, "The Center Out There: Pilgrims Goal," *History of Religions,*
vol. 12 (1973:191-230). See also Victor Turner and Edith Turner, *Image and
Pilgrimage* (1978).

18. *Hajji* refers to a title giving to a man or woman who made the pilgrimage to
Mecca at least once in their lifetime.

my thought-patterns previously held, and to *toss aside* some of my previous conclusions....During the past eleven days here in the Muslim world, I have eaten from the same plate, drunk from the same glass, and slept in the same bed (or on the same rug)—while praying to the *same* God—with fellow Muslims, whose eyes were the bluest of blue, whose hair was the blondest of blond, and whose skin was the whitest of white....We were *truly* all the same (brothers)—because their belief in one God had removed the "white" from their *minds*, the "white" from their *behavior*, and the "white" from their *attitude.*[19]

Ali Shariati:

Names, races, nor social status make a difference in this great combination. An atmosphere of genuine unity prevails. It is a human show of Allah's unity. Fear and pleasure, excitement and charm, perplexity and rapture all appear as minute particles in a magnetic field. Allah is in its center.... In this desert all the nations and groups merge into one tribe. They face one Ka'aba....Everyone "melts" himself and assumes a new form as a "mankind". The egos and individual traits are buried. The group becomes a "people" or an "Umma." All the I's have died....What has evolved is "we" (Shariati, 1980: 10-11)....You must find and select your "orbit". Enter the system and move with the others. As you circumambulate and move closer to the Ka'aba, you feel like a small stream merging into a big river. Carried by a wave, not by your feet, you are detached from the ground. Suddenly, you find yourself floating and carried on by this flood. As you approach the middle, the pressure of the crowd squeezes you so hard that you are endowed with a new life. You are now a part of the people; you are now a man alive and eternal! You move not "by yourself" but "with others." You join them not "diplomatically" but "with love."[20]

---

19. Malcolm X, *The Autobiography of Malcolm X: As Told to Alex Haley*, New York: Ballantine Press (1973:346-47); emphases in original.
20. Ali Shariati, *Hajj* (1980:31).

These two important pilgrimage experiences illustrate clearly that nationalism has neither overwhelmed, nor surpassed, the possibility of other forms of identity. They further suggest that a civilizational or religious identity can eclipse or transcend a national one. Taking the predominant literature on nationalism at face value, one can easily miss the fact that people possess identities and histories larger in scope than their national frames of reference, and that such alternate formations provide a great attraction for much of the world's population. Cities such as Rome, Mecca, and Jerusalem provide the key to a centralized location, terrestrially as well as personally, in which the multitude of members of their respective communities may re-create an identity that is at odds with the one they hold in their specific place of residence. Indeed, as Malcolm X and Ali Shariati show, this transnational identity illustrates the potential to overwhelm a nationalist one, be it Black Nationalist, as in the former, or Shiite/Iranian, as in the latter.

Moreover, a Muslim, Christian, or Jewish pilgrim from any part of the world, no matter what nationality or other affiliation he/she possesses, has the legitimate right to claim his/her respective sacred city as a personal and communal spiritual center.[21] This is a phenomenon unique to sacred world cities. Places such as Niagara Falls, for example, although visited by people the world over, belong to a specific *national* population. This is because, as John Sears argues in his *Sacred Places*, cities like Niagara have become synonymous with the land of a particular nation or people, where the land itself is made to construct a national community.[22] While a Frenchman or a Pakistani may get much satisfaction from visiting such a place, his/her identification with it is voided by the fact that his/her nationality belongs elsewhere. A pilgrim coming from Indonesia, or the United States, visiting Rome, Mecca, or Jerusalem for religious purposes, on the other hand, feels as intimate a connection

---

21. In practical terms, however, states can and do limit access to these shrines. This is especially apparent for Palestinians attempting to visit Jerusalem from the Occupied Territories of the West Bank and Gaza, or for Shiites attempting to make the pilgrimage to Mecca and Medina. But what is most important here is the fact that grievances of such blockages are viewed by the international community as an issue of great concern and pit the state in a negative light. Sometimes this criticism yields positive results, even causing a state to open its borders, as Saudi Arabia did to Iraqis after the Gulf War.

22. John Sears, *Sacred Places: American Tourist Attractions in the Nineteenth Century*, New York: Oxford University Press (1989).

with the site as might an Italian, Saudi, or Israeli/Palestinian; the pilgrim's national origin, unlike in the former case, does not in any way invalidate a cultural identification with the sacred place. In other words, while meanings attributed to places like Niagara Falls are identified with a national population, those ascribed to a sacred world city extend to an entire creed no matter what the national background.

The ability of sacred cities to attract the religious sensibilities of their larger communities to a given, fixed sacred center is thus an additional feature of their status as world cities. These cities transcend the popular consciousness of a given nation-state and serve as a sort of "cultural anchor" for an entire world civilization. The city itself belongs to a community that is *transnational*, both by virtue of being dispersed and as a result of belonging to a number of different national communities. In this way, as some anthropologists have recognized, these sacred cities have generated entire civilizations and seem to condense the cultures and values of those civilizations in one place. Milton Singer and Robert Redfield describe such cities as "orthogenetic," creating and sustaining the identity of an entire civilization.[23] Diana Eck characterizes them as such:

> Their names become virtually synonymous with that culture, for they have gathered together the energy of a wider civilization and converted that energy into culture. Rome, Jerusalem, and Mecca come immediately to mind as orthogenetic cities....Sacred cities [are] ceremonial centers. The proper site is ascertained by divination, its center and perimeters are staked out, its quadrants and gates are designated, and it is in due course consecrated. Such sacred centers are deliberately built, and the self-conscious energy and symbolization of the culture is brought to bear upon their layout, their architecture, and their iconography.[24]

Thus, the sacred world city clearly represents the sharpest global example of paradigmatic divergence between radically different methods of identity formation. Although, as might be inferred from Eck's architec-

---

23. Robert Redfield and Milton Singer, "The Cultural Role of Cities," in *Man in India*, vol. 36, no. 3 (1966:161-94).
24. Diana Eck, "Introduction," in Bardwell Smith and Holly Baker (eds), *The City as a Sacred Center: Essays on Six Asian Contexts*, Leiden and New York: Brill (1987:2-3).

tural description of how a sacred world city is formed, such spaces share cosmetic and functional qualities with other types of world cities, they are clearly distinct in that they serve as a civilizational and transnational center and, moreover, they articulate the potential for an undifferentiated global citizenship that supersedes and renders irrelevant the nationalist imagination.

II
Imagined Communities:
National versus Civilizational

The notion of a sacred world city aims at opening up the "world city hypothesis" to cities that are qualitatively different from those that receive most of the attention, in both temporal as well as thematic terms. By far, the majority of essays about world cities describe the economic organization and role of their respective cities, focusing largely on their financial functions within the international division of labor. As a result, a limited number of cities tend to comprise the case studies, the majority of which typically focus on New York, London, and Tokyo. When other cities, such as Cairo, Rio de Janeiro, or Istanbul find their way into this literature, the analysis is usually made only to demonstrate their larger relationship to the core capitalist cities.[25] The problem with this literature is not so much that it does not include cities outside the core, but rather that it misses the opportunity to include cities that are of such global dimension that only a truly limited definition of the term would fail to recognize their significance.

Anthony King, moving the hypothesis outside of its typically narrow perimeters of application, invites us to consider a range of other criteria by which cities assume the power attributed to the status of a "world city":

---

25. For a good example of this, see the essay by John Friedmann and Goetz Wolf, "World City Formation," in Paul Knox and Peter Taylor (eds.), *World Cities in a World-System*, Cambridge, New York: Cambridge University Press (1995) in which he develops a layout for a hierarchy of world cities; see also "The World City Hypothesis," in Paul Knox and Peter Taylor, *World Cities in a World-System*, New York: Cambridge University Press (1995).

[C]ities also exist under scores of quite different meta-
phors: sin city, holy city, drug city, city of angels, and
many more. In this context the number of meanings
which "world city" might have are infinite. The problem
with the term "world", or "global city", is that it has
been appropriated, perhaps hijacked, to represent and
also reify not only just one part of a city's activity...but
also has been put at the service of only one particular
representation of the "world"—the world economy....
An argument can and, indeed, has been made...that a
particular world city has, in relation to a particular economic and administrative sphere, global control capabil-
ity: but this neither exhausts the function or meaning of
the city in relation to the world economy, in relation to
"the world" nor, more importantly and pointedly, the
significance or meaning to "the world" to the city.[26]

As King seems to suggest, early proponents of the world city hypothesis originally articulated the need for a rich and varied exploration
of the terminology, yet subsequent "appropriations" of it left cultural and
religious features, as well as symbolic aspects of cities, virtually untouched. Sadly, much is lost within such a limited scope of reference as
is afforded by economic and financial indicators, for while the capitalist
world system is undeniably a political and economic reality, cities within
its reach also operate through a wide range of other cultural processes.[27]

Benedict Anderson's conceptual framework of "imagined communities" aptly expands the range of possibility embodied in the world city
hypothesis. While he and others have explored a notion of "nationalist
imagined communities," it seems fitting in juxtaposition to speak of
global or civilizational imagined communities, particularly as applied to

---

26. Anthony King (ed.), *Re-presenting the World City: Ethnicity, Capital and
Culture in the 21ˢᵗ Century Metropolis*, New York: NYU Press (1995).
27. Fortunately, a group of innovative scholars is emerging who are attempting
to develop a perspective that moves toward a more inclusive field of inquiry
(King 1995; Grosfoguel 1994; Zukin 1995). Ramon Grosfoguel, for example,
argues that the most interesting aspect of world cities like Miami and San Juan is
not reducible solely to their economic dominance over a given region, in this
case the Caribbean. What is more illuminating about these two cities, he argues,
is their ideological and symbolic functions within the Caribbean region, a function that in the end turns out to be their greatest cultural capital (1994:378).

Islam and Christianity, in order to illustrate the tensions that arise when the two types encounter one another. Within such a framework, conflicts that emerge around sacred world cities can be understood as deriving from the inherent expression of two different forms of imagined communities: nationalist and civilizational. Nationalist aspirations are limited to specific imagined communities that develop territorial limits to their claims. By contrast, sacred world cities, as penultimate expressions of the civilizational imagination, have consistently been in direct conflict with national projects aimed at appropriating such cultural and historical landmarks. This is so because communities respective to these cities experience them as state-free and identify themselves as universalistic communities that function radically differently from their nationalist counterparts. Therefore, the rigid notions of spatial property found in the discourse of modern nationalism act as a disconfirming force against the civilizational imagination.

As Benedict Anderson argues in his seminal work, *Imagined Communities*, "the nation is imagined as limited, has finite, if elastic, boundaries, beyond which lie other nations."[28] At its most basic level, "state sovereignty is fully, flatly, and evenly operative over each square centimetre of a legally demarcated territory," and most significantly for the current study, "no nation imagines itself coterminous with mankind."[29] Hence, these identities are *place* oriented and incorporate an absolute claim of membership to a very specific and precise portion of mankind. John Lie, in his *Modern Peoplehood*, characterizes this clearly:

> Modern state boundaries are definite and determinate.... In modern polities, frontiers disappear, boundaries are meaningful, and border surveillance is the norm.... Modern geography and cartography inscribe exact borderlines, inventing the very idea of territoriality as classified, bordered, and controlled area....People cannot come and go as they please without state-sanctioned mechanisms of identification and permission. The term foreigner comes to refer to non-nationals and noncitizens.[30]

---

28. Benedict Anderson, *Imagined Communities* (1995:7).
29. Ibid. (1995:19).
30. John Lie, *Modern Peoplehood*, Cambridge, Massachusetts: Harvard University Press (2004:100).

The civilizational identity, on the other hand, such as the Islamic *umma* and the Christian *oikoumene*, is transnational and universalistic in character, belonging to a radically different vision of the world than its nationalist counterpart. Such forms of identity are not conceived as finite with clear boundaries, but as expansive bodies that seek to encompass all of humankind. Preceding the modern concept of a nation, this form of imagination, according to Anderson, has historically identified states by their centers, ascribing permeable and imprecise borders through which sovereignties would overlap without notice.[31] Anderson further dramatizes the comparison: "The most messianic nationalists do not dream of a day when all the members of the human race will join their nation in the way that...Christians...dream of a wholly Christian planet."[32]

Exploring this contrast in identity formation, John Lie employs the conceptual scheme of "peoplehood," asserting that "modern state making...transformed people in itself (population) to people for itself (peoplehood)."[33] In Lie's view, the modern notion of statehood transformed the consciousness of populations in a way that fashioned a wide reaching and radically new sense of identity within them. Prior to the emergence of the modern state, the infrastructural limits of earlier regimes did not have the capacity to nationalize their populations whose identification was either limited to the village level or to the abstract and supranational (religious) level. Not until the state assumed total political and military authority was it capable of superseding local and ecclesiastical establishments. Lie explains further:

> This presupposes a new conception of political space. The realm of the early modern European state or empire was geographically indeterminate and historically fluctuating. Much of the periphery constituted frontiers where central rule was nominal in character. Ecclesiatical and local authorities competed with royal power. Linguistic and cultural variation reigned.[34]

Thus before the age of the modern state, with its production of a nationalized peoplehood, people were not identified in an official manner as belonging to particular and sharply defined territories.

---

31. Benedict Anderson, *Imagined Communities* (1995:19).
32. Ibid. (1995:7).
33. John Lie, *Modern Peoplehood* (2004:99).
34. Ibid. (2004:99-100).

As civilizational imagined communities have ascribed a sense of fluidity that exists in sharp contrast to national territorial logic, state efforts to capture and nationalize the sacred spaces designed to serve such communities have consistently been eluded, failing to block the fine streams of religious consciousness that slip through the state's net. From this vantage point, sacred world cities have over time come to represent the one place where a religious community plants itself in an otherwise inhospitable modern landscape. They are the physical enshrinement of a super-terrestrial order.

A graphic analogy may illustrate this further, in which the civilizational identity is represented by a horizontal line and the national identity by a vertical one. The former integrates its identified community across a number of national spaces—potentially all of them—and is in this sense transnational. Borders and national differences are effectively suppressed and restructured to provide an open ended system in which spatial configuration is not bound by geographical markers, but is instead experienced as a fluid stream of spiritual consciousness that may encompass the whole horizontal field on which all communities are located. By contrast, the national identity constructs a community vertically and thus effectively blocks its integrative mechanism by imposing spatial limits on the horizontal field. Hence, its ability to integrate communities horizontally across a long geographical space depends upon its capacity for vertical reproduction across the horizontal field. In this sense, the vertical quality of national structure acts to contain the identity of a given community within solid and indisputable perimeters.

To clarify how this process works we can employ the concept of a global ethnographic map. Ernest Gellner, for instance, describes two such maps: one an ecumenical representation of the globe, the other a nationalist depiction. The first map is an intersection of "diverse points of color such that no clear pattern can be discerned in any detail."[35] The globe's composition is a complex expression of a universal spatial representation of humankind, where no clear lines of demarcation are neatly expressed and a sense of region is indistinct. The nationalist version presents a wholly different image, in which "there is very little shading; neat flat surfaces are clearly separated from each other, [and] it is generally plain where one begins and another ends, and there is little if any ambiguity or overlap."[36]

---

35. Ernest Gellner, *Nations and Nationalism*, Ithaca, New York: Cornell University Press (1983:139).
36. Ibid. (1983:139-40).

For the nationalist imagination, the national order of things passes as the norm, for it is self-evident that "real" nations are fixed in space and "recognizable on a map."[37] As Anthony Smith demonstrates, such a representation is akin to "any school atlas with yellow, green, pink, orange, and blue countries composing a map with no vague or 'fuzzy spaces' and no 'bleeding boundaries.'" Regions are distinctly defined as countries that are inherently other to one another and nations assume the function of partitioning spatial territory.[38]

Victor Turner, exploring symbolic constructs that inform patterned ritual behavior, views these competing conceptions as two major representations of the world, juxtaposing and alternating.[39] In his view, the nationalist vision is characterized by its rigid structural rules, based on formal political-legal distinctions and qualifications that separate men and women into watertight compartments, whereas the transnational civilizational vision, characterized by the Islamic *umma* and the Christian oikoumene, keeps the structural properties of locality and nation at bay, disregarding formal allegiances to any political-legal authority. It is a vision that is "an unstructured or rudimentarily structured and relatively undifferentiated *comitatus*, community, or even communion of equal individuals who submit together to the general authority of the ritual."[40] Regarding the major monotheistic religions, Mecca, Jerusalem, and Rome represent the concrete locations in which this vision is activated and realized.

Belonging to the universal community of believers and to an ecclesiastical vision of the world, Mecca, Rome, and Jerusalem are thus not bound to the finite imaginary map of the state on which they reside. Their past belongs to a world community over which the state has little, if any, moral or cultural hold. In a sense they are "state-free"—the space they occupy being qualitatively different from that which surrounds them. The physical land on which they stand is not the property of the state, but belongs to the cosmos—literally. Furthermore, they still, for all

---

37. Anthony Smith, *The Ethnic Origins of Nationalism*, New York: Oxford University Press (1986:1).

38. The analogy of a school atlas is borrowed from Lissa Malkki, "National Geographic: The Rooting of Peoples and the Territorialization of National Identity Among Scholars and Refugees," *Cultural Anthropology,* vol. 7, no. 1, February (1992:26).

39. Victor Turner, *The Ritual Process: Structure and Anti-Structure*, Chicago: Aldine de Gruyter (1995:96).

40. Ibid. (1995:96).

practical purposes, belong to the old empires of the classical period and are regarded in some metaphysical sense as supranational, representing the global perspective of empires which, in the eyes of many believers, have never died.

Historically, Rome and Mecca embody this struggle clearly, having become entangled in fierce confrontations with nationalist movements that nearly swallowed them up whole. As a result, the empires of Islam and Christendom gradually became fragmented, pluralized, and territorialized, leaving in their wake supranational, a-temporal, and spiritually connected communities that became largely concerned with notions that were alien to land-based enterprises. In a sense, these communities reimagined their empires as having taken flight from the soil and become property of the cosmos.

However, in the case of Jerusalem, a convergence rather than a conflict with nationalism accounts for a more complex and radically different historical development in the modern period. Christian and Islamic sectors of Jerusalem's population follow the historical patterns of their respective global communities, but Jewish segments arrive at the scene having adopted nationalism, as expressed in its contemporary Zionist version.

One of the general arguments presented here is that the Jewish religion is unlike its Islamic and Christian variants in that it has, for reasons that must be contextualized, a particularistic quality that the other two do not share. Notions of *covenant* and *chosen people*, both as originally conceived and as applied today, are much more at ease within a world of nationalism than are the universalistic abodes that Christianity and Islam both inhabit.[41] Indeed, while the covenant concept has historically not mixed well in the ancient world of empires, where it is regularly seen at odds with the universalistic empires that surround it, it has fared much better within the context of a state in the modern world. Conversely, while Islam and Christianity have succeeded fabulously in the age of empire, quickly engulfing massive territories, their reach has diminished, *temporally speaking*, in the modern period of nation-states, as their universalistic qualities are at odds with the particularistic visions of present-day nationalism.

---

41. The Jewish notion of covenant is at ease with an *internal* reading of a Jewish state, not necessarily with nationalism in general, as anti-Semitism and fascism make all too clear. Moreover, Judaism has also been expressed in non-nationalist terms, especially before the rise of Zionism in Europe. See Stephen Steinberg, "Reform Judaism: The Origins and Evolution of a Church Movement," *Review of Religious Research*, vol. 7 (1965:1-8).

The Zionist vision of Jerusalem exemplifies an interesting and unexpected resolution to the otherwise wholly conflicted relationship between civilizational and national imagined communities. It seeks, for the purposes of nationalizing a transnational community, to highlight particularistic elements of its parent religion, whose communities are scattered throughout the world and whose practice has, throughout the period of empires and into modernity, largely incorporated universalistic rudiments of its variant faiths. Proponents of Zionism generally, in their official accounts anyway, see no internal ideological contradictions in their nationalist vision for Jerusalem. This view ascribes total legitimacy to the nationalist orientation in stipulating that it is fully within the state's right to encapsulate Jerusalem—a contemporary sacred *world* city and a universalistic symbol of the civilizational imagination—and enshrine it with a nationalist stamp. Thus, Zionists see the state's appropriation of Jerusalem not as contradicting but as fulfilling their ideological claims, as they equate the antiquated and only *recently* restored Jewish sense of a biblical nation with the state itself. As a result, the Jewish community identifies Jerusalem in a manner that neither transcends nor negates the nationalist vision of the state of Israel.[42] Zionism illustrates that the religious peculiarities of Judaism can be made to fit a nationalist project that aims to place the identity of an imagined community onto the structural boundaries of the state.[43]

In the cases of Islam and Christianity, their shared universalistic and transnational character seems thus far to have overwhelmed any nationalist vision, creating a cultural and political contradiction that is difficult to resolve. As a result, no single nation-state possesses the legitimate cultural and ideological resources to hold a monopoly of power over their central sacred cities. For the Palestinian movement (composed of Muslims *and* Christians spread over self-identified and "official" Muslim states), the nationalist vision of a Palestinian state and the identity of Jerusalem cannot be reconciled as they are for Zionists. This is due to the fact that for Muslims and Christians, in a world of multiple Islamic and

---

42. This was not always the case. During Zionism's formative years, Theodor Herzl and his contemporaries faced serious competitors who had opposing religious views regarding the return of Jews to the Holy Land. In time, Zionists formed alliances with religious Jews, transforming the notion of *return* in the process. See Aviezer Ravitsky, *Messianism, Zionism, and Jewish Religious Radicalism*, Chicago: University of Chicago Press (1996).
43. For a fuller discussion of this process, see chapter 4 of this book.

Christian states, Jerusalem is the property of no single political authority, but of the *umma* and of the *oikoumene*, respectively. Hence, any attempts by a Muslim or Christian state to nationalize Jerusalem would encounter tremendous political and religious obstacles, not only on behalf of Zionists, but also from Muslim and Christian communities within *and* outside of Palestine. As the empires constructed by Islam and Christendom in the Middle Ages have been shattered into multiple states in the modern period, having been forced to further develop non-terrestrial and cosmological aspects of their representative faiths, any effort on behalf of Christians and Muslims to nationalize Jerusalem seems, in any event, unlikely.

By contrast, the Jewish historical experience during the period of empires illustrates and embodies an "exiled" community scattered the world over with no formally political unifying structure. The community's recently imagined "return" concentrates its identity into a single political authority. Although the Jewish community is dispersed throughout the world, once it has attained a state, no other legally sanctioned Jewish unit has been able to claim Jerusalem as its own. The state, however, holds a monopoly over the city only *within* a community of believers. Therefore, exterior to the Zionist vision of Jerusalem, no worldview is bound by the same rules.

Another more obvious facet of Jerusalem that sets it apart from Rome and Mecca is that while the latter two are imagined as belonging to only one religious community, Jerusalem has been claimed by three such communities, each of which has historically wavered across a continuum of acknowledging and disavowing the authenticity of its counterpart faiths. While Rome and Mecca have posed political obstacles to the territorial claims of Italian and Saudi nationalist movements, Jerusalem complicates the picture further, in the case of the Zionist movement, by introducing *multiple claims.* This is felt viscerally upon entering the walled portion of the city, as the shrines of different faiths are literally stacked on top of one another. However, while the question of Jerusalem does not seem to be as clearly resolved as that of the other two cities, it nonetheless illustrates, as do Rome and Mecca, the incongruity between nationalist movements and sacred world cities. In one way or another, all three of these cities share in common the fact that they are territorially conceived as belonging to civilizations that escape and transcend the reach of the respective states in which they reside, and each city embodies a reality which suggests that concepts of conflict and of community arise from the source of human imagination.

III
The Limits of the
Time-Immemorial Perspective

The time-immemorial myth, as espoused by current proponents of a view that is antagonistic to religious forms of identity, embodies a notion that such conflicts as are witnessed today in the Middle East and around secular bastions of modernity evolve naturally from civilizational, religious, or cultural differences. Many who employ this naturalized construct of difference pose it as the root cause of conflict between peoples of the Middle East and those of the West. Such theorists are quick to embrace modernity as the cure for a system inherently skewed toward violent resolution of differences—based upon foundational texts, religions, or cultures that do not recognize the legitimacy of any system exterior to them. From this perspective, such issues as the conflict between Arab and Jew, or Islam and the West, are garbed in essentialist language with minimal, if any, regard for modern social, institutional, and organizational contributions to the construction of these conflicts.

Such a view conjures a world in which conflict appears to stem from characteristics innate to a specific civilization or religion. For instance, the present eruption of violence between, on one side, the United States and Israel and, on the other, portions of the Arab and Islamic world, is analyzed through the discourse of dysfunctionality, a character-type that can only be understood through the lens of "cultural environment" and/or religious (read: Islamic) influences. For example, two influential advocates for this position, Bernard Lewis and Samuel Huntington, argue that Muslims have learned to hate the West because Islam represents a cultural universe that is, by its essence, anti-modern and anti-Western.[44] Muslims, they argue, have learned traits and mentalities from their seventh-century predecessors in Mecca that are intrinsically anti-modernist. Further, they posit and answer the question "Why do they hate us?" in terms of an "Islamic mind" located deep within doctrinal ideas that call for a "return" to "the classical Islamic view," in which "the duty of God's soldiers is to dispatch God's enemies as quickly as possible to the

---

44. Samuel P. Huntington, *The Clash of Civilizations: Remaking of World Order*, New York: Simon & Schuster (1996); Bernard Lewis, "The Roots of Muslim Rage," *The Atlantic Monthly* 266, September (1990).

place where God will chastise them—that is to say, the afterlife."[45] As Ali Mirsepassi explains further:

> ...the venturing of the "clash of civilization" thesis depends upon the assertion that the hatred felt by Muslims has relatively little to do with any violation on the part of the West, and a great deal more to do with an ancient and almost supernatural form of enmity.[46]

Hence, for Bernard Lewis and Samuel Huntington, Muslims have acquired seventh-century cultural baggage that is at odds with Western civilization.

These types of essentialist perspectives may explain why many in the United States hold the view that missteps in the twentieth- and twenty-first-century Islamic world stem from a genetic defect in the cultural DNA of Muslims.

Attending to the question of violence around sacred spaces, Peter van der Veer argues that many accounts commonly make the misleading assumption that "the passions are 'natural' and that violent struggle is an explosion of pent-up feelings." Instead, he offers a much more compelling line of reasoning, noting that "although passions are certainly involved, their very 'naturalness' is produced by a political process."[47] Similarly, Mark LeVine, in his analysis of Jaffa and Tel Aviv, contends that one flawed characteristic common to many contemporary analyses is the failure to portray motives and dynamics of emerging ideologies and the events they have inspired during the tumultuous era of modernity, particularly "the role of the precise time-space zoning of social life as the source of modernity's 'dynamic nature.'"[48] LeVine's time-space zoning presents the image of a nation constructed from the ground up, as opposed to earlier templates in which a population could not recognize itself as forming a nation. In other words, in order for a collective, unified body to identify as a "national citizenry," it must first be made aware of itself as a nation that only the state can forge into existence. As Massimo

---

45. This summary is taken from Ali Mirsepassi, *Intellectual Discourse and the Politics of Modernization: Negotiating Modernity in Iran*, Cambridge, UK: University of Cambridge Press (2000:41-43).

46. Ibid. (2000:44).

47. Peter van der Veer, *Religious Nationalism: Hindus and Muslims in India*, Berkeley: University of California Press (1994:7).

48. Mark LeVine, *Overthrowing Geography: Jaffa, Tel Aviv, and the Struggle for Palestine, 1880-1948*, Berkeley: University of California Press (2005:18).

d'Agelio proclaimed upon the unification of Italy: "We have made Italy, now we have to make Italians."[49]

It is this modern fabrication of national time-space zones that must be contextualized in order to make sense of the contemporary violence that occurs around sacred spaces. Hence, our inquiry aims to examine the nature of political processes involved in restructuring populace imaginations and how the production of new forms of identity shapes those very passions behind violent conflicts that have frequently been characterized as natural, even primordial.

Browsing the shelves of any bookstore, it is clear that many contemporary scholars make the assertion that religion is the main culprit of the current world disorder, with a large number of publications boasting such titles as Hector Avalos's *Fighting Words: The Origins of Religious Violence*, Steve Bruce's *God Is Dead: Secularization in the West*, and Sam Harris's *The End of Faith: Religion, Terror, and the Future of Reason*. Such accounts often pose an underlying assumption that religion has become static within a modern social context, thus wavering "between a sterile conservation of its pre-modern characteristics and a self-effacing assimilation to the secularized world."[50] The linear, narrative model of history that modern scholars use lends itself to the notion that modern and secular identities have replaced obsolete and dangerous religious systems that belong to a "pre-modern" world. In this view, religion and modernity, as Anthony Smith illustrates, "figure as two terms in the conventional distinction between tradition and modernity, and in an evolutionary framework that sees an inevitable movement—whether liberating or destructive—from the one to the other."[51] Such a reading of modernity is thus one of increasing rationality and progress, heralding an age of secularism, while simultaneously replacing the old and decrepit politics of religion. In turn, religious social dynamics are understood as preceding those of a secular modernity insofar that the former characterizes "the 'traditional society' from which the transition to modernity began and [modern] nations later emerged."[52] The logical conclusion of this view, in which religion becomes inherently antithetical to modernity, is

---

49. Cited in John Lie, *Modern Peoplehood* (2004:124).
50. Peter van der Veer and Hartmut Lehmann (eds.), *Nation and Religion: Perspectives on Europe and Asia*, Princeton, New Jersey: Princeton University Press (1999:10).
51. Anthony Smith, *Chosen Peoples*, New York: Oxford University Press (2003: 9).
52. Ibid. (2003:10).

that only secular and rational scholars can legitimately resolve conflicts that are based upon irrational scriptures. As Hector Avalos forcefully proclaims: "Our final mission, as scholars of these scriptures, must be to help humanity close the book on a long chapter of human misery."[53] And further:

> A sound foreign policy...must include an educational program that convinces world citizens that violence about resources that do not exist [namely religious], or that cannot be verified to exist, is against their own interest.[54]

This school of thought, in no uncertain terms, credits religion as possessing an inherent bias toward intolerance and violence. One year after September 11, for instance, Andrew Sullivan, in an essay for the *New York Times Magazine*, entitled "This *Is* a Religious War," makes the claim that monotheistic religion inherently contains within it a tendency toward what he calls a "terrorist temptation," and he further insists that any view of the current violence that does not see it as rooted in religion is in denial.[55] Similarly, Sam Harris, in a book that purports to use logic and reason, finds it unacceptable that his culture has developed a taboo for "criticizing a person's faith," especially since he believes that such faiths "are leading us, inexorably, to kill one another."[56]

Many others, varied in their political persuasions, have reached similar conclusions, from critical accounts such as Benjamin Barber's *Jihad vs. McWorld*, Regina Schwartz's *The Curse of Cain*, and Jack Nelson-Pallmeyer's *Is Religion Killing Us?* to the anti-Muslim polemics of Bernard Lewis's "The Roots of Muslim Rage," Samuel Huntington's *Clash of Civilization and the Remaking of World Order*, Roger Scruton's *The*

---

53. Hector Avalos, *Fighting Words: The Origins of Religious Violence*, Amherst, New York: Prometheus Books (2005:378).
54. Ibid. (2005:378).
55. Andrew Sullivan, "This *Is* a Religious War," in *New York Times Magazine* (2001:46).
56. Sam Harris, *The End of Faith: Religion, Terror, and the Future of Reason*, New York: W.W. Norton & Company (2005:12-13).

West and the Rest, and Robert Spencer's *Islam Unveiled*.[57] The former tend to cluster around being critical of *all*, but especially monotheistic, religious traditions, providing a discursive reply to the latter group, which focuses exclusively and with great bias on Islam. But they all share an essentialist, time-immemorial perspective, which posits that some—and in a few of the accounts, all—religions are inherently violent, as evidenced in Nelson-Pallmeyer's contention that "exclusive claims to truth at the heart of the monotheistic religions made violent conflict likely if not inevitable."[58]

Lewis, Huntington, Spencer, Harris, and Barber take this one step further by characterizing Islam as more inherently violent than any other religion, contrasting it with a depiction of the West as a largely secular entity:

> [A]lthough it is clear that Islam is a complex religion that by no means is synonymous with Jihad, it is relatively inhospitable to democracy and that inhospitability in turn nurtures conditions favorable to parochialism, antimodernism, exclusiveness, and hostility to "others"—the characteristics that constitute what I have called Jihad.[59]

Perspectives that presume this sort of clash of civilizations create a dichotomy where the West is seen as secular and postcolonial societies are depicted in contrast as "religious," making possible Bernard Lewis's and Samuel Huntington's highly problematic proposals, which posit Islam as the antithesis of everything that is modern and Western. Huntington argues that "conflicts between Western and Islamic civilizations have been going on for 1,300 years," and he concludes that such cultural differences led a unified "crescent-shaped Islamic bloc, from the bulge of

---

57. Benjamin Barber, *Jihad vs. McWorld*, New York: Ballantine Books (2001); Regina Schwartz, *The Curse of Cain: The Violent Legacy of Monotheism*, Chicago: University of Chicago Press (1997); Jack Nelson-Pallmeyer, *Is Religion Killing Us? Violence in the Bible and the Qur'an*, Harrisburg, Pennsylvania: Trinity Press International (2005); Roger Scruton, *The West and the Rest*, Wilmington, Delaware: ISI Books (2002); Robert Spencer, *Islam Unveiled*, San Francisco: Encounter Books (2002).
58. Jack Nelson-Pallmeyer, *Is Religion Killing Us?* (2005:xii).
59. Benjamin Barber, *Jihad vs. McWorld* (2001:205).

Africa to central Asia" to experience continuous "bloody borders."[60] Sam Harris, leaning almost exclusively on Bernard Lewis's account, proclaims, "Islam, more than any other religion human beings have devised, has all the makings of a thoroughgoing cult of death."[61]

In Edward Said's view, such binary construction of "Islam" and the "West" is inextricably tied to the colonial experience.[62] That is, binaries of this sort allow colonial powers to portray themselves, in the words of Peter van der Veer and Hartmut Lehmann, as "an enlightened and rational race of rulers who had to lead and develop the [colonized], who were steeped in ancient prejudices and communal violence."[63] Perhaps the crudity of this binary is most clearly expressed by Sam Harris: "It is not merely that we are at war with an otherwise peaceful religion that has been 'hijacked' by extremists. We are at war with precisely the vision of life that is prescribed to all Muslims in the Koran..."[64]

From our perspective, the most significant aspect of the current debate is how it has impacted the study of sacred spaces, for although much of the literature has arisen in response to both the Palestinian-Israeli conflict and violence surrounding secular, rather than sacred, world cities, this wave of publications scrutinizing the link between religion and violence is unsurprisingly finding its way into discussions over the legitimacy of sacred spaces. Hector Avalos sums this up in his analysis of violence within Jerusalem, arguing that the "repeated recorded conflict over that space since at least the Assyrian siege in the eighth century B.C.E."— a staggering three thousand years of violence—"is almost entirely the creation of religion."[65] Indeed, many histories of Jerusalem, beginning at least in the 1950s, with the early works of Mircea Eliade,[66] pose the premise that violence around sacred spaces is somehow outside of time, space, and context, and is the logical result of the separation of space into the sacred and the profane—"a cosmic clash of religions, cultures, and civilizations," which, in the words of Meron Benvenisti, are rooted in a

---

60. Samuel Huntington, "The Clash of Civilizations?" in *Foreign Affairs*, vol. 72, no. 3, Summer (1993:31, 34-35).
61. Sam Harris, *The End of Faith* (2005:123).
62. Edward Said, *Orientalism*, New York: Vintage Books (1979).
63. Peter van der Veer and Hartmut Lehmann (eds.), *Nation and Religion* (1999: 10).
64. Sam Harris, *The End of Faith* (2005:109).
65. Hector Avalos, *Fighting Words* (2005:261).
66. Mircea Eliade, *The Sacred and the Profane: The Nature of Religion*, San Diego, California: Harcourt Brace Jovanovich ([1957] 1987).

"primordial, irreconcilable, endemic shepherd's war."[67] Eric Cline, in his *Jerusalem Besieged*, contributes to this line of reasoning, noting that "military occupations and religious conflicts continue in Jerusalem, as they have done unrelentingly for four thousand years, with no end in sight."[68] And further:

> Today the struggle for Jerusalem and for all of Israel continues with respite, perpetuating four thousand years of confrontation in the heart of the land once called Canaan. Where once the ancient weapons were bronze swords, lances, and battle-axes, they are now stun grenades, helicopter gunships, remotely detonated car bombs, and suicidal young men and women armed with explosives. *Although the individuals and their weapons may have changed, the underlying tensions and desires have not.*[69]

This time-immemorial perspective makes an assumption that requires a significant leap of faith, insisting that conflicts occurring in the vicinity of sacred spaces have not substantially changed in form and that they are built into sacred space, emanating naturally from its center. Oblivious to the great political and economic transformations that the world has experienced over the past two centuries, this a-historical argument fails to interrogate current methods and motivations for devouring and slicing up landscapes, seeming to give a free pass to such media as nationalism, nation-states, and more recent exclusivist forms of identities. Instead, sacred spaces, functioning like totems, are understood as symbolic locations of primordial religious passions, a nuisance to "our" modern and secular ways of negotiating national space. This sort of reasoning allows Hector Avalos to claim that in order to relieve humankind from the type of violence that takes place around sacred spaces, scholars must not only conclude that "desacralizing space is ultimately the best solution,"[70] but they must also make clear recommendations for action.

---

67. Meron Benvenisti cited in Norman G. Finkelstein, *Beyond Chutzpah: On the Misuse of Anti-Semitism and the Abuse of History*, Berkeley: University of California Press (2005:7).
68. Eric Cline, *Jerusalem Besieged: From Ancient Canaan to Modern Israel*, Ann Arbor: University of Michigan Press (2004:2).
69. Eric Cline, *Jerusalem Besieged* (2004:2), emphasis added.
70. Hector Avalos, *Fighting Words* (2005:367).

The explicit assumption is that only a modern, secular concept of politics and space can correct the inherently destructive sacralization of space. In Avalos's own words:

> ...until the Abrahamic religions overthrow the master-slave model in which they were born, we see little progress to be made. Since all religious beliefs are ultimately unverifiable, the greatest scarce resource of all is verifiability. And one way to remedy or minimize unverifiability in any decision-making process, especially that leading to violence, is to eliminate religion from human life altogether.[71]

In light of this academic assault, it is critical to ask: how do sacred spaces, particularly the three sacred world cities at the heart of our inquiry, challenge the authenticity of a modernist, nationalist, and secular agenda? One aspect of clear difference is the notion of borders, which elevates the qualities of division and ownership in defining identity. Sacred world cities struggle to survive in an age that has difficulty dealing with untidy spaces. The modern age demands a clear vision of division, whereas sacred spaces offer ambiguity and the possibility to transcend or diminish such a vision. As Mark LeVine claims, "modernity is (self-) defined by its refusal of hybridity."[72] Conversely, in the words of John Lie, "the state projected itself as a unitary subject...as a Leviathan," where the nation is viewed as a single body "marching in a single step, moved by the same thought, seeming to form one being."[73] The concept of nationhood produces a narrative antithetical to the infinite variations of everyday life, in which the image of a cohesive and homogenous whole entity to which a citizen belongs exists in constant exclusion of potentially divisive markers of diversity and difference, as defined simply by virtue of not belonging to the state.[74]

The complicated cultural landscape that Jerusalem has historically embodied presents a wholly different image in which layer upon layer of new cultural and religious markers, particularly with the conquests of the first and seventh centuries, eventually culminates in a complex symbio-

---

71. Ibid. (2005:367).
72. Mark LeVine, *Overthrowing Geography* (2005:21).
73. John Lie, *Modern Peoplehood* (2004:103, 119).
74. David Theo Goldberg, *The Racial State*, Malden, Massachusetts: Blackwell Publishers (2002:10).

sis. As Zionists are discovering today, such historical intersections seem to immunize the city from the political project of glorifying one community's history at the expense of another's. The current conflict over Jerusalem can thus be understood, in Edward Said's words, as being marked by "a seamless amalgam of cultures and religions, engaged like members of the same family, on the same plot of land, in which all has become entwined with all."[75] Consequently, the Zionist attempt to seize Jerusalem and to divide a complex, intertwined population into clear and segregated communities has proven to be explosive. The resulting outbursts of violence are not surprising given that, as Mark LeVine observes, "the production of space in Palestine was governed by the [Zionist] belief that the 'new Israel' could only be erected on a *vacant* site...where all otherness [was] absent or neutralized." Zionist discourse, not unlike most other forms of nationalism, produces a cleansing mentality on behalf of its idealized social vision, in which otherness is either posed as an obstacle, or is not even acknowledged altogether.[76]

The Zionist attempt to re-write Jerusalem's symbiotic history and to create an exclusively Jewish city lies at the root of "the Question of Jerusalem," and its project of severing the city from its integrative whole, therefore, goes against the very nature of Jerusalem as an interconnected terrain of three world religions. Such an intercultural history as Jerusalem retains, in which a complex symbolic landscape holds multiple projects of strategic religious enshrinements, cannot be anything other than a field particularly sensitive to *any* nationalist movement that would attempt to appropriate the city for itself. The eradication of difference, which lies at the heart of modern nationalism, is thus the key to understanding the "Questions of Jerusalem, Mecca, and Rome."

In this sense, a time-immemorial perspective can offer little, if anything at all, to any serious inquiry that seeks to identify real political motives for violent resolutions to current conflicts. The exception occurs when those who employ it are willing to accept secularism, modernity, nationalism, and ultimately humanity as the new ritualistic symbols of communal deification and worship; part of a time-immemorial continuum and not a paradigmatic break from it, for the notions of disconfirming otherness that seem to be peppered throughout the arguments against religion are just as easily identified at the heart of the nationalist agenda.

---

75. Edward Said, "Keynote Essay," in Ghada Karmi, *Jerusalem Today,* Ithaca, New York: Cornell University Press (1996:7).
76. Mark LeVine, *Overthrowing Geography* (2005:23)

IV
Re-Imagining Sacred Spaces

We have thus far argued that it is unproductive to characterize civilizational formations of the pan-Islamic or Christendom type as the product of an archaic system of a bygone era and as decaying structures that belong to a preceding age. The linear argument produced by secular notions of logic that—even if some old formations persist—modernity will over time replace those systems of orientation with a more rational and tolerant secular conception of space seems self-aggrandizing and remarkably lacking in dimension. Contrary to such common evolutionary wisdom as proponents of the secular agenda posit, it seems clear that not only are civilizational formations surviving in the modern world, but they have been able to maintain strong affiliations, having come to pose a viable alternative to the nation-state form itself. Rather than undergoing a process of decay, they seem to be reviving and articulating their vision of the world at the expense of their nationalist counterparts. If a time-immemorial perspective is to contribute to the debate at all, it will need to be reformulated in light of the persisting transnational identities of which pan-Islam is the clearest expression.

Mark LeVine asks, "Can we uncover the 'mask' of modernity and challenge its existing spatializations?" In effect, such a question asks the inquiry to take a critical leave from modernity and its methods of reasoning, while employing them all at once. The current study will attempt to do just that, offering alternative perspectives to existing historical narratives while excavating the rich history of Jerusalem, Rome, and Mecca's collective "struggle with modernity—long buried under the debris" of nationalist symbols.[77]

Chapter 2 presents the formations of Rome, Mecca, and Jerusalem in the age of world empires, specifically considering the periods associated with the Apostle Paul and the prophet Muhammad. Chapter 3 examines how modern nationalism has attempted to undermine this rich and complex past by trying to erase symbolism incompatible with its self-imposed and pre-packaged image of identity. In the case of Rome, the War of Religions, the Reformation, and the Italian *Risorgimento* movement are explored as purification projects of other peoples' idols. In that of Mecca, the inception of Wahabism is discussed as a modern purifying movement, attempting, much like its European predecessors, to disinfect

---

77. Ibid. (2005:21, 24).

holy sites from the contamination of the "Other." Chapter 4 focuses on Jerusalem and illustrates how Zionism, Christian Fundamentalism, and Islamists today are all following a zealous path of sanitizing sacred spaces.

Concluding this study is an exploration of how people living in a modern world can re-imagine the sacred landscape. While the present project of modernity has produced clear spatial notions of Self and Other with dire consequences for those who find themselves within the latter category, it seems prudent to begin dismantling the monolith. This section will investigate the actual lived messiness of Jerusalem today, which exemplifies how differing communities with intertwining neighborhoods continue to present a picture of hope for a better future.

2

THE MAKING OF
SACRED WORLD CITIES:
HOW CHRISTIANITY AND
ISLAM TRANSFORMED
IDENTITIES

Is God the God of Jews only? Is he not the God of
Gentiles too? Yes, of Gentiles too, since there is only one God... You are
all sons of God through faith in Jesus... There is no longer Jew or Greek,
there is no longer slave or free, there is no longer male and
female, for all of you are one in Christ Jesus.[1]

Paul

There is no god but God alone; He has no associates.
He has fulfilled His promise and helped His servant. He alone has put
to fight the confederates. Oh men, we created you male and female and
made you into peoples and tribes so that you may know one another.[2]

Muhammad

I

The Foundations of
Universalistic Sacred World Cities

Christian and Islamic traditions both pose their central figures, Jesus
and Muhammad, hovering high over Jerusalem. Following the Crucifix-

---

1. Galatians 3:26-28.
2. Ibn Ishaq, *"Sirat Rasul Allah,"* cited in F.E. Peters, *Muhammad and the Origins of Islam*, New York, Albany: SUNY Press (1994:236-37).

ion, the New Testament portrays Christ through images of Resurrection and Ascension, taking flight from his tomb and ascending from Jerusalem into the heavens. Similarly, Islamic sources illustrate Muhammad journeying one night from Mecca to Jerusalem, where he ascends into the skies above to visit a number of Jewish and Christian biblical prophets, including Moses, Abraham, and Jesus.

Historically, these stories both function as much more than myths, embodying the expressions of a shared political and social project that seeks to consecrate Jerusalem anew for freshly established communities of believers. The passages are best read as statements of identity in which God's singular existence, as understood through Judaic monotheistic tradition, is no longer the privileged experience of a specific chosen few, but is revealed and made available to humankind as a whole. For Christianity, this image of ascension symbolizes a radical shift from earthly to otherworldly spaces, functioning as an allegory, in a Pauline sense, that illustrates the city of Jerusalem uprooted from its past affiliations with the Israelites to now include all of humankind. In this sense, flight into the hereafter represents the transcendence of a particularistic identity formation and the discovery of a universalistic one.

Such intentions arise in response to an Israelite tendency to view Jerusalem as a social indicator of distinctiveness and as a symbol of independence that has kept external practices and customs at a distance by reinforcing clear boundaries of separateness from imperial order. Paul and Muhammad display a clear interest in overturning the traditional Israelite identification of sacred space with a particular people, which has long been used to justify the exclusion of subjects from its fold. Following their visions and political agendas, subsequent Christian and Islamic empires would sanctify their sacred claims upon Jerusalem, Rome, and Mecca in a horizontally diffused manner, not intending to designate a marker of difference, as in the Israelite fashion, but rather aiming to absorb difference.

In this sense, Christians and Muslims alike historically formulate notions of sacred space that world empires, immense and diverse as they are, can easily appropriate or employ, simply because they are framed in a manner that can be readily diffused as imperial symbols throughout the entire geographical reach of an empire. Thus, sanctification of a city becomes meaningful for a wide array of inhabitants and its symbolism is easily transferable to every corner of the empire.

UNIVERSALIZING JERUSALEM: PAUL'S PROJECT

Ancient Israelites organized space through the lens of divine law in a manner that established degrees of holiness, as though such a quality was localized and radiated outward losing definition, as does a ripple in a pond. Accordingly, territories exterior to the kingdom were considered to be least holy and those of which it was comprised assumed greater sanctity with closer thematic or spatial proximity to the holy city of Jerusalem. Still holier sectors were to be found inside Jerusalem culminating within the Temple Mount, which dictated access according to degrees of holiness, so that a court of the Gentiles existed as its least holy area as did, on the other end of the spectrum, a sanctuary designated for the high priest alone, only to be entered one day out of the year on Yom Kippur, the Day of Atonement. The Israelites therefore arranged space in a way that measured distance from divinity,[3] while it established ethnic markers by which to separate and exclude Gentiles from divinity.

Unique to Jerusalem's Temple was the Israelite refusal to accept placement of any imperial symbols within its gates. Biblical texts clearly illustrate that the Israelites adopted Jerusalem as a symbolic rallying cry to reject any imperial religious markers within its midst. Over time, the city thus came to distinctly embody a spirit of independence and allegiance, particularly for those who wished to express opposition to their powerful neighbors. George Mendenhall, a Marxist historian of ancient Israel, describes this development as "a religious revolution" involving a "systematic, ethically and religiously based, conscious rejection of many cultural traits of the Late Bronze Age urban and imperial cultures," such as "kingship, art, professional military, temples."[4]

This message of purity and separation had become especially acute after the Babylonian conquest of Jerusalem in 597 B.C.E., in which the city had seen its First Temple destroyed. During this Second Temple period, two competing movements emerged that characterized Jerusalem in ways that were diametrically opposed to one another. The first introduced a series of religious innovations that would place the city at the

---

3. Karen Armstrong, *Jerusalem: One City, Three Faiths*, New York: A.A. Knopf (1996:85-86).

4. George E. Mendenhall, *The Tenth Generation: The Origins of the Biblical Traditions,* Baltimore, Maryland: Johns Hopkins University (1974:2); see also Herbert Schneidau, "The Hebrews against the High Cultures," in his *Sacred Discontent: The Bible and Western Tradition*, Baton Rouge: Louisiana State University Press (1976).

center of Jewish identity, employing strict and rigid notions of authenticity that extended beyond a ban on idolatry and placed a "greater emphasis on matters of ritual purity."[5] Under this faction, circumcision, as a marker of difference, became a more pronounced necessity that dictated access to the Temple. Such notions allowed for the prohibition of Gentiles and non-Jews from entering the Temple's courtyards, as those who did not observe the laws contained within the Torah were pronounced "unclean."[6]

For such isolationists, Jerusalem thus became a purely Jewish center, where strict and clearly defined markers were advanced in an effort to eliminate any foreign and, by the time of the Seleucids, Hellenistic influences. The city was thoroughly and completely identified as Jewish in character and no elements or forms exterior to Judaic practice were permitted to enter its walls. This group saw Jerusalem and its sanctuary as concrete manifestations of God's pact with a chosen people, hence, as exclusive of humankind at large.

At polar opposite to this camp were those who found such rigid distinctions difficult to maintain, who thus pursued options that were congenial to foreign influences. These Jews viewed their puritan companions as overly parochial and alienating, preferring a more cosmopolitan lifestyle, and they introduced such things as Greek baths and gymnasiums to the city. This movement refused to define Jerusalem in specifically Jewish terms. It reinterpreted the scriptural passages pertaining to the Temple in a manner that fashioned a more conciliatory position. As a result, these Hellenized Jews introduced Gentile cultural practices to the population and found no discomfort in having Greek and Hellenistic deity representations placed alongside, sometimes even replacing, Jewish forms.

The success of Hellenization, to a large degree, over the isolationist position allowed for the emergence of a figure such as Paul, a Hellenized Jew who, within such an atmosphere of assimilation, was provided a context in which to express his anxieties about Judaic exclusivity. Thus, the Christian movement took form in the first through third centuries, comprised of such characters as Paul, Origen, and Eusebius, who aggressively advanced a call to marginalize Palestine, developing a theology of Land that was hostile to anything resembling a terrestrial and worldly

---

5. Lee I. Levine, "Second Temple Jerusalem: A Jewish City in the Greco-Roman Orbit," in Lee I. Levine (ed.), *Jerusalem: Its Sanctity and Centrality to Judaism, Christianity, and Islam*, New York: Continuum Pub. (1999:55).
6. Karen Armstrong, *Jerusalem* (1996:108).

sense of holiness as was embodied by Jerusalem. As such, early Christians used the Jewish isolationist terminology of impurity and uncleanness against those who espoused it, urging the Christian community to divert its attention from any "Jewish contamination," including Palestine itself, which was too closely identified with the Jews for the taste of this new Gentile movement. Indeed, during the first three centuries of Christianity, Palestine and its Holy City were insignificant to the Christian imagination, with the exception of a few curious travelers who made rare visits.[7] Instead, what mattered were such Greco-Roman cities as Antioch, Corinth, Galatia, and, of course, Rome itself, where real power lay.

Early Christians understood quite well that in order to sell their brand of Christ flavored Judaism in a Gentile dominated empire their sect had to shed its Jewish attire and clothe itself with a more Gentile-friendly (Greco-Roman) vision. Paul perceived that a disengagement from the political entity of Jerusalem was essential to such a project and he thus led early Christianity toward a decisive break with the Land. Within such a radical context, this movement recognized a need to shatter old notions of sacred space as were practiced by Jews in the pre-Resurrection period. They viewed the protected centrality of Jerusalem as a nuisance. Thus, "Jerusalem Below," as one Gentile Christian pilgrim remarks, "was worthless now because of the Jerusalem Above."[8] These early Christians further believed that holy places were merely the domain of pagans and Jews, and that "Christians knew better."[9] In the following verse, where Jesus is having a discussion with a Samaritan woman, the Gospel of John is very explicit:

> "Sir," the woman said, "I can see that you are a prophet. Our fathers worshipped on this mountain, but you Jews claim that the place where we must worship is in Jerusalem." Jesus declared, "Believe me, woman, a time is

---

7. P.W.L. Walker, *Jesus and the Holy City: New Testament Perspectives on Jerusalem*, London and New York: Ederman Press (1996).
8. The pilgrim was one of the few early Christians to make a pilgrimage to Jerusalem. See Karen Armstrong, *Jerusalem* (1997:170-71). For pilgrimages in this early period see John Wilkinson, *Jerusalem Pilgrims before the Crusades*, Warminster, Eng.: Aris & Phillips (1977).
9. R.A. Markus, "How on Earth Could Places Become Holy? Origins of the Christian Idea of Holy Places," in *Journal of Early Christian Studies*, vol. 2, no. 3 (1994:258).

coming when you will worship the Father neither on this
mountain nor in Jerusalem."[10]

Indeed, the New Testament provided as clear a distinction as is possible,
overturning, quite consciously, one may argue, the understanding of
Land presented in the Old Testament. As Conor Cruise O'Brien notes, in
the *Old Testament* "it is God who offers land to Abraham, and Abraham
accepts (Genesis 12); in the New Testament it is Satan who offers land to
Jesus, and Jesus refuses" (Luke 4:5-8).[11] Moreover, these Gentile Christians viewed Jerusalem as a Guilty City based upon its rejection of
Christ.[12]

This Diasporic thirst to transform a Jerusalem identified solely with
the Jews into one belonging to all of humankind was an integral part of
the project to annul the Old Testament's understanding of sacred space.
Paul understood this more clearly than any other figure of his time and
he consciously negated many of the particularistic claims the Hebrew
Scriptures offered. His method gradually eroded the reign of a purely
Judeo-centered worldview of Jerusalem, producing an attitude among
followers regarding sacred space that was more akin to such notions as
were held outside of Israel.

Paul was largely motivated by a fervent personal rejection of exclusive claims to a ritualistic relationship with divinity that denied outsiders
such a privilege. As noted in the Gospels' account of Paul's struggle with
the Christians of Palestine, Jews that practiced "those rites that are special, performed by and marked in the body" were deemed misguided for
their shortsighted commitment to maintaining the religion as "an affair of
a particular tribal group, 'Israel in the flesh.'" Of this theme, Boyarin
remarks:

> The insistence on the literal, the physical, is a stubborn
> resistance to the universal, a tenacious clinging to differ-
> ence…. By substituting a spiritual interpretation for a
> physical ritual, Paul at one stroke was saying that the lit-
> eral Israel, "according to the flesh," is not the ultimate
> Israel; there is an allegorical "Israel in the spirit." The
> practices of the particular Jewish people are not what the

---

10. John 4:19-20.
11. Quoted in Conor Cruise O'Brien, *God Land: Reflections on Religion and
Nationalism*, Cambridge, Massachusetts: Harvard University Press (1987:3-4).
12. Karen Armstrong, *Jerusalem* (1997:171).

Bible speaks of, but faith, the allegorical meaning of
those practices. It was Paul's genius to transcend "Israel
in the flesh."[13]

Hence, the Law as is codified in the Torah, from circumcision and
dietary laws to Sabbath and other such practices, became invalid, as faith
in Christ had overturned all those customs that were once the property of
a particular ethnic group. In its place was a universal message for all of
humankind. Paul thus understood faith in the Resurrection of Jesus as a
revolutionary moment that theologically nullified those laws which were
applicable only to the Jews. As Boyarin provocatively observes, Paul
sought to transcend a system that "remains, after all, a valorization of
difference," which "is precisely the motivating force behind Paul's entire
conversion experience and mission."[14] Paul, zealously identifying and
eschewing the notion of difference, preached for its erasure, maintaining
a strong stand against those Jewish Christians, particularly within Jerusalem, who insisted otherwise. He perceived as essential to his mission the
ideal of human unification as a divinely inspired successor to that of division, and he believed this principle to be embodied in the uniquely
Christian event, the Resurrection of Jesus, which was "the vehicle for
this transformation of humanity."[15]

Paul's was not a voice unique to the experience of Jews living outside of Palestine; rather, it was innovative of sentiments long bubbling
under the surface. Israelite hostility toward the Greco-Roman world,
though not pervasive throughout the land, certainly placed great stress
upon Diasporic Jews. Many traveled long distances through highways
and trade routes, visiting major cities, not only in the Hellenistic East,
but "as far west as Italy and North Africa."[16] Accustomed to the larger
Greco-Roman culture, it is not difficult to imagine that many must have
felt displeased with a strictly Judeo-centered interpretation of the Law
that did not permit them to worship among the larger communities with
which they were in regular contact. Indeed, as was the case with many
cities outside of Palestine that contained a large Jewish population, there
tended to be a relaxed attitude toward Jewish Law, in which Greeks,

---

13. Daniel Boyarin, *A Radical Jew: Paul and the Politics of Identity*, Berkeley,
California: University of California Press (1994:37-38).
14. Ibid. (1994:54).
15. Ibid. (1994:106).
16. L. Michael White, *The Social Origins of Christian Architecture*, Cambridge,
Massachusetts: Harvard University Press (1990:60).

Romans, and Jews worshipped the God of Israel together and mingled in the same synagogues. These Jews, predominantly "living as aliens, as an ethnic and religious minority, in the dominant culture of urban life in the Greek east and then Rome itself,"[17] must have, to a large extent, been eager to form some degree of assimilation. A strict, separatist interpretation of the Law, especially as pertained to worship, offered them little comfort.

If the ancient Israelites were in a constant state of defending their cultural and national integrity from imperial penetration, Paul's Christian adaptation served as an accommodating alternative, making Judaic practice more palatable—sometimes quite literally, as in the negation of kosher laws—to imperial standards. This new sect would develop in the midst of Jewish civil wars and violent conflicts between the Israelites and the Roman imperial order,[18] searching for a genuine alternative to these hostilities and finding resolution of the Israelite/Imperial divide in Pauline Christianity.

In light of these complex questions of identity, it is not surprising that Hellenized Jews and their early Christian converts capitalized upon themes of inclusion and in the process refashioned the Jewish notion of one God in a manner that Greco-Roman potential followers could find more attractive. In this sense, a growing emphasis upon the universal qualities derived from monotheism at the expense of particularistic notions may be understood as an adaptation to Greco-Roman philosophical and religious ideals.[19] Thus, the uniquely Christian message that resulted from questioning the particularity of Judaism crafted a bridge for those inhabiting an already extant Greco-Roman community that held similar concepts of God.[20]

---

17. Ibid. (1990:60).
18. For an excellent account of the Roman and Jewish wars see Martin Goodman, *The Ruling Class of Judaea: The Origins of the Jewish Revolt against Rome AD 66-70*, Cambridge, Massachusetts: Cambridge University Press (1987) and his essay "Opponents of Rome: Jews and Others," in Alexander Loveday (ed.), *Images of Empire*, Sheffield, Eng.: JSOT Press (1991:222-38).
19. Daniel Boyarin, *A Radical Jew* (1994:58).
20. Ibid. (1994:58).

UNIVERSALIZING MECCA: MUHAMMAD

While early Christians traveled west from Palestine to acclimatize Judaism to their Greco-Roman environment and, in turn, Romanize Judea, the Muslims would journey southward toward Mecca, transforming the region anew, albeit in a radically different social context. In contrast to the early Christians who operated within an already existing imperial order, introducing monotheism to a world that had long developed religious and philosophical themes analogous in form to the spiritual and political concerns of Hellenized Jews, the Muslims achieved a similar end within a tribal environment that lacked such an anchor. Indeed, while Christian innovation was based upon imperial concerns, Islam would develop within the context of a tribal confederation deficient of an all-encompassing superstructure that internalized local social formations. Some semblance of universalistic concerns could be found among the multiple tribal groups in Arabia prior to Muhammad and the rise of Islam, but they had little impact upon the daily experiences of tribal members.

In contrast to the pagans of the Roman Empire at the inception of Christianity, those of Arabia at the turn of the eighth century C.E. envisioned the world through a particularistic lens. The predominant power structure to which they were subject crossed through tribal and familial lines and depended largely upon the reproduction of a social order that vertically integrated multiple communities. Under Muhammad's vision, Mecca, serving as the sacred center of tribal Arabia, would witness a power struggle very similar to the one that occurred between Palestinian Christians and their Hellenized counterparts in first century Jerusalem. In Muhammad's time, however, little support could be found for a new monotheistic movement, either within the holy land or outside of it. "Hellenized" Arabs, although they existed in pocket communities, were a weak force,[21] and figures such as Paul who were scattered throughout Greco-Roman cities in the first-century were seldom present in seventh century Arabia.

Thus, the effectiveness of such a figure as Muhammad depended upon an even more radicalized vision than that of Paul; in this case, it assumed the ancient and well-developed form of prophecy. Whereas Paul had called for a transcendence of "Israel in the flesh" to make monothe-

---

21. See the work of J.S. Trimingham, *Christianity among the Arabs in Pre-Islamic Times*, London: Longman (1979).

ism more palatable for the world of Diaspora, Muhammad would overcome the pagan tribes of Arabia. The essential element of distinction between the two can be characterized thus: while Paul appropriated a flesh-
oriented monotheism and altered it within the predominant framework of
pagan universalism, Muhammad, by contrast, negated a similarly earthly
paganism, employing an external otherworldly vision within the princi-
pal context of *pagan particularism*. In order to introduce a universalistic
notion of monotheism, Muhammad then needed to import it *into* a particularistic system, essentially a reversal of the Christian path. This effort
required a resurrection of another kind—that of a divine message forgotten or distorted by communities gone astray. Accordingly, the transformation of Mecca from a sacred center serving the spiritual needs of multiple tribal communities into one of imperial aspiration followed a virgin
path.

During the eighth century, Arabia experienced an economic transformation that would prove to contribute significantly to the disintegration of its tribal structure. Such an environment offered Muhammad the
opportunity to begin a process of articulating a radically different structural form from the one into which he was born. The injection of long-
distance trade into Arabia at the time of the prophet's birth in 570 C.E. led
to a series of institutional breakdowns in the way tribes and clans interacted with one another. This is not surprising given the fact that "tribal-
ism was the only mode of social organization, where each individual saw
himself as belonging to a kinship group claiming descent from a real or
supposed ancestor."[22] Under the "old" pre-trade system, "solidarity increased with ancestral proximity: the most immediate loyalty was to the
family; then to the clan, a small group of closely related families; beyond
that to broader groups of increasingly distant relatives" who could sometimes be called upon for support; finally reaching the tribal level,
"roughly...defined as the largest group capable of providing effective
social solidarity."[23] Such a social organization required loyalties that
were not conducive to the newly transformed environment,[24] which be-

22. Malise Ruthven, *Islam in the World*, New York: Oxford University Press
(1984:50).
23. Ibid. (1984:50).
24. Mahmood Ibrahim, *Merchant Capital and Islam*, Austin: University of
Texas Press (1990). Ibn Khaldun's concept of *'asabiyya* is intended to describe
this unifying phenomenon. For this classic observer of the Muslim world, religion is critical to the integrative forces of the *umma* and the *'asabiyya*, but according to Ira Lapidus's reading of ibn Khaldun, the *'asabiyya* more importantly

gan to collapse under a setting that required a diverse set of social groups to form far more cooperative relationships.[25] Eric Wolf, in one of his early anthropological essays, recognizes the significance of trade for the rise of Islam thus:

> The change from a type of society organized on the basis of kin relationships to a type of society possessed of an organized, if rudimentary, state...took place in an urban environment...connected with the spread of trade.[26]

Mecca's economic progress, therefore, had taken this tightly bound tribal system beyond what its institutional structure could support. The emergence of a society based on long-distance trade gradually unraveled an organization of newly formed allegiances and in the process weakened the tribal bonds that had dominated the region. As Mahmood Ibrahim cogently argues, "Mecca's tribally supported superstructure was no longer viable in the new social environment."[27] Meccan elites responded to this crisis far too little and much too late and left the region ripe for a visionary capable of foreseeing the need for complete renewal.

Thus, as Mecca's contacts with tribes outside of the *haram* area (the precinct surrounding the sacred stone known as the Ka'ba) continued to become more complex during Muhammad's lifetime, altering political and economic conditions, the city weakened further, poised for fresh institutional modifications.[28] Elaborating further, Ibrahim writes:

> A far-reaching change was needed, especially in Mecca's relationship with tribes outside of the *haram* area. A better relationship with other tribes was required so that merchants could be more secure in their travel.

"enables them to restrain themselves and cooperate in a common cause. It supplements family loyalties to create wider, more encompassing solidarities"; Ira M. Lapidus, "Tribes and State Formation in Islamic History," in Philip Khouri and Joseph Kostiner (eds.), *Tribe and State Formation in the Middle East*, Berkeley: University of California Press (1990:29).
25. Malise Ruthven, *Islam in the World* (1984:82).
26. Eric Wolf, "The Social Organization of Mecca and the Origins of Islam," in *The Southwestern Journal of Anthropology*, vol.7, no. 4 (1951).
27. Mahmood Ibrahim, *Merchant Capital* (1990:75).
28. Ibid. (1990:43).

Only then could they have access to a wider market area
and thus more opportunities for commerce.[29]

In a knee-jerk response to the economic changes that were undermining their privileges, the ruling classes of Mecca had improvised by developing broader pagan institutions based on their hold over the *haram*,
reasoning that the wider the appeal of the sanctuary was spread, the
greater would be the flow of pilgrims and merchants to Mecca. According to Ibrahim, the Quraysh, Mecca's dominant tribe, had attempted to
accommodate various pagan deities within the zone of the Ka'ba as a
show of "universality." Indeed, half a century before Muhammad, there
had already been a mixture of pagan deities represented in the sacred
precinct of Mecca.[30] Numerous old cults had existed in Arabia in connection with various shrines, of which the Ka'ba had been one of the more
important, and many of the old practices had been retained, especially in
cases for which taboos of time and place made trade easier by suspend-
ing blood feuds.[31]

Consequently, such inclusive policies had led to serious "overcrowd-
ing." As Ruthven remarks, "it seems probable that the 360 idols placed
around the Ka'ba represented various tribal totems, signifying adherence
to the sanctuary, rather as the flags of member states are ranged in the
UN Plaza in New York."[32] Although the presence of multiple symbols
around the intertribal forum of the Ka'ba had been intended to serve as a
display of unity, this renovation would fail to secure the divisive reality
of multiple deity worship from disaster. As Mecca continued to expand
and the number of traders passing through it increased, deity representation became of paramount significance for each tribe, placing a burden
upon the worthiness of each individual icon. Consequently, a competitive
element characteristic of old tribal allegiances eventually led to conflicts

---

29. Mahmood Ibrahim, *Merchant Capital* (1990:41-42); see also Eric Wolf,
"Social Organization" (1951:337-39)
30. Ibrahim, *Merchant Capital* (1990:55). The careful studies of M.J. Kister
shed much light on the *Jahiliyya* period (Muslims use this word to mean "age of
ignorance" before Islam). See especially her essays "*Labbayka, allahumma,
labbayka:* On a monotheistic aspect of a Jahiliyya practice," in her *Society and
Religion from Jahiliyya to Islam*, Aldershot, Hampshire, Great Britain: Variorum Gower Publishing Group (1990a).
31. See Ira Lapidus, "Tribe and State Formation" (1990:25-47).
32. Malise Ruthven, *Islam in the World* (1984:51).

and outright violence concerning, for instance, whose deity should be placed in the center of the Ka'ba, or above the others.[33]

In 605, approximately five years before his first revelation, Muhammad witnessed such a clash in his hometown of Mecca. Ibn Ishaq, writing a few generations after the Prophet's death, gives an account of the event:

> The Quraysh decided to rebuild the Ka'ba when the Apostle was 35 years of age....They were planning to roof it and feared to demolish it, for it was made of loose stones above a man's height, and they wanted to raise it and roof it because men had stolen part of the treasure of the Ka'ba which used to be in a well in the middle of it....Now a ship belonging to a Greek merchant had been cast ashore at Jidda and became a total wreck. They took its members and got them ready to roof the Ka'ba. It happened that in Mecca there was a Copt who was a carpenter, so everything they needed was ready at hand...
>
> The tribes of the Quraysh gathered stones for the building, each tribe collecting them and building by itself until the building was finished up to the black stone, where controversy arose, each tribe wanting to lift it to its place, until they went their several ways, formed alliances and got ready for battle. The Banu Abd al-Dar brought a bowl full of blood, then they and the Banu Adi ibn Ka'b pledged themselves unto death and thrust their hands into the blood. For this reason they called themselves the "blood-lickers." Such was the state of affairs for four or five nights, and the Quraysh gathered in the mosque and took counsel and were equally divided on the question.
>
> A traditionist alleged that Abu Umaya ibn al-Mughira, who was at that time the oldest man of the Quraysh, urged them to make the first man to enter the gate of the mosque umpire in the matter of the dispute. They did so and the first one to come in was the Apostle of God. When they saw him they said, "This is the trustworthy one. We are satisfied. This is Muhammad."

---

33. On the complexity of tribal representation preceding Muhammad's reforms, see M.J. Kister, "*Labbayka, allahumma, labbayka*" (1990a:33-57).

When they came to him and informed him of the matter,
he said, "Give me a cloak," and when they brought it to
him, he took the black stone and put it inside it and said
that each tribe should take hold of an end of the cloak
and they should lift it together. They did this so that
when they got it into position he placed it with his own
hand, and then building went on above it.[34]

Such occurrences must have demonstrated to Muhammad that the
tribal social structure had not only failed to resolve ever-escalating numbers of social conflicts, but in fact had aggravated them. This disequilib-
rium posed several threats to society, especially to merchant-clan leaders,
who had the most to lose from social violence. It is in this milieu that
Muhammad appeared as a man "singularly inspired, a prophet who articulated the problems of his society and in the process founded a new
religion with an institutional framework relevant to the solution of the
social, political, and economic problems that impeded the progress of
Mecca's merchants."[35] To this end he would introduce the so-called Constitution of Medina in which he would outline his vision of the *umma*.[36]
Here, he would propose to do away with the tribal order once and for all,
replacing it with a system that, unlike the existing one, was not based on
exclusivity.

Muhammad designed his platform with the specific intention of tear-
ing down such barriers between rival tribes and replacing adherence to
the antiquated social unit with a deeper and universal loyalty to the Islamic *umma*.[37] Having been raised precisely within this crisis period of
Arabia, Muhammad emerged organically from within it with a forceful
capacity for introducing relevant solutions to current dilemmas. He thus
formally advanced, through his conception of Islam, an ideological and

34. Ibn Ishaq's account as cited by F.E. Peters, *Muhammad and the Origins of
Islam*, Albany, New York: SUNY Press (1994:139-40). The account given by
al-Azraqi is more concise: "The four factions among the Quraysh each built its
own side. It was on that occasion that the door, formerly on ground level, was
raised. When it was time to replace the stone they had to summon 'Amin,' the
trustworthy Muhammad, to adjudicate. He used his mantle as described by ibn
Ishaq and all were satisfied," cited in Peters (1994:140).
35. Mahmood Ibrahim, *Merchant Capital* (1990:75).
36. On the significance of the Constitution of Medina, see Hamid Dabashi, *Authority in Islam: From the Rise of Muhammad to the Establishment of the
Umayyads*, New Brunswick, New Jersey: Transaction Publication (1989).
37. Malise Ruthven, *Islam in the World* (1984:100).

institutional superstructure that invoked substantial transformations of the society in a manner that was consonant with these new circumstances.[38]

Upon an examination of the Qur'an and the excellent biographical accounts written shortly after Muhammad's death, two important details surface in characterizing him: first, as discussed, is his role as a mediator of tribal conflicts in Mecca, prior to his conversion; second, is his birth into a Meccan tribe that was well placed in the caravan trade of Arabia (the Quraysh) and his marriage to a woman of wealth (Khadija).

As Ruthven has noted, little is known about Muhammad's early life that is of historical value, distinct from such mythically or theologically significant material as "stories of impressive encounters with holy men who instantly recognized the young Muhammad's spiritual destiny, and tales about the angelic surgeons who opened up his breast and 'cleaned his heart' before replacing it with a purified one."[39] Nonetheless, such anecdotes provide interesting details. One of Muhammad's reported encounters with holy men, for instance, occurred near Bostra with a Syrian Christian hermit, the monk Bahira.[40] Of interest here is not the monk's prediction of Muhammad's destiny to become the next prophet, but the fact that Muhammad is to be found as far north as Syria,[41] which may provide a clue regarding exposure in light of his conversion to monotheism.

At the age of twenty-five, he married a wealthy forty-year-old Qurayshi woman who provided the means for his future business efforts. By marrying up on the tribal ladder, Muhammad had gained the opportunity to assume a vocation that was central to the changing tribal land-

---

38. Mahmood Ibrahim, *Merchant Capital* (1990); see also Maxine Rodinson, *Muhammad*, New York: Pantheon (1990), Tor Andrae, *Mohammed: The Man and His Faith*, New York: Harper (1960), and Marshall Hodgson, *The Ventures of Islam: Conscience and History in a World Civilization*, 3 vols., Chicago and London: University of Chicago Press (1974) for relevant discussions on this theme. Hodgson, in particular, examines an "Axial Age" that marks a period in which a "cumulatively increasing geographical network of commercial and cultural interchange" (vol. 1:114) emerges. Of interest is his discussion of its effect upon the Afro-Eurasian *oikoumene* and upon the life of Muhammad.

39. Malise Ruthven, *Islam in the World* (1984:55).

40. For the accounts of this meeting see Maxine Rodinson (1980:46-47).

41. His actual physical presence in Syria has never been verified, but the mere fact that his contemporaries suggest such a possibility hints at the likelihood that Meccans were in regular contact with the northern regions.

scape. Involvement in trade afforded him a view of the current crisis
from within its very heart, a vantage point without which he might never
have been in a position to respond to it the way that he did. His travels,
during this time of transition, had on many occasions placed him in precarious situations, some quite dangerous, ultimately leading him to consider the tribal structure under which he functioned as an obstacle to the
current regional developments that marked his profession. Illustrating
this further, Montgomery Watt relates the following story:

> Shortly before 590 we have an account of an event that
> Muhammad was involved in which demonstrates the
> kind of conflicts he must have experienced on his cara-
> van routes. In that year there was a series of battles,
> known as the Wicked War, and at one or more of these
> Muhammad was present accompanying his uncles. This
> war began with a quarrel between two nomadic chiefs,
> one of whom was convoying a caravan from Iraq
> through the territory of the other to a great twenty-day
> fair held annually at Ukaz, not far from Mecca. The sec-
> ond felt slighted, and ambushed and killed the first. Be-
> fore long the Meccans were dragged into this conflict
> and a series of violent battles occurred.[42]

Of interest here is the fact that the conflict arose on the caravan route
over the movement of goods through *tribal territory*. Although he seems
not to have been a participant in this dispute, such episodes provided
Muhammad with a firsthand experience of the fragility of doing business
in this environment and must have led him, as a merchant himself, traveling across long stretches of territory, to question the quality of the tribal
and clan system as it was.

Muhammad would later use a variety of methods to transcend such
markers of division. One of his most innovative practices, for example,
was the *salaat*, or prayer. As Ruthven observes, the old kinship groups of
Arabia had been reinforced by all sorts of subtle physical traits so that an
individual's membership in a particular tribe might be determined by a
special gesture. Muhammad introduced the *salaat* as a way of breaking
the link between the individual and his tribe. "By subjecting itself at

---

42. Montgomery Watt, *Muhammad: Prophet and Statesman*, London: Oxford
University Press (1974:8). For a slightly different account of this event, see F.E.
Peters, *Muhammad* (1994:135).

regular daily intervals to a series of identical and physical actions," Ruthven argues, "the *Umma* subsumed the particularism of tribal or racial identity in a common physical discipline."[43] Muhammad instituted this interruption of ordinary activities at least three times daily (later to become five), which served believers as a reminder of the superior claims of God and community over those of tribal allegiance. The institution of the *salaat*, therefore, was intended to provide a new field of loyalty that would smooth out the transition to a more universalistic consciousness. A further method of distinction came in the implementation of a complete ban and removal of idolatry. In this area, Muslims would express a closer identification with similar Jewish views and practices than with Christian ones, relatively tolerant of iconography, but while the ancient Israelites had banned deity representations in resistance of universalistic world empires, Muhammad did so in a transcendental fashion, negating particularistic Arab social formations in order to establish a new universalistic social order.

Such practices as the *salaat* were essential to the creation of the supertribal *umma*, loyal only to Allah. In its intended capacity to overcome particularistic, flesh-centric systems of identity, the role of the *umma* was equivalent to that of the church, in its Pauline form, as it subsumed all other allegiances symbolized by tribal rituals and customs within a new superseding loyalty to a universal community. Bringing them into the liturgy, Muhammad freed local rituals from their seasonal connections, instituting the *Hajj*, for example, as a rite to be performed at any time of the year, based upon the simple principle of a single ·cosmic deity that remained consistent throughout the passage of time.[44] Even the use of the word *Allah* to signify God fits this pattern of appropriation: as an abstract term, it was common to all pre-Islamic tribes, each having referred ·to its own deity as "the god,"[45] while ascribing it a specific qualifying name and distinct representative symbols. Muhammad thus stripped the multiple specificities attached to this term to unmask its deeper universal significance as an analogy that suggested allegiance to the *umma* over the tribe. Muhammad seems to have had an intuitive sense for transforming known rituals in such a manner that could potentially form a universal language composed of orchestrated bodily movements (*salaat*), shared practices (*Hajj*), and a synchronized calendar.

---

43. Malise Ruthven, *Islam in the World* (1984:83).
44. Ibid. (1984:47).
45. Ibid. (1984:113).

During his final years, in 630 and again in 632, after finally defeating the Qurayshi tribe, Muhammad made a pilgrimage to Mecca, completing his mission. Upon entering the renewed Holy City, the Prophet walked up to the Ka'ba and touched it with his stick, proclaiming out loud "Allahu Akbar" (God is Great). Immediately upon entering the sacred *haram*, he ordered the idols to be thrown down from their pedestals. Then, according to ibn Ishaq's account, he gave one of his last great sermons:

> "There is no god but God alone; He has no associates. He has made good His promise and helped His servant. He alone has put to flight the confederates. Every claim of privilege or blood or property are abolished by me except the custody of the shrine and the watering of the pilgrims... O Quraysh, God has taken from you the haughtiness of paganism and its veneration of ancestors. Man springs from Adam and Adam from dust." Then he recited them this verse: "O men, we created you male and female and made you into peoples and tribes that you may know one another; in truth, the most noble of you in God's sight is the most pious."[46]

Rejection of the idols not only entailed a denial of their divine attributes, but also of the authority that had developed around them in Mecca. Hence, "distinctions based on lineage, with the elimination of idolatry, would wither away because the values inherent in the system itself were based on virtues and values inherent in group lineage."[47] According to the respective Qur'anic passages, a value system free from notions of lineage clearly was to be applied universally, because Allah was the God of all creation.

As a result of Muhammad's efforts, for the first time in its history, Arabia had been unified: "This unprecedented political unity was the first fruits of the new religious system, under which allegiance to Allah and his Prophet overrode all prior allegiances based on tribal or family ties."[48] All aspects of the community's life were synchronized, from the movements of bodies as represented in the *salaat*, to the multiple reli-

---

46. Ibn Ishaq, "*Sirat Rasul Allah*," cited in F.E. Peters, *Muhammad* (1994:236-37).
47. Mahmood Ibrahim, *Merchant Capital* (1984:83).
48. Malise Ruthven, *Islam in the World* (1984:91).

gious acts members were required to perform, most significantly the *Hajj*. The new practices served in unison to generate an orderly and co-ordinated *umma*, restructuring the space-time concepts of localized towns, villages, and regions to produce one massive and unified social entity. This new solidarity embodied by the *umma* ignited the way to what would be the most remarkable of Islam's historic achievements— the overnight conquest of the Sassanid Empire in its entirety and of portions of the Byzantine Empire, including Syria and Egypt.[49]

PAUL AND MUHAMMAD DE-CENTER JERUSALEM

The clearest expression of transcending "Israel in the flesh" can be found in both Paul's and Muhammad's marginalization of Jerusalem in favor of Rome and Mecca, respectively. Transplanting Jerusalem from its soil in Palestine and transferring it to Rome and Mecca was first and foremost a political project designed to address the needs of Paul's and Muhammad's communities.

In the case of Paul, a reformulation of notions of Land was essential to his effort. The Jews of his day inextricably bound their conception of Land with the city and Temple of Jerusalem. Paul, disturbed by the exclusive policies that accompanied this model, envisioned an a-territorial derivative of the Temple with his formulation of a divine Church. In his scheme, space as a territorial divide was rendered immaterial to a true understanding of holiness, in which terrestrial claims of ownership became "transubstantiated," so to speak, into an open community of persons that comprised the Body of Christ.[50]

His momentous decision to bring an uncircumcised Greek into the Temple courts was central to this endeavor, as it called into question the utilization of circumcision as a basis for the exclusion of Gentiles from the Temple. As a result of his intentional violation, he would be attacked, ridiculed, arrested, and finally, executed:

> When the seven days were nearly over, some Jews from
> the province of Asia saw Paul at the temple. They stirred
> up the whole crowd and seized him, shouting, "Men of
> Israel, help us! This is the man who teaches all men

---

49. Ibid. (1984:91).
50. See W.D. Davies, *The Gospel and the Land: Early Christianity and Jewish Territorial Doctrine*, Berkeley: University of California Press (1974:185-86).

everywhere against our people and our law and this place. And besides, he has brought Greeks into the temple area and defiled this holy place.".…The whole city was aroused, and the people came running from all directions. Seizing Paul, they dragged him from the temple, and immediately the gates were shut.[51]

As a Hellenized Jew, born and raised in Tarsus, Paul was exposed to sacred sites that were open to public use and rarely the property of a single people. The spread of sacred sites throughout the Greco-Roman world was an intricate web of power symbols that served to connect peripheral elements with an imperial center. The Temple in Jerusalem thus posed a thorn in this network that discomfited not only Greeks and Romans but, more importantly, Hellenized Jews such as Paul himself. As Jews were diffused throughout the Greco-Roman urban centers, they faced a radically different, far more cosmopolitan social and political environment than did Jews living in Palestine.[52] Paul was a product of this environment and his early exposure to various Greek cities seems to have been a major contributing factor to his acceptance of Christianity.[53] By the time of Paul's birth, several centuries of increased interaction between Jewish and Greco-Roman, Hellenistic culture had produced many unforeseen innovations of which Pauline Christianity would later become the most striking example.[54]

The religious and mythic symbols that the early Christians used, as exemplified by Paul, allowed them to define and negotiate a relationship with the larger Greco-Roman community. An elastic and incorporative approach to defining sacred space provided a significant formula for this

---

51. Acts 21:27-30.
52. Daniel Boyarin, *A Radical Jew* (1994:25); Rodney Stark, *The Rise of Christianity*, San Francisco: Harper (1997).
53. See Alan F. Segal, *Paul the Convert: The Apostolate and Apostasy of Saul the Pharisee*, New Haven, Connecticut: Yale University Press (1990).
54. Rodney Stark places supreme emphasis on this thesis: "Jews had adjusted to life in the diaspora in ways that made them very marginal vis-à-vis the Judaism of Jerusalem. As early as the third century B.C.E., their Hebrew had decayed to the point that the Torah had to be translated into Greek. The Jews outside Palestine read, wrote, spoke, thought, and worshiped in Greek. Many in the diaspora had taken Greek names, and they had incorporated much of the Greek enlightenment into their cultural views. In short, large numbers were no longer Jews in the ethnic sense and remained only partly so in the religious sense." Stark, *The Rise of Christianity* (1997:57-58)

process in that it navigated the Christian community of the first two centuries to come to terms with its surrounding environment and to find its place within it.

For people living within the bounds of the Roman Empire, a sacred sense of geography in the form of "mental maps" served as a predominant form of social orientation, maintaining boundaries between persons "inside" and "outside" a given zone. Such forms acted as negotiating agents in a local community's relationship with imperial, regional, and cosmic networks of power.[55] The further outward symbolism radiated from its local environment and the more groups it encompassed within the empire, the more prestige and power it received in the imperial hierarchy of deity worship. As Douglas Edwards observes:

> When a symbol transcended its geographical location, it could interact with ancient society through the promotion of insiders or from the recognition of outsiders. Fundamental was the degree of power (local, regional, imperial, cosmic) that a religion or cult was perceived to wield by its promoters, its adherents, and outsiders.[56]

Sacred geography, therefore, was an important component of this imperial cult complex, allowing local elites to "participate in the divinely sanctioned power of Rome."[57] It was the symbolic vehicle by which power flowed both into and out of the imperial center, linking the periphery with its core. Rome was thus accorded validating representations at its peripheral reach, while simultaneously distributing prestige and status to local elites who put them in place. Aphrodite of Aphrodisias, Artemis of Ephesus, Mithras, Isis, Men, and Dionysus are all good examples of deity localization that served to legitimate peripheral communities while establishing Roman imperial authority.

---

55. On this issue, see the work of Douglas R. Edwards, *Religion and Power: Pagans, Jews, and Christians in the Greek East*, New York: Oxford University Press (1996). See also S.R.F. Price, *Rituals and Power: The Roman Imperial Cult in Asia Minor*, Cambridge, Massachusetts: Cambridge University Press (1984); Gerhart B. Ladner, *God, Cosmos, and Humankind: The World of Early Christian Symbolism*, Berkeley: University of California Press (1992); Susan E. Alcock, *Graecia Capta: The Landscapes of Roman Greece*, Cambridge and New York: Cambridge University Press (1993).
56. Douglas Edwards, *Religion and Power* (1996:73).
57. Ibid. (1996:79).

The most outstanding feature of these symbols of power is the fact that they were not site specific, possessing an anti-territorial quality essential to holy sites that were intended to receive dedications from regions far from their initial source, a quality Christians would later exploit. An inscription of Artemis, for example, dated at 162-164, demonstrates that such deities were in fact distributed throughout the *oikoumene*:

> The deity over our city, Artemis, is honored not only in her city which she has made more famous than all other cities through her own divinity, but also by Greeks and foreigners; everywhere shrines and sanctuaries have been dedicated, temples founded and altars erected to her because of her vivid manifestations.[58]

The widespread presence of such deities as Artemis suggests that the proponents of each deity were very interested in transcending their locality, preferring to create symbols that were flexible rather than spatially or socially limited. Thus unsurprisingly, the deities that were distributed throughout the empire were those that stressed traditions and customs commonly held by all, while, conversely, those attributes that were peculiar to a small sector of the population were marginalized, if not eliminated all together.

Paul and his followers drew upon such dynamics, creating the basis for a community whose existence itself embodied an a-territorial Church that could potentially be represented anywhere and that anyone could join or visit. Whereas many Jews of his time viewed the Temple in Jerusalem as the central dwelling place of God, Paul stressed that the Divine presence was not confined within the Temple, but to be found in every place.[59] Hence, his notion of Church shared the pagan quality of worship as nonspecific regarding location and, more importantly, as free of any affiliation with an ethnic group. His novel departure from the politics-as-usual deity worship of the Roman Empire, however, was in locating the presence of Divinity not within a spatial representation, a quality that the Temple of Jerusalem actually shared with the Roman-pagan system of shrines, but instead, within the community itself as a whole.

---

58. Translated in S.R.F. Price, *Rituals and Power* (1984:130-31) and Douglas Edwards, *Religion and Power* (1996:74).
59. W.D. Davies, *The Gospel and the Land* (1974:188).

Paul's vision of a Heavenly Jerusalem, free from its false, earthly and ethnically dominated representations, served as the initial step in this direction, although it was the cause of many conflicts between the Apostles.[60] Early in its life, the Church would struggle greatly in its efforts to characterize a unified vision and mission. Many would follow in the tradition of Paul, Origen (185-253) of Alexandria being a prominent example as one of the first great theologians of Christianity. Over time, these early Christians would come to develop a route that led not to Jerusalem, but further yet from their Jewish prototype, straight into the heart of that other sacred center, imperial Rome.

***

From the perspective of understanding intention and motive, Muhammad's decision, expressed in the Qur'an, to uproot "the House of God" from its Palestinian soil in Jerusalem and re-plant it in Mecca shares several characteristics with that of the parallel Christian experience. However, it is largely misunderstood today, viewed through the lens of modern conflicts. Historians of Islam, especially those of Jewish and Christian background, such as Montgomery Watt and H.A.R. Gibb, usually situate this modification in the context of Muhammad's struggle with the Jewish tribes of Medina. Such arguments are built upon the fact that the Jews of Medina would not accept Muhammad as an authentic prophet, mocking him at times for making such claims. These accounts portray a reactive and defiant Muhammad, diverging from Jewish tradition by changing the direction of prayer from Jerusalem to Mecca.

As an alternative to this interpretation, it seems as easily conceivable that Muhammad's decision to de-center Jerusalem in favor of Mecca fit neatly into his grand strategy to usher monotheism into Arabia. In this sense, it is his desire to persuade Mecca to accept his vision that serves as a primary motivating factor, rather than his strategizing a break with the local Jews.

In his book, *Islam*, Fazlur Rahman contends that the argument advanced by many Western historians, "simply exaggerates the role of Medinese Jewry on Islam's development and on this point particularly fails

---

60. For more on this theme see the interesting overview of early Christianity by W.H.C. Frend, *The Rise of Christianity*, Philadelphia: Fortress Press (1984), especially chs. 3-4; Paula Fredriksen, *From Jesus to Christ: The Origins of the New Testament Images of Jesus,* New Haven, Connecticut: Yale University Press (1988).

to distinguish cause from effect."[61] Rahman insists that the change in direction of prayer is primarily instituted within the context of Muhammad's larger project of unifying the Arab tribes and that the dispute between the Jews of Medina and Muhammad is marginal, at best, to his intentions. Most tribes of his time, including those of Medina, centered their religious activities within the Meccan sanctuary, not the one in Jerusalem. Retaining Jerusalem as the sacred center of Islam would have alienated many of the tribes. In this respect, the magnetic hold that Mecca had over most Arabs is thematically far more important to his project than is his dispute with the Medinese Jewish tribes. A keen observer of his surroundings, Muhammad must surely have understood that an incorporation of Mecca into the Islamic project would receive substantially greater support from other tribes and that situating Mecca at the heart of the new faith would generate far greater respect and acceptance than would a distant Jerusalem.

Muhammad's decision to change the direction of prayer receives extensive treatment, both in the Qur'an and in later commentaries. The Qur'an illustrates the following interaction between God and Muhammad:

> The foolish among the people will say, "What has turned them away from the direction of prayer toward which they formerly prayed?" Say: "To God belongs the East and the West, and He guides whom He wills in the straight way"...Thus we have made you a community of the middle path in order that you may witness over humankind and that the Messenger be a witness over you. We appointed the prayer-direction to which you formerly prayed only to make known those who follow the Messenger and those who would turn back on their heels....We have seen you turning your face about toward heaven. We shall therefore direct you toward a prayer-direction which would please you. Turn your face toward the Sacred House of Worship; wherever you may be, turn your faces toward it. As for those who were given the Scriptures, they know well that it is the truth from their Lord, nor is God unaware of what they do. (Qur'an 2:142-44)

---

61. Fazlur Rahman, *Islam*, Chicago: University of Chicago Press (1979:20).

Later commentators wrote much about this change. Al-Tabari takes the many versions available to him and condenses them into one:

> The first injunction which was abrogated in the Qur'an was that concerning the direction of the prayer. This is because the Prophet used to prefer the Rock of the Holy House of Jerusalem, which was the prayer-direction of the Jews. The Prophet faced it for seventeen months in the hope that they would believe in him and follow him. Then God said: "Say, 'To God belong the east and the west....'"[62]

According to Ruthven, Muhammad could not accept the biblical texts as they stood in their Christian and Judaic formulations. The accounts and details of the Old and New Testaments seemed too remote from the daily concerns of the Arabia he knew. In this respect, he understood the need to "Arabize" them by deriving a form that would speak to local interests, addressing such issues as family, divorce, inheritance, and business ethics in a manner relevant to his time and place.[63] Hence, even though there were plenty of Christian and Jewish communities from which he could have directly "borrowed" in formulating his universalistic paradigm shift, this likely would not have been enough. Ruthven elaborates further:

> For a thinking man, of course, there was the alternative of religion. There is evidence that some of Muhammad's contemporaries, or near contemporaries, adopted Christianity.... Many former nomads adopted Judaism....Both Christianity and Judaism, however, entailed adherence to scriptures in foreign languages, involving an admission of cultural inferiority which most Arabs, who were rightly proud of their linguistic heritage, found unacceptable.[64]

If Muhammad had left the central symbolic source of monotheism in Jerusalem, the impact of his message upon the imagination of local inhabi-

---

62. Al-Tabari as cited in F.E. Peters, *Muhammad and the Origins of Islam* (1994:209).
63. The spiritual journey that Muhammad undertook is captured brilliantly by Maxine Rodinson, especially the chapter "The Birth of a Prophet" (1980:38-68).
64. Malise Ruthven, *Islam in the World* (1984:58).

tants would have seemed bland to say the least. The characters and story-lines found in biblical scriptures were intended to inspire the cultures of ancient Israel and the Greco-Roman world, not those of the Arabian heartland. Muhammad directly adapted monotheism to Arabia by liter-ally locating the characters and settings of biblical stories in an Arabian context. In his account, for instance, the House of God is removed from its Judean setting and placed within Mecca; Abraham, his maidservant, Hagar, and their son, Ishmael, at God's command, are recorded to have left Egypt only to show up in Mecca. In the process of introducing mono-theism into the Arabian landscape, therefore, he not only revised biblical scriptures, but physically relocated their sacred center at his town's door-step.

Theologically speaking, his approach toward biblical texts required a degree of caution. Like his predecessor, Muhammad devised a variety of allegorical stunts, some of which were exceptionally similar to Paul's. For instance, in the context of his effort to permit the entry of Gentiles into the Church without having them first undergo a conversion to Juda-ism, Paul argues the following:

> Is this blessedness only for the circumcised, or also for the uncircumcised? We have been saying that Abra-ham's faith was credited to him as righteousness. Under what circumstances was it credited? Was it after he was circumcised, or before? It was not after, but before! And he received the signs of circumcision, a seal of the righteousness that he had faith *while he was still uncir-cumcised.* So then, *he is the father of all who believe but have not yet been circumcised*, in order that righteous-ness be credited to them. And he is also the father of the circumcised who not only are circumcised but who also walk in the footsteps of the faith that our father Abraham had before he was circumcised. (Romans 4:9-12; empha-sis added)

By comparison, in the Qur'an, Muhammad declares:

> O people of the Book, why dispute about Abraham? The Torah and the Gospel *were sent down after him*: Do you not understand? Neither was Abraham a Jew or a Christian, but upright and obedient. (Qur'an 3:65-67; emphasis added)

Common to both of these accounts is the attempt to link Abraham, the father of the faithful, to a religious doctrine that is all-encompassing. Paul chose circumcision, because it epitomized "Israel in the flesh" for him and if he could demonstrate that even Abraham was uncircumcised when God had spoken to him, then he could logically posit that any uncircumcised Gentile could become a believer in Christ and directly connect with God. Similarly, Muhammad suggested that if Abraham had received his Divine message prior to the existence of Scripture, then it followed that neither Jewish nor Christian doctrine enjoyed a monopoly of God, and that anyone who thus submitted to Divinity could receive God's message. Muhammad elaborates further on this theme:

> They say: "Become Jews or become Christians, and find the right way." Say: "No. We follow the way of Abraham the upright.".…Say: "We believe in God and what has been sent down to us, and what had been revealed to Abraham and Ishmael and Isaac and Jacob and their progeny, and that which was given to Moses and Christ, and to all other prophets by the Lord. *We make no distinction among them*, and we submit to Him." (Qur'an 2:135-36; emphasis added)

While Muhammad and Paul share methodical similarities in interpreting the Old Testament, Muhammad begins to diverge radically from Christian innovation in his transformations of the stories contained within it. The Qur'an, explicitly identifying them as the builders of God's House, locates Abraham and his son Ishmael in Mecca, fulfilling God's commandment to construct the Ka'ba there:

> Remember We made the House a place of assembly (*mathaba*) for the people and a secure place; and take the station (*maqam*) of Abraham as a prayer-place (*musalla*); and We have made a pact with Abraham and Ishmael that they should sanctify My House for those who circumambulate it, those using it as a retreat (*'aqifun*), who bow or prostrate themselves there . . . And remember Abraham raised the foundations of the House, yes and Ishmael too, saying accept this from us, for indeed You are All-hearing and All-Knowing. (Qur'an 2:125-27)

This is an obvious departure from the original scriptures. In Genesis, Abraham, Hagar, and Ishmael are last seen together in Egypt. Sarah, Abraham's wife, is growing old and cannot seem to bear a child, so she offers Hagar, her maidservant, to Abraham and shortly thereafter, his first son, Ishmael, is born. Then, surprisingly, Sarah conceives Isaac and a dispute emerges over who will receive the inheritance. Concerned with her son's future, Sarah demands that Hagar and Ishmael be banished from the town. Abraham then, at God's command, takes them into the desert of Beersheba, where God promises Abraham: "I will make the son of the maidservant into a nation also, because he is your offspring" (Genesis 21:13). Here ends the story, leaving no clues as to what will happen to Ishmael and Hagar.

From this account, an arrival in Mecca seems mysterious. Muhammad must have understood the need to fill this gap. According to an account provided by the Islamic historian Ibn al-Tabari (923), Abraham, Hagar, and Ishmael embark upon a lengthy journey to Mecca through the Hijaz of Western Arabia:

> Sarah said to Abraham, "You may take pleasure in Hagar, for I have permitted it." So he had intercourse with Hagar and she gave birth to Ishmael. Then he had intercourse with Sarah and she gave birth to Isaac. When Isaac grew up, he and Ishmael fought. Sarah became angry and jealous of Ishmael's mother....Sarah said, "She will not live in the same town with me."

At this point, the account diverges radically from its original:

> God told Abraham to go to Mecca, where there was no House at the time. He took Hagar and her son to Mecca and put them there....When God pointed out to Abraham the place of the House and told him how to build the sanctuary, he set out to do the job and Gabriel went with him. It was said that whenever he passed a town he would ask, "Is this the town which God's command meant, O Gabriel?" And Gabriel would say: "Pass it by." At last they reached Mecca...The House at that time was but a hill of red clay. Abraham said to Gabriel, "Was it here that I was ordered to leave them?" Gabriel

said, "Yes." Abraham directed Hagar and Ishmael to go to the Hijr, and settled them down there.[65]

In this manner, then, Qur'anic modifications of ancient accounts coupled with later interpretive renditions form the basis for a clear vision of Mecca's origins and that of its Ka'ba, offering a comprehensive context for the redirection of prayer and the centrality of Mecca to Abrahamic, monotheistic tradition.

II
Christians and Muslims Transform Jerusalem

Under the watchful eye and intimidating designs of the Roman Empire, prior to its marriage with a maturing Christianity, Jerusalem entered an age of dramatic transformation. Renamed Aelia Capitolina, following the destruction of its Temple in 70 C.E., the Romans wasted little time renovating Jerusalem, quickly eliminating the very symbols ancient Israelites had used to keep the empire at a distance. In place of them, Romans arrogantly exhibited their own imperial symbols at important Jewish sites.[66] The Old Temple Mount, for example, became the location of a temple dedicated to Jupiter; a temple to Aphrodite was built "beside the western forum on the site of the Golgotha hill."[67] Officially, the Romans declared their own religion as that of the city's, delivering the unmistakable message that Rome was here to stay. Aelia quickly became "an entirely pagan, gentile city, indistinguishable from any other Roman colonial settlement,"[68] where imperial, universalistic, and image-ready gods supplanted the tribal, particularistic, and abstract God of the Hebrews.

The Roman Christian Empire would later continue this policy with the exception that the God of the Old Testament would once again be welcomed as a legitimate Deity; albeit with a new look not all too unfamiliar to the pagans of Rome. Thus, although the process of enshrining Jerusalem and the Holy Land with the symbolism of the old Jewish Deity

---

65. Al-Tabari's *Tarikh al-Muslimiin* is an extensive and fascinating multivolume history of Islam. This citation is from F.E. Peters, *Muhammad* (1994:2-3).
66. See Doron Mendels, *The Rise and Fall of Jewish Nationalism: Jewish and Christian Ethnicity in Ancient Palestine*, New York: Eerdmans Publishing (1992:333-84).
67. Karen Armstrong, *Jerusalem* (1996:165).
68. Ibid. (1996:166).

seemed to reflect continuity with Judaic traditions, it was not expressed as a return to Jewish roots. Instead, Christian rulers strategically conducted this endeavor in such a manner as to eliminate any sense of Jewish flavor that lingered in the city. Indeed, the Christian remapping of the Holy Land was a process based upon the negation of traditional Jewish sites. The Old Temple's remaining walls, for example, were intentionally left to deteriorate and the entrance that came to be known as the "Dung Gate" was used not as a sacred space, but as a center for waste deposit. The Church of the Holy Sepulcher, the Stations of the Cross, and all the new sites of this now imperially sponsored religion were strategically located so as to demonstrate that the Jews had been superseded by a superior community. Illustrating this further, one of the oldest known maps of Jerusalem (the Madaba map, dated 570 C.E.) found in present-day Jordan fails to include the Temple Mount and its remaining Western Walls, a clear expression of the deeply rooted antipathy that Christians felt toward the Jews.

This "return" to a worldly Jerusalem, in light of earlier notions of the city advanced by such figures as Paul and Origen, represented a theological obstacle. Christianity, as one biblical scholar notes, "originally had no holy places and for some three centuries continued to have none."[69] Such theological shifts as are found in the trading of a heavenly Jerusalem for a worldly one are suggestive of a larger paradigmatic shift embodied by imperial concerns of conquest. Consequently, a new rationalization emerged during this period of imperial absorption that silenced the New Testament's account of a Jewish Guilty City and, instead, placed the responsibility of guilt for the events surrounding Jesus's last days squarely on the shoulders of the Jews. Cyril, the bishop of Jerusalem in the fourth century, for example, made the deliberate distinction that *God had rejected the Temple, not the City of Jerusalem.*[70] Eusebius, heavily influenced by the emperor Constantine's wishes to claim Jerusalem as the empire's new sacred center, likewise spoke of a New Jerusalem composed of new Christian sites and Constantinian complexes that were "built over and against the old." In this way, as Karen Armstrong elucidates, "the New Jerusalem gave Christians yet another vantage point from which to contemplate the defeat of Judaism." This image was a visceral expression intended to "sanitize" Jewish presence, make the city

---

69. R.A. Markus, "How on Earth?" (1994:258).
70. See Robert Wilken, *The Land Called Holy: Palestine in Christian History and Thought*, New Haven and London: Yale University Press (1992:65-125).

wholly Christian, and free it from its Jewish past. As such, it captured the imagination of an emerging Christian identity that had at its center "a violent uprooting...a demonization of older traditions, and a contemptuous assertion of superiority over Judaism."[71] Empiric logic required that the city maintain a universalistic appeal and repress anything that smacked of a particularistic nature. Following Constantine's rule, the Roman Christian Empire remained loyal to this old imperial practice. Indeed, it went one step further by not permitting any local deity representations whatsoever.

Of paramount importance to the New Christian Jerusalem was an emphasis on the Resurrection of Christ. In fact, the Christian Empire's first major archeological dig was the "True Cross." Constantine had found in Christ's death and subsequent rise an attractive and dramatic marker that stimulated Christian focus upon the New Jerusalem, while blurring the Old Testament's hold over the Christian imagination. From the time of Constantine's conquest until that of the Muslim period, all of the archeological excavations that took place in the city would serve a similar function, unearthing bodies of saints in a manner that validated the current articulation of the region. Even when such digs retrieved figures from the Old Testament, Christians would remove them from their Jewish locations and place them within the topography of the New Jerusalem. By the sixth century, events traditionally ascribed to Mount Zion had been relocated to Golgotha and other significant New Jerusalem sites, a dramatic example having been the displacement of the altar upon which Abraham had intended to sacrifice his son Isaac.[72] Christian conversion of the city did not only reflect conquest in the abstract, but also a further de-fleshing of remaining ethnic and tribal affiliations with the Jews. In essence, the message of this New Jerusalem made it unmistakably clear that the sacred city was home to a universal, imperial Deity, not a particularistic one that belonged exclusively to the Jews.

Islam's conquest of Jerusalem in the seventh century provides a stark contrast to the Christian model. Muslims did not project a New Jerusalem onto an already extant sacred map of the city; in fact, they neither distanced themselves from Jerusalem's Jewish (or Christian) past, nor did they attempt to transcend "Israel in the Flesh" as had their Christian predecessors. To the contrary, in planting Islamic seeds there, Muslims

---

71. All the quotes in this paragraph are from Karen Armstrong, *Jerusalem* (1996:174-93).
72. Ibid. (1996:212-13).

worked diligently to revive Jerusalem, searching for ways of connecting with its ancestral past. Upon their very first years within the city, Caliphs resurrected many sites that had been wounded by the Christians and insisted upon the continued presence and viability of both Jewish and Christian sites. In essence, Muslims allowed space for notions of both "Israel in the spirit" and "Israel in the flesh," *as long as they were monotheistic in nature*, steering Jerusalem toward a more radical universalism than had yet been imagined.

An early example of this is a story about the Muslim Caliph 'Umar, in which, upon his entry of the newly conquered city in the mid-seventh century, he visited the Church of the Holy Sepulcher and opted not to pray inside it, fearing that the prayer inside might be interpreted as a sign to transform the church into a mosque. Instead, he exited the church and prayed in the courtyard. Soon thereafter, he dictated a charter which forbade the seizure or disturbance of any Christian or Jewish site.[73]

Still more telling is the Muslim resolve to build the al-Aqsa Mosque on top of the Temple Mount. Many contemporary Western scholars, particularly of Christian Fundamentalist and Zionist leanings, have mischaracterized this gesture as "an attack by Muslims" designed to replace the Temple Mount "with an Islamic shrine."[74] Such views describe an arrogant act that desecrated the holiest of sites with the intention of undermining its Jewish significance by generating a powerful symbol of the new Islamic Empire. Writings contemporaneous to the construction of this Mosque, however, reveal sentiments inconsistent with such an interpretation. Al-Walid ibn Muslim, documenting an early encounter of the Temple area, portrays 'Umar, horrified by the filth that filled it, ordering an immediate sanitization of the site, after which he renames it "the dungheap," as if to shame the Christians for their sacrilegious behavior. A fourteenth-century account elucidates further:

> There was over the Rock in the Holy City a great dung-heap which completely masked the prayer niche of David and which the Christians had put there in order to offend the Jews; and further, even the Christian women were wont to throw their (menstrual) cloths and clouts in place so that there was a pile of them there.... Now when Umar came to the Holy City and conquered it, and

---

73. S.D. Goitein, "Jerusalem in the Arab Period," *Jerusalem Cathedra*, vol. 2 (1982:168-96).
74. S.R.F. Price, *Rituals and Power* (1984:90).

saw how there was a dungheap over the Rock, he regarded it as horrible and ordered that the place be entirely cleaned....When Umar first exposed the Rock to
view by removing the dungheap, he commanded them
not to pray there until three showers of heavy rain should
have fallen.[75]

A few decades following the cleansing of the Temple Mount, the Caliph, Abd al-Malik, built the Dome of the Rock. Several accounts suggest
that this enterprise was not intended as a symbol of condescension toward the Jews, but as a *securing of Islam's continuity* with its Jewish
heritage. Muslims and Jews had acknowledged alike that the rock upon
which the Mosque was built marked the site of the Holy of Holies within
the Old Temple, an expression not of faiths colliding as in the previous
relationship between Jews and Christians, but of merging. Most stun-
ningly revelatory of this view are the chronicles of the Jewish Rabbi
Simeon ibn Yohai who approved of the construction. As Karen Armstrong persuasively argues,[76] he saw the building as a prelude to the messianic age and went so far as to praise the Caliph as "a lover of Israel"
who "had restored the breaches of Zion and the breaches of the Temple."
According to this Rabbi, the Caliph 'Umar "hews Mount Moriah and
makes it all straight and builds a mosque there on the Temple Rock."[77]

To further appreciate such developments, under Muhammad, Islam's
predominant concern was its conflict with local pagan tribes. Although
disputes had existed with Jewish tribes, Muhammad was thematically
moving toward them and away from tribal paganism. His Islam envisioned the creation of an empire at the expense of a paganism that was
naturally hostile to its central principle—a radically anti-tribal and universalistic entity as was the *umma*. Islam's greatest obstacle, therefore,
was neither Jew, nor Christian, but the tribal paganism of Arabia. By
contrast, Christianity had been formulated from its inception as a break
with "Israel in the flesh" and as a rebellion against Jewish exclusivity.
Early Christianity had been developed within a context of Jewish assimilation into an imperial culture that was hostile toward its basic principles.
Paul, exemplifying this reality, widened the doctrinal gap between Juda-

75. Quoted in F.E. Peters, *Muhammad* (1994:187-88).
76. Karen Armstrong, *Jerusalem* (1996:240).
77. Quoted in Ibid. (1996:240). Also see S.D. Goitein, "The Historical Background of the Erection of the Dome of the Rock," in *Journal of the American
Oriental Society* (1950:104-8).

ism and Christianity in order to attract non-Jews.[78] In this respect, Paul and "Christianity challenged the Jews' claim to divine election."[79] As Cohen further explains, Muslims had no reason to create a New Jerusalem:

> Genealogically, Arabs traced their descent from Ishmael, Abraham's first born son, the brother of Isaac. Chronologically, Arab peoplehood paralleled the peoplehood of Israel: Arabs and Jews had the same ancestor. The Ishmaelite branch simply had been dispersed for centuries, awaiting its revival and the fulfillment of its claim to centrality in history. This came with the advent of the Prophet Muhammad. Unlike Christianity, Islam felt no need to establish its identity at the expense of the Jews.[80]

Theologically, therefore, in contrast to Christianity, Islam did not represent itself as the divine fulfillment of Judaism. On the contrary, it viewed itself as a return to Abraham—the original pure monotheist. Indeed, the Qur'an (3:67) depicts Abraham as the first "Muslim" to submit to God.

This important distinction inspired within the Muslim imagination a notion of sacred space that was inclusive of its counterpart faiths. Logically then, its theological dictums could thus be conceived so as to allow the coexistence of the three Abrahamic religions on the same sacred ground. Islam shared the city of Jerusalem, providing each community with its own district and allowing them all to worship at their own special shrines, a sign of its vision of continuity and harmony with all rightly guided religions.[81] In this spirit, the Mosque built atop the Temple Mount in which stood the Holy of Holies demonstrated Islam's veneration of Abraham and, thus, its inextricable link to the other People of the Book, as Muhammad had referred to both Jews and Christians. Similarly, the great churches of Christianity and the remaining Jewish sites were not only guaranteed protection by the new conquerors, but were, in some

---

78. Marcel Simon, *Verus Israel: A Study of the Relation between Christians and Jews in the Roman Empire, 135-425*, New York: Oxford University Press (1996: 71-77).

79. Mark Cohen, *Under Crescent and Cross: The Jews in the Middle Ages*, Princeton, New Jersey: Princeton University Press (1994:18).

80. Ibid. (1994:25).

81. Karen Armstrong, *Jerusalem* (1996:245).

cases, viewed by the Muslims as an essential element of Jerusalem's sacredness.

Nowhere is this better illustrated than in Muhammad's famous Night Journey to Jerusalem. In the annals of the early Muslim commentator, al-Tabari describes the scene in which two angels approach Muhammad in his sleep and prepare him for the spiritual journey:

> At the time when the Prophet became a Prophet, he used to sleep around the Ka'ba [in Mecca]....On one occasion two angels, Gabriel and Michael, came...upon him as he slept, turned him on his back, and opened his breast. Then they brought water from Zamzam and washed away the doubt, or polytheism, or pre-Islamic beliefs, or error, which was in his breast. Then they brought a golden basin full of faith and wisdom, and his breast and belly were filled with faith and wisdom.[82]

After this purification, Muhammad was ready for passage:

> Then he was taken up to the earthly heaven. Gabriel asked for admittance, and they said, "Who is it?" "Gabriel," he said. "Who is with you?" they said. "Muhammad," he answered. "Has his mission commenced?" they asked. "Yes," he said. "Welcome," they said and called down God's blessing upon him.[83]

In this account of Muhammad's Ascension to heaven, he encounters a line of prophets that stem from both Hebrew and Christian Scriptures: first Adam, then John and Jesus, the Patriarch Joseph, the Prophet Idris (Enoch), Aaron and his brother, the Prophet Moses, and finally, Abraham, after which he is permitted to enter Paradise itself where, as the Qur'an (53:7) explains, he "reached the highest pinnacle."

As in the Resurrection of Christ from his Tomb, in which Jesus is said to have stayed in Jerusalem for forty days appearing several times to his Apostles and followers before entering heaven, Muhammad's spiritual form similarly soars above the Holy City. In the figure of Aisha, the Prophet's youngest wife, Islam shares with Christianity the notion of witness to spiritual movement, as she is known to have said: "the Apos-

---

82. Al-Tabari, *Annals*, vol. 1 (1988:1157), quoted in Peters, *Muhammad* (1994: 146).
83. Ibid. (1994:146).

tle's body remained where it was but God removed his spirit by night."[84] Here, however, thematic similarities between the two narratives diverge with Muhammad's introduction to his predecessors and with the subsequent return to his community in Mecca.

In Paul's understanding, the Resurrection symbolizes the end of "Israel in the flesh" and the beginning of "Israel in the spirit," such that a decisive break takes place between the Ancient Israelite notion of covenant and the newly envisioned Church. Circumcision, laws pertaining to *kashrut* (Jewish dietary laws), and other such practices that concern the body are thus deemed invalid. Further, the Temple and Jerusalem, seen as extensions of the body, suffer the same fate, superseded by a "Heavenly Jerusalem." By contrast, Muhammad's Ascension seems to necessitate, through contact with essential traditional figures, continuity with ancestral forms. The spirit does not negate and supersede the body through a spiritual rebirth; rather it unites those who have traveled upon the same path alongside God. Additionally, the earthly realm is validated through Muhammad's journey, as he descends from heaven and returns to Mecca, linking it directly with Jerusalem. Despite the central role of Mecca over Jerusalem in Islam, this remarkable story offers an unmistakable message of gratitude toward the prototypical Holy City for its historical development of lineage, without which the Prophet might never have possessed a context upon which to base his reception of Islam. Thus, Jerusalem, as both a heavenly and an earthly form, remains integral to the expression of Islam, suggesting a critical sense of continuity.

In this manner, early Islam not only demonstrates a far greater tolerance of Jews than has its predecessor, but it advances a universalist path greater than has previously been articulated. Sacred space is no longer the right of the Church at the expense of any who deny it, but it has been unfastened to include and validate all People of the Book (*'ahl al-Khataab*), thus granting legitimacy not only to rightly guided Muslims, but to all who proclaim the Oneness of God, regardless of the perceived accuracy of their liturgy and tradition.

---

84. Ibid. (1994:147).

III
The Crystallization of Empire:
Rome and Mecca in the Classical Period

Common to both the Christian and Islamic Empires, once firmly established, a migration took place that relocated each imperial administration far from its original location, launching a new imperial capital. Imperial Rome moved east to Constantinople, having left Rome to the Papacy; the Islamic Empire deserted Mecca for Damascus and Baghdad up north. As empires exercised direct rule over faraway colonies in the premodern world, strategizing distance was an essential component of maintaining control. Both empires thus, desiring a firm hold over Jerusalem, chose locations that were closer to the vicinity of Palestine than they were to their cities of origin.

In the case of Constantinople, its incorporation of Jerusalem into the empire came at the expense of a Rome that slowly seemed to be slipping away. As possession of Jerusalem grew to be much more secure, the city became an alternative claim to supremacy over that of Rome. From the perspective of the Papacy, as the eastern portion of the empire became a distant reality, its only claim to power centered on the assertions of the Apostles, and it would therefore develop a body of doctrine with the intention of maintaining its spiritual hegemony. From the perspective of Constantinople, it became apparent that with time Rome would be lost. Jerusalem thus became the central agent of splitting the empire's eastward focus from its westward one. As a result, the Byzantines, challenging Rome's traditional guardianship of heavenly access, would enshrine the True Cross and the remains of saints in churches throughout the Holy Land and Constantinople, while Rome continued its aggressive campaign to concretize its saintly origins.

Islam, by contrast, generated a centralized authority in Damascus and Baghdad, embodied in the Caliphate, which incorporated its spiritual qualities with its imperial ones. Thus, no competition existed in Islam between spiritual and secular power and Mecca, unlike Rome, did not possess an agency that could make counterclaims to the authority of Damascus/Baghdad. In this sense, Islam would not only diverge from Christianity theologically, but also in its imperial development.

ROME'S LONG ROAD TO SPIRITUAL HEGEMONY

*And I tell you that you are Peter, and on this rock I will build
my church....I will give you the keys of the kingdom of heaven;
whatever you bind on earth will be bound in heaven.*[85]

The great irony to be found in Rome's transformation into its Christian incarnation is that Christianity was not the initial cause of its conversion, as it can be more accurately argued that pagan Rome first converted
its Jews to Christianity, who in turn embarked on a mission that would
encapsulate pagan Rome. As five million Jews lived outside of Palestine
while only one million resided within at the time of the Crucifixion of
Jesus,[86] the influence of Greco-Roman culture upon the Jews was immense. This was especially the case in such major urban centers of the
empire as Alexandria, Corinth, Athens, Galatia, Antioch, and Damascus,
but by all accounts, the pressure upon Jews to assimilate was probably
felt most powerfully within Rome itself, which had a significant Jewish
population. Pagan symbols surrounded Jews across the empire's span,
but the scale of influence must have been most greatly inflated in Rome.
The pressure, even the need many Jews felt, to accept some of these
powerful symbols must have placed a tremendous burden on their Judaic
identities. Living in Rome, no space existed for the worship of Deities
that were defined in ethnic and exclusionary forms. Jews thus had to remain flexible, cosmopolitan, and, most of all, open to participating in the
synchronous style of worship that was the hallmark of imperial pagan
religion.

It was in the city of Rome that the imperial web of symbols, in magnificent variety, came together as in no other urban center. Rome was,
after all, the city that ruled the empire, which meant it was responsible
for upholding a universalistic appeal. "The city," as Lewis Mumford
elaborates, "[was] the point of maximum concentration for the power and
culture" it symbolized, a "place where the diffused rays of separate

---

85. Matthew 16:18-19.
86. Rodney Stark, *The Rise of Christianity* (1997:7). The original sources he
uses to calculate these numbers can be found in Paul Johnson, *A History of the
Jews*, New York: Harper Collins (1988), and Wayne Meeks, *The First Urban
Christians: The Social World of Apostle Paul*, New Haven, Connecticut: Yale
University Press (1983).

beams of life [fell] into focus."[87] It was there that the symbols of empire were joined together, giving expression to its unity; there that peripheral signs were collected and displayed, transforming them in the process to provide an ordered system. A pagan text contemporary of these early years of Christianity in the city further characterizes Rome:

> As her valor conquered cities and won her famous tri-
> umphs, Rome got herself countless gods; amid the
> smoking ruins of temples the victor's armed right hand
> took her enemies' images and carried them home in cap-
> tivity, worshipping them as divinities. One figure she
> seized from the ruins of Corinth by the two seas, another
> she took for booty from burning Athens; the defeat of
> Cleopatra gave her some dog-headed figures, and when
> she conquered the sands of Ammon there were horn
> heads among her trophies from the African desert.[88]

Accepting the deities of conquered territories, Rome stood out as the representative head of the *oikoumene*, a city "where the issues of civilization are focused.[89] Its hold and hegemony over the empire depended upon its ability to maintain such an image. Of course, other competing cities existed, such as Alexandria, but while Alexandria "was enmeshed in the egocentricity of Egypt...only Rome could aspire to be a truly universal city... the place of empire and the gods."[90] Mumford notes,

> ...the capital was the "one single home for all earthborn
> divinities," the focus of all the sacred forces within the
> empire, an "assembly of gods," "a deme of heroes, a
> tribe of guardians...the ocean of beauty," "the temple of
> the whole world."[91]

---

87. Lewis Mumford, *The City in History*, New York: Harcourt, Brace and Company (1961).

88. Quoted in Garth Fowden, *Empire to Commonwealth: Consequences of Monotheism in Late Antiquity*, Princeton, New Jersey: Princeton University Press (1993:45-46).

89. Lewis Mumford, *The Cultures of Cities*, New York: Harcourt, Brace and Company (1938:3).

90. Ibid. (1938:45).

91. Ibid. (1938:46).

Roman Jewish culture, hence, of necessity and utter immersion, developed a variety of innovative reinterpretations of Jewish culture and practice that fit more neatly into the atmosphere of Rome, providing a context for the emergence of such radical forms as would be found in Christianity. From this perspective, such Jews, actively imagining themselves out of the box—particularly those that would become Christian—were positioned extremely well to internalize the political culture of empire, learning from those powerful forces so close at hand. Nowhere else, in fact, could such an aspiring movement have learned to mimic patterns of complete authority. Everything, from its organizational structure of the Church, its style and pattern of deity worship, to its philosophy and rhetorical adaptations, came in time to be informed by its simple presence in this imperial center of power.[92] The success, then, of an imminent Christianity in overwhelming its contemporary imperial religious system depended upon how well the Roman Jewish population internalized the imperial schemata to which it was subject. Such a process entailed a complete immersion in the surrounding pagan culture if Christianity was to be formulated in a manner viable of eventually converting the Gentile population. These factors, then, form the trajectory that would firmly conjoin the notion of empire with monotheism.[93]

Thus, when Christianity had begun its lengthy and complex penetration of this metropolis, Rome's function as the sacred center of the empire (and of the world, as imperially envisioned) had long been established. If Paul had raised Jerusalem above the earth's orbit, the dense gravitational pull of Rome would force Christianity's plummet back to earth, rooting its universalistic character within Rome's extant and material template. By its time of imperial notice as a viable alternative to the pagan system of power distribution, Christianity offered a tidier house than its established counterpart, with its more uniform gestures, its methods of mass gathering, its language of worship, prayer, and purpose, and its simplified notions of unity; and in the fourth century, Rome had become a strictly uniform Christian reality. It would be here that the Holy See was built and the tomb over which its great Church would materialize would not be the one ascribed to Jesus back in Jerusalem, but rather those of Peter and Paul.

---

92. On this theme, see the work of Averil Cameron, *Christianity and the Rhetoric of Empire: The Development of Christian Discourse*, Berkeley: University of California Press (1991).
93. Garth Fowden, *Empire to Commonwealth* (1993:5).

The newly emerging Christian Church naturally focused its efforts on forming its strongest bonds within Rome. Contacts with the imperial government were easily established, which allowed the greater Christian community to intervene with the authorities on behalf of other churches. It is important to note, however, that Rome only became a Christian city after an extended period of mutual reconciliation with both the local pagan community and, upon the emperor's move to Constantinople, with a competing Byzantine Church. Four centuries would pass following Constantine's conversion to Christianity before the Church of Rome would finally become the religious and spiritual center of Christianity. The causes that led to this are many and complex; they would include the Byzantine emperor's typically weak hold over the western half of his empire and the sudden seventh-century expansion of Islam in the region. Ironically, such developments would strengthen Rome's religious identity and would eventually lead to the established primacy of its Holy See.

It was already evident at the time of Constantine's conversion to Christianity in 312 that the imperial shift would be a long and drawn out process. Having been convinced that his victory in battle was due to Christ's intervention, Constantine made up his mind to protect and favor the Church, but he was well aware of the fact that he could not transform Rome overnight. Indeed, throughout his reign, as would also be the case for many of Rome's subsequent emperors, Constantine instinctively knew that he would have to advance lightly, particularly in Rome. As Krautheimer illustrates, the Senate and Rome's leading strata of society wielded power for some time after Constantine's reign and it remained bound to the classical cultural traditions of religious belief.[94] Even though Constantine saw himself as God's instrument, entrusted with the mission of spreading the Christian faith and creating a homogeneous, centrally ruled empire with one God and Christ as its fundamental tenet, he was careful not to offend the ruling pagan families of Rome.

Constantine's cautious nature was most evident in his building projects within the city. Rome's pagan temples, theaters, and administrative structures were all grand showpieces of the pagan aristocracy. They were magnificent buildings, "glittering with marble and mosaic, rising high, splendidly furnished and richly endowed."[95] Constantine carefully constructed his new Christian structures on the outskirts of the city, making

---

94. Richard Krautheimer, *Three Christian Capitals: Topography and Politics*, Berkeley: University of California Press (1983:31).
95. Ibid. (1983:28).

certain at all times that his new Christian shrines, basilicas, and palaces never visually competed with the older pagan monuments. The martyr's churches were placed outside of the Aurelian Walls, as was the marvelous cathedral of Rome, situated at the very edge of the city, "hidden away in the greenbelt...where the location could hardly have been more inconvenient."[96]

This strategy would change dramatically by the seventh century, when new basilicas would loudly proclaim the newfound standing of the established Church. Suddenly, at this time, the skyline of Rome would become dramatically altered by the new Christian structures that were brought into the very center of the city.[97] Rome would unmistakably become a Christian city in which the Church's position as a public institution was no longer in question.

This dramatic shift occurred as a result of the increasing power of the Holy See, which by the seventh century had become the spiritual center of the West. The decline of imperial power in the West after the barbarian invasions of the fifth century and the Islamic conquests of the seventh strengthened the position of Rome's religious authorities in a manner that allowed them to shape the city's religious and symbolic character. As a deliberate effort to demonstrate its newfound powers over the West, the Papacy had, during this period, successfully made Rome the religious and symbolic center of Western Christendom.

Many factors help to explain Rome's essential centrality to the development of the office of bishop as Christianity's most important religious agency. The immense prestige attached to the city upon its emergence as the Christian Eternal City and the spiritual center of the Holy Roman Empire was due to external forces that were scarcely informed by the legal claims or individual ingenuities of Rome's bishops, most significantly: the imperial transfer from Rome to Constantinople that gave rise to a competition between two imperial visions; and the Islamic conquest of much of North Africa, including its old religious centers, and of Jerusalem. Lacking such developments, the city of Rome would surely have dwindled in import from its great past and would have perhaps become relegated to ancient history.

---

96. Ibid. (1983:28).
97. Ibid. (1983:35).

THE COMPETITION BETWEEN ROME AND
"THE NEW ROME"

Once Constantine had moved the seat of government to Constantinople a few years after having become emperor, the bishopric of Constantinople had begun to advance its own claims of centrality. The emperors who would follow were naturally in favor of such efforts, simply because it was easier to control and direct local bishops than it was to maintain authority over those situated in a Rome that was becoming more and more independent and less easily subject to imperial influences. Indeed, by the end of the fifth century, the patriarch of Constantinople declared himself "prince of the whole church" and began to use the title "ecumenical" or "universal patriarch."[98] Constantinople's Council of Chalcedon stated yet more clearly in 451 that the city was "to enjoy the same primacy" in the East as Rome had exercised in the West, and in doing so, the council had placed Rome and Constantinople on a level of parity that the pope found unacceptable.[99]

Further complicating this relationship was the descent of the Lombards into Italy in 568 C.E. and their expansion southward toward Ravenna and Rome. Yet more significant was the victorious advance of a new monotheistic religion, Islam, which, shortly after the death of its herald, Muhammad, in 632, burst out of its Arabian homeland, overrunning Syria and Egypt, turning against Byzantium itself in the East, and dominating its North African provinces in the West.[100]

The existence of the Lombards in the West had driven a wedge between imperial East and West, further isolating Rome and loosening Constantinople's grip of supremacy over it. Rome's Church by this time had developed great resources: the Papacy had already become a territorial power, which enabled the pope to act with renewed vigor; while the bishop of Rome directly supplied provisions to the city and paid the troops of the Roman duchy.[101] As a result of serious imperial failures to instill a sense of protection and security, Rome's bishopric increasingly distanced itself from the Eastern, Greek Church of Constantinople. Herrin further illustrates the pressing concerns that Rome felt:

---

98. Geoffrey Barraclough, *The Medieval Papacy*, New York and London: W.W. Norton & Company (1979:27, 29).
99. Ibid. (1979:27).
100. Ibid. (1979:30).
101. Ibid. (1979:32-33).

The rise of Constantinople continued to pose a threat to
Rome's standing throughout the fifth and sixth centuries.
This was coupled with the barbarian invasions of the
western portion of the dwindling empire, leaving Rome
with concern for the See of St. Peter. Local issues, predominantly the Lombard threat, drew attention constantly to such issues as inadequate protection provided
by Constantinople, including inadequate military forces
and food supplies and other grave concerns.[102]

Such urgent anxieties stimulated religious leadership throughout
these early years of Christianity to define and assert its privileges and to
advance a doctrine of Papal primacy. As Barraclough argues, the challenge issued from Constantinople was "the main incentive driving the
bishop of old Rome to formulate his rights":

The pretensions of Constantinople had propelled Rome,
with sudden force along the road to primacy; they compelled it to gather together its earlier titles and combine
them into a single claim to be the "exclusive inheritor of
all that the New Testament tells us of the prerogative of
Saint Peter."[103]

As a result, Rome began to develop the "Petrine Doctrine" by which it
claimed that the Roman Church derived its "primacy" from the powers
assigned to Peter by Christ. The Papacy rested its case upon an indisputable notion that Rome was the first see, indeed the "apostolic see," of the
Apostle Peter, which culminated in Pope Leo I's (440-461) decisive intervention, asserting that the martyr (Peter) city's residing Papacy was
the only legitimate institution. The See of Rome thus became the sole
seat of Peter, who "rightly rules all who are ruled in the first instance by
Christ."[104] This doctrinal declaration formed a major development for
Christianity, as it positioned the pope as the direct representative of Peter, and, through Peter, of Christ himself.

But the most dramatic effect of the Petrine Doctrine was the manner
by which it characterized Rome in the popular imagination of Western

---

102. Judith Herrin, *The Formation of Christendom*, Princeton, New Jersey:
Princeton University Press (1987:141).
103. Geoffrey Barraclough, *Medieval Papacy* (1979:23-24).
104. Ibid. (1979:26).

Christendom. Centering Western imperial Christianity definitively within Rome involved a conscious rejection of Byzantine political and ecclesiastical claims. It was the existence of St. Peter's tomb that inspired in believers a visceral link between the immanence of heaven and the Church as its earthly domain. The historical certainty, for the believer anyway, of Peter's bodily presence in Rome as an indicator of authenticity would thus have a major impact upon the sacred topography of the Christian world.

Especially significant to the expanded image of the Papacy was the firmly established perception that "even the pope, whatever theoretical claims were made for him, in practice owed most of his authority to the fact that he was the guardian of the body of St. Peter";[105] the implication being that St. Peter spoke directly through the pope. Papal documents throughout this period never tired of reiterating this fact and continuously reminded competing centers that the active force in Rome was that of St. Peter himself.

As a result, Christianity gravitated toward visible sources of supernatural power, which, as the seventh century approached its end, drew increasing numbers of pilgrims to Rome from Anglo-Saxon England, forming large and newly captivated crowds.[106] The Donation of Constantine, exemplifying the importance of Peter in linking imperial authority with the Church, described a scenario in which the emperor, placing a gift upon the Apostle's body, swore an oath to St. Peter to sustain and protect it. By the eighth century, St. Peter had become such a part of Rome's identity that the council of 731 assembled for the first time "before the most holy burial place of the most blessed body of St. Peter," instituting a tradition of physical contact between councils and the source of their authority that would frequently be recalled.[107] Southern aptly describes the power of St. Peter mythology upon the popular imagination:

> The rulers and pilgrims from the newly converted peoples of Europe, who came to Rome to be baptized and if possible to die in the presence of the Apostle, were not drawn by any sophisticated theories of papal authority but the conviction that they could nowhere find such safety as in the physical presence of the keeper of the

105. R.W. Southern, *Western Society and the Church in the Middle Ages*, London: Penguin Books (1990:30).
106. Geoffrey Barraclough, *Medieval Papacy* (1979:47).
107. R.W. Southern, *Western Society* (1990:94-95).

keys of heaven....They did not ignore the pope but they
quite simply looked through him to the first occupant of
his throne. It was possible to say in a quite practical way,
without any thought of metaphor, that men met in Rome
"in the presence of St. Peter."[108]

Facing the challenge posed by Constantinople, the Papacy's focus on
instituting its Petrine Doctrine became such an essential part of Western
conscience that it gradually championed the city of Rome as the source
of Western unity during those troubling centuries. From the eighth century onward the spiritual hegemony of Rome and the apostolic see, endowed with the keys of Heaven, went uncontested as a separate and independent Western counterpart to the declining and exhausted Eastern
Empire. Brown depicts a Papacy that "emerges for the first time as a
temporal power in its own right, no longer just de facto or as the agent of
the Eastern Empire."[109]

The Petrine Doctrine's counterpart in upsetting the imperial balance
of power in favor of Rome came in the form of a religious movement
from a region irrelevant to imperial concerns, far south of Constantinople
in the dry deserts of Arabia. Islam's conquest over a large portion of the
Byzantine Empire would be the final and decisive moment in rebalancing
the power locales of the ancient world. As a result, two new political and
spiritual authorities would resonate from Rome and Damascus, while
Constantinople steadily weakened.

It was not until after the middle of the seventh century, when the
Arab fleet controlled the Mediterranean and the Slavs had cut off the
land route from Constantinople to the West, that the consequences became obvious. Henri Pirenne's imagery of the "lost Roman lake to the
Muslims" illustrates further:

The familiar and almost "family" sea which once united
all the parts of this commonwealth was to become a barrier between them. On all its shores, for centuries, social
life, in its fundamental characteristics, had been the
same; religion, the same; customs and ideas, the same or
very nearly so. The invasion of the barbarians from the
North had modified nothing essential in that situation.

---

108. Ibid. (1990:94-96).
109. R. Allen Brown, *The Origins of Feudalism*, London: Allen & Unwin
(1973:71-72).

> But now, all of a sudden, the very lands where civiliza-
> tion had been born were torn away; the Cult of the
> Prophet was substituted for the Christian Faith, Moslem
> law for Roman law, the Arab tongue for the Greek and
> the Latin tongue.[110]

Although this characterization is contested by scholars today, it is clear that the onslaught of Islam profoundly affected the position of the imperial government in Constantinople, forcing it to attend to the problems of its eastern frontier and limiting its capacity to interfere in the West. Pirenne's memorable dictum—"without Mohammed, Charlemagne would have been inconceivable"—is correct if it is interpreted to mean that Charlemagne's coronation by Pope Leo III on Christmas Day, 800, would have been unthinkable had not Islam reduced the Byzantium Empire to a novel position of weakness. But for the Muslim conquest of key strategic seaports of the Mediterranean that connected Rome with Constantinople, the reinstatement of an emperor in the West could not have occurred.[111]

Nevertheless, the imperial structure in the West crumbled and the Church of Rome was forced to increasingly bind its spiritual authority with additional requirements of temporal power. As J.M. Roberts demonstrates, "the collapse of imperial government in the West had as a matter of necessity imposed new secular and administrative responsibilities on the popes."[112] The fact that the Church, inheriting such a feeble feudal structure, would be able to not only maintain itself, but prosper under these conditions is a testimony to its powerful hold on the imagination of the people. In remaining viable, it would provide the West with the semblance of a coherent unity that otherwise could not have existed. However, its triumph was hard won. The Church faced serious challenges from powerful adversaries, some of whom preferred a dispersed, splintered society to the centralizing thrust of Rome. Many local rulers and dynasties looked unfavorably upon Rome's desire to maintain tight control over cardinals and bishops, as they believed such a sphere of influence belonged to them. Not until the eleventh century had Rome successfully suppressed these voices of opposition, reaching heights of power unimaginable a century earlier.

---

110. Henri Pirenne, *The Medieval Cities: Their Origins and the Revival of Trade*, Princeton, New Jersey: Princeton University Press (1974:24-25).
111. Judith Herrin, *Formation of Christendom* (1987:134).
112. J.M. Roberts, *The Triumph of the West* (1998:62).

The Benedictines of Cluny helped to place the Church at the heart of a new, revitalized Europe by launching a campaign that set forth an extremely effective mechanism for limiting the authority of lay powers, while simultaneously empowering the Church of Rome. The Roman Curia, established by the highly disciplined Order, was the Church's single most important institutional innovation during this period, as it embodied a structure that constrained local leaders who were now forced to obtain the confidence of Rome. The Church grew in strength, deeply influencing lay and ecclesiastical structures alike,[113] which had tremendous effects upon political, social, and economic conditions:

> From all over Europe, first parchment and then paper flowed in a rising flood to Rome, all in the international language which bound the continent together, Latin. Churchmen and pilgrims circulated endlessly along the appalling roads, many leading to Rome, and this, too, testified to a new unity in the continent's life, for all its local diversity....Architecture underwent a great blossoming; a great era of cathedral building began in the twelfth century.[114]

Having finally limited lay influence, the Church, once again, turned its full focus upon the heavens and began to substitute a sense of spiritual unity for the political harmony characteristic of the Carolingian era. After the fall of the Frankish state, what could have become a fragmented West composed of local magnates and dynasties, independent of one another and divided along political, social, and economic lines, was in fact held together by that mysterious power long known as the keepers of the keys to Heaven. As such, the Church of Rome's universal appeal, with its ecclesiastical structure spanning throughout the continent, prevented lay political entities from blossoming into nationalized communities. Christianity, in the late Middle Ages, therefore, represented a genuine sense of transnational identity, one which surfaced more from religious bonds than from any clear political or temporally localized sense of identity. In his remarkable statement of 1302, Boniface VIII, only a year before Rome would be sacked by French troops, made the following claim:

---

113. J.M. Roberts, *The Triumph of the West: The Origin, Rise, and Legacy of Western Civilization*, New York: Barnes & Noble Book (1998:67).
114. Ibid. (1998:69).

We are obliged by faith to believe and hold...that there is one holy, catholic and apostolic church, and that outside this church there is neither salvation nor remission of sins....In which church there is one Lord, one faith, one baptism....Of this one and only church there is one body and one head–not two heads, like a monster–namely Christ, and Christ's vicar is Peter, and Peter's successor, for the Lord said to Peter himself, "feed my sheep." "My sheep" he said in general, not these or those sheep. Thus, concerning the church and her power, is the prophecy of Jeremiah fulfilled, "See, I have this day, set thee over the nations and over the Kingdom," etc.[115]

The authority of the Church evidently was not solely concerned with spiritual power, but extended itself deeply into earthly concerns. This statement by Giles of Rome in 1301 illuminates this theme quite clearly:

We intend to explain...that all things are placed under the dominion and power of the church....The power of the supreme pontiff governs souls. Souls ought rightly to govern bodies....But temporal things serve our bodies. It follows then that the priestly power which governs souls also rules over bodies and temporal things.[116]

The Church's intention could not be more lucidly stated, overtly implying that analogous to the soul's dominion over the body is the pope's rule over kings and other temporal powers.[117] Yet more explicitly, some one hundred years earlier, Pope Innocent III (1198-1216) had made similar pronouncements:

To me [the pope] is said in the person of the prophet: "I have set you over nations and over kingdoms, to root up and pull down and to waste and to destroy and to build and to plant" (Jeremiah 1:10). To me also is said in the

115. Quoted in Denis R. Janz, *The Reformation Reader*, Minneapolis: Fortress Press (1990:13-14).
116. Quoted in Brian Tierney, *The Crisis of Church and State: 1050-1300*, Englewood Cliffs, New Jersey: Prentice-Hall (1964:199).
117. Steven Ozment, *The Age of Reform (1250-1550): An Intellectual and Religious History of Late Medieval and Reformation Europe*, Westford, Massachusetts: Yale University Press (1980:147).

person of the apostle: "I will give to you the keys of the kingdom of heaven. And whatsoever thou shalt bind upon earth it shall be bound in heaven, etc." (Matthew 16:19)...[T]hus the others were called to a part of the care but Peter alone assumed the plentitude of power. You see then who is this servant set over the household, truly the vicar of Jesus Christ, successor of Peter, anointed of the lord, a God of Pharaoh, set between God and man, lower than God but higher than man, who judges all and is judged by no one.[118]

By the thirteenth century, therefore, the pope was truly, as he claimed, supreme. He ruled from his central headquarters in Rome over the European continent, his spiritual power resonating in its every corner. The Church, its cardinals, bishops, lower clergy, and the monastic orders were all subordinate to him. Even such rising powers as France, England, Hungary, and the Spanish and Scandinavian kingdoms were considered Papal vassal states; the powerful Hohenstaufen emperors, including the rebellious Henry VI and his son, Frederick II, and the Normans all were constrained by a Rome always prepared to discipline any who opposed its interests.[119]

The concept of placing the "Church over nations" was thus more than a Papal rhetorical notion empty of content; it expressed a real enterprise that was made manifest on many fronts. In Rome it took inimitable form as the Papacy, identifying itself as an international, universal institution, not merely a regional one, wasted no time injecting itself into the topography of Rome. Krautheimer describes the comprehensiveness of the Church's expression of power, posing Rome as:

The head of the world, caput mundi through the papacy, a power center in politics, in law, in finances. All legal business of importance in Western Christendom, whether or not within the Church or even temporal powers alone, came to the papal court at some point.[120]

---

118. Quoted in Brian Tierney, *Crisis of Church* (1964:131-32).
119. See, for example, Geoffrey Barraclough, *Medieval Papacy* (1984:193-246).
120. Richard Krautheimer, *Rome, Profile of a City, 312-1308,* Princeton, New Jersey: Princeton University Press (1980:118).

In endorsing itself as the head of the world, Rome would in time be described by its thirteenth-century contemporaries as "mistress of the nations, domina gentium, queen of cities, regina urbium,"[121] and its Papal reach would extend, though altered in form, to the great power structures of the modern world.

MECCA IN THE CLASSICAL AGE OF ISLAM

The displacement of secular power from Rome in the fourth century did not leave the city without a power base. Indeed, the Papacy quickly adapted itself to its new situation and succeeded in maintaining, even enhancing, the spiritual prestige of its host city. A very different scenario occurred in Mecca. Shortly after Muhammad's death, Islam's political head, the Caliphate, moved north of Mecca leaving behind no power structure independent of external secular authority that could speak for the city. The Caliphate, functioning both as a spiritual and as a secular institution, left Mecca with no agency to act independently of Islam's newly established northern base. The city thus was neither equipped to generate complex spiritual treatises and theological statements as did Rome, nor to develop such earthly bureaucracies as the Curia, composed of spiritual representatives conspiring to enhance the city's standing. Instead, as Mecca saw its power source drawn northward toward the richer and more populous lands of Syria and Iraq, the newly established empire viewed the city merely as a place to perform the obligatory ritual of *Hajj*, prescribed by the Qur'an to all Muslims. Strictly speaking, Mecca did not require advocacy as did Rome; its sacred status was inscribed within Islam's instant canon. However, its spiritual centrality would not translate terrestrially in the young imperial language of Islam as did Rome under Christian designs.

Ironically, the northerly migration was due in part to Islam's success in conquering the Byzantine and Persian empires, returning stability to the old Mesopotamian trade routes used by the local tribes. Mecca had initially risen during the sixth and seventh centuries in response to the volatility of these northern regions and its effect upon economic interests. Due to Islam's triumphs, trade would proceed as it previously had, although it left Mecca with little more than its *haram*.

---

121. Ibid. (1980:144).

Mecca's development is so distinctly different from that of Rome that few firsthand sources exist from within the city other than those of visiting pilgrims and of officials appointed the responsibilities of maintaining pilgrimage routes. Indeed, with Muhammad's death, all of the great Islamic historians of the classical period shift their attention to the "conquests" (*futuh*) "and then...abruptly to the 'chronicles and times of the Caliphs' at a period when those lives and times are unfolding chiefly in Baghdad."[122] Even modern-day historians of Mecca have little to say about this period in the city's history, with most of the content dedicated to the period of Muhammad and then jumping into the nineteenth and twentieth centuries.

Despite this lack of attention, Mecca remained significant to the Islamic world empire. With Islam's extension into areas far from its origins, Mecca's importance became ever clearer to the Caliphs and to the greatly expanded, scattered community, as it quickly became apparent during the *ridda* (civil wars in early Islamic history) wars that expansion came with a cost. The Caliphate faced practical concerns regarding complex intellectual and social tensions that surfaced overnight: how was it possible to maintain unity within a world empire that included such newfound diversity; and who would rule this great empire in accordance with the Prophet's wishes? Indeed, during its phoenix-like flight from Mecca, Islam had instantly ignited its engulfed regions with a conflict between two factions, the Shi'ite and Sunni, concerning the question of rule transfer. The northern regions were unwilling to embrace lineage traced directly to Muhammad as the indicator of power and they resented the reign of the third Caliph, 'Uthman ibn Affan (644-656), appointed by a small group of members of the Quraysh from Mecca. Soldiers were dispatched from Egypt in an effort to undermine Meccan rule and urbanite families aided other local tribes resulting in the Caliph's murder in 656.[123] Gerald de Gaury illustrates the depth of this conflict:

> Even today the sectaries of Ali (Shi'ites), the followers of anti-Sunni creeds, are, with the exception of Persia, more numerous in their communities and in their proportionate numbers in Arabia than elsewhere....Behind this defection, this adherence to Shiahism, was deep seated

---

122. F.E. Peters, *Muhammad* (1994:92).
123. Albert Hourani, *A History of the Arab Peoples*, New York: Warner Books (1992:24-25).

resentment at incapacity to retain control of the Faith
and Empire to which Arabia gave birth.[124]

With the death of Muhammad, therefore, the first and second Caliphs, Abu Bakr (632-634) and 'Umar ibn al-Khattab (634-644), saw
their original alliances with tribal chiefs threatened, as the Meccans perceived a loss of power to their northern brethren. This sense of injury
only increased when 'Umar expanded the reach of Islam to include not
only all of Arabia, but also a part of the Persian Empire as well as the
Syrian district and Egyptian provinces of the Byzantine Empire, as it became evident that the leading families of Mecca and Medina were becoming marginalized. The rise of the Shi'ite branch of Islam, concerned
primarily with preserving lineage, thus, can only be understood in the
context of this geographical expansion and its resultant power shift.

Once the empire had consolidated its power by the ninth and tenth
centuries and began to feel more secure, it introduced a unique system of
cultural signs and symbols. By the turn of the eight century it had already
introduced a new type of coinage that replaced the old human figures of
Byzantine and Sasinid currency with Islamic words.[125] Throughout the
empire, spread across Jerusalem, Damascus, Aleppo, Baghdad, Iran,
Cairo, and eventually as far west as Cordoba, the Arab capital of Spain,
monumental buildings were erected and places of worship called *masjids*
assumed new architectural styles that distinguished them from earlier
Christian and Jewish designs. Such symbols were not only intended to
consolidate the power of the new rulers, but also to provide a sense of
unity for a world marked by diversity, in which millions from a variety
of locations were converting to Islam and, more precisely, assimilating
Islamic rituals into their local religious practices. Even as the Caliphs
attempted to indirectly impose a uniform system of signs throughout the
empire, local practices resisted a total incorporation of the new faith, en-
gendering Islamic rituals and customs that, while bearing certain formal
resemblances to one another, remained idiosyncratic to their specific
communities.[126]

---

124. Gerald de Gaury, *Rulers of Mecca*, London: George G. Harrap & Co. LTD
(1951:53).
125. Albert Hourani, *History of Arab Peoples* (1992:27).
126. See the work of Clifford Geertz and Richard Eaton for an interesting discussion of this process: Clifford Geertz, *The Interpretation of Culture*, New
York: Basic Books (1973); Richard Eaton, *The Rise of Islam and the Bengal
Frontier*, Berkeley: University of California Press (1993).

It is within this context that the significance of Mecca could be fully appreciated and exploited. Ruling over such vast territories, Caliphs were challenged to find innovative ways to engage the issue of social integration. While palaces, mosques, and works of art were useful to a certain degree, they formally comprised a limited semblance of unity that quickly dissipated within communities that lay distant from a given capital. Thus, the generation and nurturance of sacred sites, particularly of the Holy City of Mecca, counterbalanced all those elements existent within the lifestyles of towns and villages which made for extreme localization. Lacking such modern tools as mass media and the printing press, Islam, of necessity, devised informal systems of communication, advancing cultural integration over long stretches of territory and maintaining the mutual involvement of cities, regions, and social groups. Markets, roads, canals, and educational institutions (the *madrasa*) all served such incorporative systemic functions, but the unique assertion of sacredness embodied by such cities as Mecca, Medina, and Jerusalem maintained a presence within the imagination of even the empire's most remote regions. *Hajjis* (designating those that made the pilgrimage to Mecca) would return to their villages and provide oral testimonies of their mystical experiences in distant Mecca, inspiring a wondrous sense of the *umma* as a divine necessity.

The Caliphate, as spiritual leaders of the Islamic community, had a vested interest in providing for these sacred sites. The Ummayad and Abbasid dynasties, ruling from 661-750 and 750-1258 respectively, claimed the protection of pilgrims as both a duty and a right, a responsibility that, as Suraiya Faroghi contends, served to either legitimize a ruler or to trigger a negative image of his throne:

> The failure of a pilgrimage caravan to reach Mecca and return home safely constituted a severe political liability to the [Caliphate]....The same applied to major Bedouin attacks or uprisings in the Holy Cities. To put it differently, such events occasioned a crisis of legitimacy.... Many [of the rulers] were surely motivated by reasons of personal piety when they put up magnificent buildings in Mecca and Medina. But, in addition, they were also staking their claim to a preeminent political position in the Holy Cities.[127]

127. Suraiya Faroghi, *Pilgrims and Sultans: The Hajj under the Ottomans, 1517-1683*, London: I.B. Taurus & Co. (1994:7-8).

The Caliph, as a generous benefactor of the inhabitants of Mecca and Medina and as the organizer and protector of pilgrimages, "constituted a dominant image…impart(ing) a special colouring to even mundane matters such as the clogged water pipes leading from 'Arafat to Mecca."[128]

The all too evident reality of such dramatic regional variants within Islam must have put great emphasis upon the significance of Mecca from the perspective of the Caliphate. Indeed, every Caliph, no matter how far he resided from Mecca, devoted enormous amounts of effort to promoting the upkeep of the city and carefully planning and subsidizing the elaborate pilgrimage routes that ran not only from the capital city to Mecca, but throughout the empire extending to West Africa, Egypt, and the Indian Ocean. Each newly built *masjid* along these routes included a *mihrab* on its wall marking the direction of the *salaat* (prayer), facing toward Mecca; and it included a platform, also facing Mecca, on which *imams* would lead the *salaat*.

Despite the absence of any central imperial authority contained within Mecca, such a grand and consistent project as the preservation of the *hajj* as an essential and mandatory component for each and every able-bodied member of the *umma* would sustain a political as well as spiritual centrality embodied in the city, fixing it as a polar magnet impervious to power shifts and populace distances.

IV
Two Competing Empires at a Crossroads:
The Crusades and the Contest over Jerusalem

Before the launch of the First Crusade in 1095, Jerusalem had remained, for Western Christendom, the heavenly, otherworldly abode of which Paul had spoken in his letters. Westerners, made familiar with Jerusalem only through scripture, had rarely made pilgrimages to the actual city, as Rome had always been much more accessible and the Papacy had successfully demonstrated its sacred legitimacy.[129] By contrast, Constantinople and the Byzantine Empire had developed a much more earthly

---

128. Ibid. (1994:9).
129. See, for example the careful study of John Wilkinson, *Jerusalem Pilgrims before the Crusades* (1977). For the period during the First Crusade see his *Jerusalem Pilgrimage, 1099-1185*, London: Hakluyt Society (1998).

and tactile relationship with Jerusalem. From Constantine's reign to the era of Islamic conquest, the city had been securely Byzantine. It had attracted a healthy flow of pilgrims from its surrounding Christian population and emperors had dutifully shown respect by investing admirably in its infrastructure, building churches around important shrines and maintaining such sites as the path that Jesus had walked on the way to his crucifixion. Even after Jerusalem had fallen to the Muslims in the seventh century, Byzantine pilgrimages had continued on an impressive scale. Diplomatic ties and political negotiations between Constantinople and Baghdad, Damascus, and Cairo had insured safe passage for Christians. The original Holy Land, for these pilgrims, was a vivid reality, available to all the senses, not an otherworldly kingdom—as it had been for Western Christians—only to be entered upon flight from this world and ultimately upon God's return.

The Crusades would change this scenario, ushering in Europeans, en masse, who would build new settlements in Jerusalem. Suddenly, churches sprang into existence on a grand scale in a style that was unmistakably Latin. As the pilgrim experience grew and became memorably vivid, Jerusalem's heavenly mystique began to acquire definitive details and qualities. An account by a contemporary Crusader demonstrates this:

> Here is the Mount called Sion. Here the Lord had supper with his disciples. There He washed their feet. There was the place where the Apostles took refuge for fear of the Jews. There the Holy Spirit descended in fire on the Disciples. There they composed the creed. There also Blessed Mary died to the world....Now let us go in the city itself. There is the Tomb of Him who was Crucified for us, over which a Temple is built. Next to this are the steps by which people come up to the temple. Next to these steps a stone cross stands, of the same size as the Cross that was carried by the Lord...[130]

The Crusades, moreover, marked a turning point regarding Western claims upon the Holy Land, newly perceived as a city abducted by the Muslims from its rightful owner. Crusaders, therefore, understood their siege of Jerusalem in 1099 to be a remedy for this historical imbalance, utilizing such manners of justification as referencing biblical accounts

---

[130] Crusader quoted in Michael Foss, *People of the First Crusade*, New York: Arcade Publishing (1997:190).

and biographies of beloved religious figures, and exploiting historical memory. This violent venture moved the Western Christian imagination for the first time toward a property-based identification with Palestine, in which the earthly city, by divine right, belonged solely to the children of Christ.

Robert the Monk, a famous activist of the First Crusade, made the argument, for example, that the liberation of the Holy Land was a just and honorable objective for Christians to pursue. He viewed violence as a legitimate and necessary act for the recovery of lost property. In his own words:

> The land is not theirs, although they have possessed it for a long time, for from the earliest times it was ours and your people attacked it and took it...and so it ought not to be yours just because you have held it for a long time; for by heavenly judgement it is now decreed that that which was unjustly taken from the fathers should be mercifully returned to the sons.[131]

Men hurried from all over Europe, even from as far as the fringe regions of Ireland and Scotland, to share in this great spiritual venture of arms. It was "the beginning of an enterprise which would continue for centuries, and whose moral ambiguities would deepen with the passing years."[132] The Crusades engendered a renewed sense of purpose that awoke and sharpened the focus of European consciousness upon a geocultural element of its identity, informing the Crusader experience to be understood as a "reconquest" of the once wholly Christian Mediterranean.[133]

What made this possible? A century earlier no one would have imagined such a turn of events. Before the eleventh century, Western Christendom lacked the power it would have needed to launch such an enterprise. Since the expansion·of Islam in the seventh century, the balance of power had been tilted in favor of Islam, largely at the expense of the Byzantines, providing Rome the opportunity to develop independently of Constantinople and culminating in the Gregorian reforms of the eleventh

---

131. The quote has been attributed to Robert the Monk, but the source is unknown.

132. Eamon Duffy, *Saints and Sinners: A History of the Popes*, New Haven, Connecticut: Yale University Press (1997:105).

133. Jan Pieterse, *Empires and Emancipation*, Cambridge, Massachusetts: Cambridge University Press (1989:93).

century. Nevertheless, the lingering struggle between Constantinople and Rome had continued throughout this Crusader era. The Crusades thus had been conceived as an opportunity for the Papacy to definitively settle this rivalry, with the intention of finally subjugating Byzantium to its spiritual hegemony.[134]

With the decline of Byzantine power, the Holy Roman Empire, headed by the Papacy, and the Islamic Empires would be the remaining superpowers of the region. As Constantinople began to look to the West for assistance once the Seljuks had begun an assault on its frontier, Rome, in response, mobilized its forces. However, the city in its view would not be Constantinople, but Jerusalem. Rome had long been limited by its primary claim of spiritual legitimacy and a conquest of Jerusalem suddenly appeared on the horizon as an undeniable vision of grandeur.

The growing strength of Western Europe, as these developments unfolded, was not limited to Rome and the Papacy; a revival of commercial activity, especially for the Italian city-states of the north, began to emerge as a leading factor in this period. The expansion of Islam into the Mediterranean had long rendered the western portion of the Roman Empire a landlocked region. Its merchant class, having little access to the rich trading lands of the East, had dwindled in number and communities had been forced to develop a livelihood through agriculture. However, there had remained a few locations in the Mediterranean that continued to be linked to the riches of the East. Neither the Lombards nor Charlemagne's conquests of the Italian peninsula, for example, had been successful in overtaking some of the key trading centers and such cities as Venice had continued to trade and interact with the East, particularly with Constantinople and to a lesser degree with Muslims. Even "the south of the peninsula beyond Spoleto and Benevento was still," according to Pirenne, "under the power of the Byzantine Empire,"[135] which included, among others, the Amalfi port, a lively center of trade not only for Constantinople, but for Damascus and Baghdad as well. The Venetians and the southern peninsula centers were far more concerned with business than with religion and were thus quite willing to trade with Baghdad and Damascus, but other rising centers, such as Genoa and Pisa, embraced the zealous attitudes of the Papal-dominated West, making peaceful trade with Muslims difficult. Their growth thus followed a mili-

---

134. For an excellent discussion of this see Friedrich Heer, *The Medieval World: Europe from 1100 to 1350*, London: Sphere (1967:123).
135. Henri Pirenne, *Medieval Cities* (1974:88).

taristic path that would duly ally itself with the Papacy and would help to finance the Crusades. The Genoese and the Pisans would shortly be joined by the Venetians in accommodating the Papacy's call for holy war and as the Crusade unfolded, these Italian trading cities would mobilize their resources in an effort to "re-secure" the Mediterranean from the Muslims. Although Islam would, a century later, drive out the Crusaders from Jerusalem and from the other territories of greater Syria under Saladin, the Mediterranean would remain an open sea for these Italian traders.

From within Jerusalem, meanwhile, Europe's growing power could be felt several decades prior to the Crusades. With the exception of the crazed Caliph al-Hakim early that century, by the mid-eleventh century Christian pilgrims had been reporting that Muslims and Christians had "dwelt together indifferently."[136] But in 1055, a radical turn of events would begin to unfold, as Constantinople, having negotiated with the current Caliph, funded the exclusive Christian development of a city square named the Quarter of the Patriarch, as no other figure, with the exception of the emperor, would make decisions pertaining to that sector. Accordingly, the Fatimid Caliph ordered all Muslims residing within the quarter to move elsewhere, leaving it cleared for a fully Christian population.[137] The Byzantines, in essence, "had managed to achieve a protectorate of sorts, a Christian enclave that was separate from the Muslim city and backed by a foreign power." Such foreign influence, in fact, directly took form within the quarter, as locals of Amalfi, Italy, for example, built such institutions as a hospice and the Hospital of St. John.[138]

However, the most radical changes to Jerusalem would take place as the Crusaders entered Jerusalem at the turn of the century. Immediately, the city saw the two mosques upon the Temple Mount, the Haram al-Sharif and the al-Aqsa Mosque, converted into churches renamed "Temple of the Lord." Built alongside them was a residence for house officials. The Qur'anic inscriptions that had encircled the Haram Mosque

---

136. Mustafa Hiyari, "Crusader Jerusalem: 1099-1187 AD," in Kamil J. Asali (ed), *Jerusalem in History: 3000 BC to the Present Day*, London and New York: Kegan Paul International (1997:134).
137. Ibid. (1997:134). See also F.E. Peters, *Jerusalem: The Holy City in the Eyes of Chroniclers, Visitors, Pilgrims, and Prophets from the Days of Abraham to the Beginnings of Modern Times*, Princeton, New Jersey: Princeton University Press (1995:271-73).
138. Karen Armstrong, *Jerusalem* (1996:264); Mustafa Hiyari, "Crusader Jerusalem" (1997:134-35).

were covered with Latin texts[139] and a variety of Christian structures
were erected throughout the city,[140] but the most cherished prize would
be the Church of the Holy Sepulcher, which the Crusaders diligently refurbished and reconstructed, making it the heart of the city. A Christian
traveler by the name of Daniel the Abbot, visiting the Church in 1106,
described it this way:

> The Church of the Resurrection is of circular form; it
> contains twelve monolithic columns and six pillars and
> is paved with very beautiful marble slabs. There are six
> entrances and galleries with sixteen columns....The mo-
> saic above the arch represents the "Ascension of our
> Lord."...The place of the crucifixion is toward the
> east....It is here that the cross of the Lord was erected....
> Beneath the place of crucifixion there is a small chapel,
> beautifully decorated with mosaic, and paved with fine
> marble, which is called Calvary, signifying the place of
> the skull. The upper part, the place of crucifixion, is
> called Golgotha.[141]

Even more radical, was the sudden shift in population, as the old Muslim
and Jewish inhabitants were swiftly slaughtered. One contemporary observer notes:

> The streets were littered with heads, hands, feet, and bits
> of bodies. We were slipping on the gory mess of dead
> humans and horses. But these were small matters com-
> pared to what happened at the Temple of Solomon, a
> place holy to all religious people. If I tell the truth, it will
> exceed your powers of belief. It is enough to say this
> much at least–in the Temple and the porch of Solomon,
> men rode in blood up to their knees and bridle-reins.[142]

The Crusaders confiscated homes and redistributed them among themselves in an arbitrary manner, as the following account describes:

---

139. Karen Armstrong, *Jerusalem* (1996:280).
140. Mustafa Hiyari, "Crusader Jerusalem" (1997:141).
141. Quoted in F.E. Peters, *Jerusalem: The Holy City in the Eyes of Chroniclers*
(1995:312).
142. Quoted in Michael Foss, *People of the First Crusade*, New York: Arcade
Publishing (1997:177).

After this great slaughter they [the Crusaders] entered the houses of the citizens, seizing whatever they found there. This was done in such a way that whoever first entered a house, whether he was rich or poor, was not challenged by any other Frank. He was to occupy and own the house or palace and whatever he found in it as if it were entirely his own. In this way many poor people became wealthy.[143]

Thus, the Crusaders cleansed the city of its old inhabitants, appropriating in totality the spoils of communities once composed of Muslims, Jews, and Byzantine Christians.[144]

Islam, however, would not lay dormant and would return to the Holy Land once again under the Kurdish general Yusuf ibn Ayyub Salah al-Din (Saladin). The Crusaders had been able to penetrate so deeply into the Islamic ruled world, primarily because the Seljuk conquest of Constantinople had seen multiple *amirs* competing for supremacy over the region, each attempting to create a new political order. The Crusaders, thus, had exploited a severely divided front. Within the following century, the Muslim Empire would regroup, beginning with the re-capture of Armenia in 1144 by the *amir* of Mosul and Aleppo, Imad al-Din Zangi, and in 1187, Saladin would take a yet greater stride, bringing not only a handful of small cities, but also, with great ease, Jerusalem back into the orbit of Islam.[145] Muslims, with the exception of one very short period in the thirteenth century, would henceforth retain the city until 1917, when Great Britain would march triumphantly through the Jaffa Gate.

Saladin immediately embarked upon a complete reversal of the structural changes that the Crusaders had imposed upon the city, first ordering that the noble Sanctuaries, the Haram al-Sharif and the al-Aqsa Mosque, be "cleansed." Statues, pictures, and other Christian images were removed, and the Latin Christian texts encircling the top of the Mosques were pealed away, exposing anew the old Qur'anic words that had been hidden behind them. Finally, the *mihrab* indicating the direction of

---

143. Fulcher of Chartres, full citation in F.E. Peters, *Jerusalem* (1995:286).
144. Mustafa Hiyari, "Crusader Jerusalem" (1997:140-41).
145. For an excellent depiction of Saladin's conquest of Jerusalem see the novel by Tariq Ali, *The Book of Saladin*, London: Verso Press (1998:239-324).

Mecca, over which the Crusaders had laid bricks, was uncovered.[146] A contemporary Islamic historian of Saladin recounts the scene:

> Once the city was taken and the infidels had left, Saladin ordered that the shrines be restored to their original state....He ordered the prayer niche (in the Aqsa) to be uncovered....The Qur'an was raised to the throne and the Testaments cast down. Prayer mats were laid out, and the religious ceremonies performed in their purity; the canonic prayers were heard and pious orations given continually; benedictions were scattered and sorrow was dispersed. The mists dissolved, the true directions came into view, the sacred verses were read, the standards raised, the call to prayer spoken and the clappers [of the Christians] silenced, the muezzins were there and not priests, corruption and shame ceased, and men's minds and breaths became calm again.[147]

However, despite the recent memory of Crusader mercilessness, Saladin's restoration of the city's former Islamic topography would not follow a similar path. Following much debate over whether or not to demolish the Christian churches in other parts of the city, he invoked the memory of 'Umar's original conquest:

> When Umar, Prince of the Believers, conquered Jerusalem in the early days of Islam, he confirmed to the Christians the possession of the place [the Church of the Holy Sepulchre], and did not order them to demolish the building on it.[148]

Exhibiting a show of tolerance and generosity, he mandated the creation of two new quarters, the Maghrabi Quarter and the Jewish Quarter, the latter designed to house returning Jews who had been banned from the city under the Crusaders.[149]

---

146. Karen Armstrong, *Jerusalem* (1996:296-97); Mustafa Hiyari, "Crusader Jerusalem" (1997: 166-67); F.E. Peters, *Jerusalem* (1995:348-52).
147. Quoted in Franceso Gabrieli, *Arab Historians of the Crusades*, Berkeley: University of California Press (1969:144, 164).
148. Quoted in Francesco Gabrieli, *Arab Historians* (1969:175).
149. Mustafa Hiyari, "Crusader Jerusalem" (1997:170).

Saladin's conquest of Jerusalem solidified its Islamic status and character for centuries to come. Muslims would, with a fair degree of consistency, allow all Peoples of the Book to retain residency and to practice their faiths. The Caliphs that followed would maintain a cautious balance that ensured the centrality of the city's Islamic character. Jewish and Christian sites, although welcome and seldom threatened, would never be permitted to shine above Islamic ones. In essence, the city retained a historically multicultural flavor, well tolerated, even nurtured to some degree, an improvement over its Christian contemporary in the West.

3

ROME, MECCA, AND THE COMING OF MODERNITY

*Times are changed. The poor old Pope has now no one on earth
upon whom he can rely. Relief must come from heaven.[1]*

Pope Pius IX, 1870

*How is it that the Saudi police attack Muslims with
jackboots and weapons, beat them, and send them to prisons from
inside the holy mosque, a place which according to the teaching of God
and the text of the Qur'an is refuge for all, even deviants?*

Ayatollah Khomeini, 1987

Thus far we have explored the *longue durée* that accompanied the emergence of Rome, Mecca, and Jerusalem as universalistic sacred centers and we have illustrated how the Christian and Islamic Empires appropriated the monotheism of the ancient Israelites, removing its particularistic features and extending it to include universalistic concepts of humankind. As this lengthy period encounters the sweeping transformations that will herald the coming of modernity, powerful particularistic forces are revived that are antithetical to the universalistic visions of the older world empires. Ironically, while the old social compositions of both Islam and Christendom have thus far remained bound by their respective historical and geographical reaches, limiting their "worlds" to a relatively small portion of the world, the new system will "liberate" them from their old frontiers, providing them new means to achieve universalistic ends.

---

1. Quoted in Francis Sugree, *Popes in the Modern World*, New York: Thomas Y. Crowell Company (1961:21).

With the sixteenth-century expansion of a European system that would encompass the entire globe just a few centuries later, the world, as Christendom and Islam had known it, had become radically altered. The freshly conceived State, a fledgling nested and developing within this new world, sat ready to displace the old world empires as they steadily lost their temporal grips to the new forces at hand. As a result, these suddenly antiquated leviathans took to the seas, finding refuge upon the vast merchant ships that were traveling the globe, and shortly thereafter they would resurface, anchored at seaports the world over. While Christendom, wooing commerce and exercising capital, had found favor with the new, inter*national* empire of capitalism, Islam had ridden the lower deck with the immigrant laborer, the new barbarians. All the while, as the religious empires were forced off their soil, their elders returned to contemplate anew otherworldly strategies, replacing land with images of seas, heavens, and cosmos.

This process formed the culmination of a lengthy historical sequence that Europe would come to share with the entire world, beginning as early as the thirteenth century with the emergence of the Italian city-states and continuing into the Reformation, the Treaty of Westphalia in 1648, and the French Revolutionary Wars. One of the most critical results of this extensive period was the consolidation of the nation-state form and the final disintegration of those large bodies of territory known as the world empires of past. As Immanuel Wallerstein suggests, it was in the thirteenth century "that not only were the boundary lines decided but, even more important, it was decided that there would be boundary lines." Paraphrasing Edouard Perroy, he notes further that this represented a "fundamental change in the political structure of western Europe."[2] Similarly, John Ruggie argues that beforehand, the idea of "external" and "internal" political realms differentiated by clearly marked borders made little sense.[3] In pre-modern times, he explains, "(t)here were only 'frontiers,' or large zones of transitions," as the world "had none of the connotations of possessiveness and exclusiveness conveyed by the modern concept of sovereignty."[4] Further, the pre-modern period was sustained by visions of unity and enforced by common bodies of

---

2. Immanuel Wallerstein, *The Modern World System I: Capitalist Agriculture and the Origins of the European World-Economy in the Sixteenth Century*, New York: Academic Press (1974a:32).
3. John Ruggie, "Territoriality and Beyond: Problematizing Modernity in International Relations," *International Organizations*, vol. 47, no. 1, Winter (1993).
4. Ibid. (1993:150).

law, religion, and custom, all of which were devised to embody an inclusive, universal moral community.[5] This would change with the rise of the nation-state.

Rome, Mecca, and Jerusalem as sacred centers of universal faiths that stretched over multiple states had come to embody the pre-modern ideal by incorporating and condensing a universalistic ethos within their walls. The new forces of nationalism, however, would represent a split from this ideal. As we will see in this chapter and the next, this rupture would pose some very difficult questions whose resolutions would entail unusual departures in the respective national consolidations of Italy, Saudi Arabia, and Israel/Palestine. From the perspective and designs of state formation, the enduring reality of universalistic sacred centers would not fit the equation neatly and would thus pose a threat to newly fashioned states by hindering their plans of territorial consolidation. Consequently, the three sacred cities would share similar fates of tension and struggle in relation to their respective nationalist movements.

Having traced the trajectory of the *longue durée* in which the cities of Rome, Mecca, and Jerusalem were transformed into universalistic sacred spaces, we will now visit the conjunctural context in which nationalism, with its new notions of space and territory, will be conceived and developed, giving rise to unavoidable conflicts within the spheres of these three sacred spaces.

I

The City That Floats above Nations:
Rome amid a Fractured Europe in the
Age of Reformation and Nationalism

Observing Rome in the 1890s, one would be likely to notice two very contrasting images of the city. Clergymen and Church employees running the day-to-day operations of the immense and impressive Church bureaucracy abounded; international pilgrims continued to pour in regularly, visiting the mythical sites of St. Paul and St. Peter; city streets were filled with a variety of Christian structures, providing a splendid visual display of significant religious symbols; and such ani-

---

5. Ibid. (1993:150).

mals as goats and sheep mingled amid the city folk in public spaces, wandering through the large numbers of scattered ruins left over from classical antiquity. This Rome seemed a city frozen in time, captive of its glorious past, but alongside this impressive show of ancient splendor stood new monuments and buildings that were steadily changing its landscape. Having become the capital of the Unification movement shortly following the Italian seizure of the Papal States in 1870 under Victor Emmanuel II, Rome had seen extensive modernization in its midst as it became the newly established state's administrative center. Northern factions envisaging a new, nationalist Rome had constructed an alternate landscape that would position such a vision at the center of public attention. New architectural and artistic innovations were introduced, "designed to send hostile signals in the direction of the Vatican."[6] Important figures and events attributed to the *Risorgimento*, the Italian nationalist movement, were depicted throughout the city in honor of the recent unification, some, such as a statue of Garibaldi, towering over city squares as if to challenge the glory of traditional religious sites.[7]

This struggle between the Papacy and Italian nationalists over Rome's symbolic imagery was not only based upon the production and manipulation of the city's cultural landscape, but more importantly, it embodied a struggle between two very different notions of space, identity, and territory. For nearly two thousand years, the city of Rome had served its universalistic empire as an administrative as well as a religious and theological center. As such, it had functioned since the foundation of Christendom as the instrument of a religious universalism that regarded humankind as one people, one *ecclesia universalis*. Its foundation was based upon an *oikoumenical* notion that in effect internalized its exterior, aspiring to a notion of sacred space that would bind humankind in its entirety to a religious conception of the cosmos. What thus made Rome a sacred world city, if not in terms of ritual at least then in its sense of imagined community and transnational space, was its encompassing and inclusive nature, which operated through the logic of fuzzy space and weak markers of distinction. By contrast, the central characteristic of a nation-state, as represented by the *Risorgimento*, enveloped a much shorter time span, providing "a peculiar and historically unique configuration of territorial space."[8] Here, community membership would be

---

6. John Cornwell, *Hitler's Pope: The Secret History of Pius XII*, New York: Viking Press (1999:16).
7. Ibid. (1999:16).
8. John Ruggie, "Territoriality and Beyond" (1993:144).

based on clear and distinct borders that legally demarcated spatial territory and posed definitive notions of internal and external. Hence, the right to exclude others from entrance into the community would become one of the chief characteristics of the modern state[9] and principles regarding the internalization and integration of external elements, as existed within the former imperial context, would become inactive under the newly defined domain.

THE GREAT BREAK

By the beginning of the fourteenth century a significant change had occurred in Christendom that would greatly affect not only the Church of Rome and its Papacy, but the whole of Europe. The transfer of the Papacy and the Curia from Rome to the "French" province of Avignon signified its declining power at the hands of the rising nation-states of northern Europe. Beginning with France and extending into England, Germany, and finally Italy itself, these new territorial states quietly laid siege upon the earthly domains of the Church, rapidly transforming it into a pawn of the emerging lay powers. As these states assumed greater power, in quest of full independence and autonomy from the affairs of the Church, they acted decisively "to curtail the traditional pre-eminence of Peter and, so far as possible, to transform the medieval church into a docile department of the inchoate sovereign state."[10]

Despite its eventual return to Rome, this traumatic experience left the Papacy in a sustained crisis that would last to the present age. As new national entities sprang to life, surrounding the Church and leaving it little ground upon which to set firm anchor, the Papacy began to revisit the spiritual and heavenly emphasis that had once colored its host city. Within this defensive context of retreat, the Papacy, accentuating transcendental, otherworldly imagery, stressed its independence from any national power and its allegiance to all who looked upon Rome as the City of the Apostles. Reduced to a small plot of land, the ground on which the Church stood would thus come to be differentiated in quality from that of its neighbors, as though it had been cut of a unique sub-

---

9. John Ruggie, "Continuity and Transformation in the World Polity," *World Politics* (1983:275).
10. Steven Ozment, *The Age of Reform (1250-1550): An Intellectual and Religious History of Late Medieval and Reformation Europe*, New Haven and London: Yale University Press (1980:137-38).

stance. Heavenly Rome, in its Pauline allegorical sense, had thus come full circle.

This process had already begun to unfold with the Papacy's northern push toward Avignon in the fourteenth century, as it had been facing the growing powers of northern Europe. With the exception of the Italian city-states, most of the revolutionary changes in the organizational structure of states had occurred north of the Mediterranean, especially in France, Amsterdam, England, and later, in Germany.[11] The whole of the Mediterranean and the surrounding southern regions of Europe, where Rome had been most dominant, had felt this shift in influence. As northern forces had gained an upper hand over these regions, the gravity of their power literally uprooted the Papacy from its southern location toward a region more in line with the new political environment of the fourteenth century.[12] As Pirenne observes:

> At the very moment when triumphing over the Empire, it [the Papacy] believed itself in a position to assume the control over Europe, to unite the Continent...and to impose its tutelage on all peoples, the economic and political transformations which had taken place, almost unno-

---

11. Arrighi provides a useful analysis of how these states captured the logics of the Italian city-states, becoming efficient territorial powers themselves: "[T]he quantum leap in the European power struggle since the middle of the fifteenth century had taken the disintegration of the medieval system beyond the point of no return. Out of that struggle new realities of power had emerged in northwestern Europe which, to varying degrees, had subsumed the capitalist logic of power within the territorialist logic. The result was the formation of compact mini-empires, best exemplified by the French, English, and Swedish dynastic states, which...collectively, could not be subordinated to any old or new central power authority." Giovanni Arrighi, *The Long Twentieth Century: Money, Power, and the Origins of Our Times*, London and New York: Verso Press (1994:41).

12. For an excellent discussion on the growing power of the north, see Immanuel Wallerstein, *Modern World-System I* (1974a). Also, the repercussions of this change as it pertains to the Church can be found in Michael L. Budde, *The Two Churches: Catholicism and Capitalism in the World-System*, Durham, North Carolina: Duke University Press (1992).

ticed by Rome, rendered the realization of the papal designs impossible.[13]

The significance of this can already be foreseen as early as 1303, when French troops sacked Rome and humiliated the pope at his own palace. Shortly thereafter, the Papacy would travel north to Avignon, a province much more in reach of the French Crown, becoming in the process an instrument of the Crown's own liking. Indeed, the extent of this reach of power became so pronounced that even when the pope returned to Rome in 1378, the French cardinals elected their own pope, resulting in a lengthy conflict between two competing claimants that lasted until 1417.[14]

The seventy-year exile of the popes at Avignon was a disaster for the Church and the Papacy returned to its historic home having learned a few lessons about modernity that it would not soon forget. By then, it had become fairly clear that the old Church, as it had defined its jurisdiction since Charlemagne's reign centuries ago, would inevitably be forced to challenge what had quickly become modernity's most powerful agent: the territorial state. Immanuel Wallerstein illustrates further:

> It is because the Church as a *transnational* institution was threatened by the emergence of an equally transnational economic system which found its *political* strength in the creation of strong *state* machineries of certain (core) states, a development which threatened the Church's position in these states, that it threw itself wholeheartedly into the opposition of modernity.[15]

Further, the Papacy had come to understand that only by retaining its hold over Rome could the Church maintain the universalistic quality on which would rest its claims of autonomy and its resistance to state absorption. Immediately upon its return to Rome, the Papacy took steps to re-root itself as firmly as possible within its soil, intending to prevent the storms of the north from ever again causing it to drift from its home. It is within this context that the Papacy began its quest to build its own state

---

13. Henri Pirenne, *A History of Europe: From the Thirteenth Century to the Renaissance and Reformation*, Vol. 2, Garden City, New York: Doubleday Anchor Books (1958a:90).

14. David Chidester, *Christianity: A Global History*, San Francisco: Harper Press (2000:295).

15. Emphasis in the original, in his *The Modern World-System I* (1974a:156).

in central Italy, aiming to create a territorial base of its own, uncontaminated by the secular territorial powers that had come to encircle it.

Facing such enormous institutional structures as the Reformation and nationalism that were inherently organized around premises antithetical to the universalistic aspirations of the Church, the city of St. Peter would find itself in a bind unlike any it had ever experienced. As the Papacy restored its gaze upon the heavens, it would invoke its root imagery in ways that would baffle the secular powers at large.

THE REFORMATION AND ROME

One area in which Rome found itself under attack was the issue of indulgence. As Barbara Abou-El-Haj asserts, these criticisms came mainly in the form of protests against "priestly hierarchy, sacraments, and the veneration of saints with all its paraphernalia."[16] The controversy that would arise from this dispute went well beyond theology and extended into the power struggles revolving around the institutional legitimacy of the sovereign state. As the north searched for ways to free itself from Rome as well as Spain, it encouraged any reform movement that was critical of the Church. The Papacy countered by re-emphasizing the central position that Rome had played in the sacred cosmology of Christianity. In so doing, it mobilized its most popular relics, highlighting those very things that the newborn Protestants found offensive. This conflict over indulgence was itself embedded in the larger power struggles taking place in Europe. The rising states of the north found in Martin Luther's clash with the Roman Church a situation extremely beneficial to their cause.[17] As Steven Ozment observes, the Reformation that Luther had helped to spark indirectly affected "the larger political landscape of Europe, for as religious and political loyalties became territorially intertwined, opposing groups identified its religious message, positively or negatively, with their own economic or political self-interest."[18] Luther's Reformation movement thus served as a significant link with the rising

---

16. Barbara Abou-El Haj, *The Medieval Cult of Saints: Formations and Transformations*, Cambridge, UK: Cambridge University Press (1997:4).

17. On Luther's struggle with the Church see the fine work of Heiko A. Oberman, *Luther: Man between God and the Devil*, New York: Doubleday Anchor Books (1989).

18. Steven Ozment, *Protestant: The Birth of a Revolution*, New York: Doubleday Image Books (1993:71).

demand for sovereignty of local rulers and princes in their attempts to break away from the hegemony of Rome.[19] As Carlos Eires contends, "(b)y attacking the images, the people were also attacking the pope.... The cultic objects represented not only false religion, but also subjection to an ecclesiastical system that was resented."[20]

This plays out most clearly in the life of Martin Luther. In 1511, several years before Luther's famous posting of his *Ninety-Five Thesis*, he made a pilgrimage to Rome in which he "sought to avail himself of the unparalleled opportunities afforded at Rome to visit sacred shrines and to view sacred relics..."[21] He performed mass at the holiest of sites and observed traditional acts of penance, but he found no sense of redemption. Although he had made every effort "to obtain spiritual merit from the rituals, including the papal indulgences that bestowed forgiveness from the church's 'treasury of merit,' Martin Luther continued to feel unworthy of divine mercy."[22] What is more, Roland Bainton adds, "(a)lthough [Luther] climbed on his knee, the sacred stairs of Pilate's judgment hall, believed to have been transferred from Jerusalem to Rome, at the top [of which] Luther straightened himself and ejaculated, 'I wonder if it is so.'"[23] This questioning of Rome's sacredness would lead him to a radical rejection of Rome and especially of its sacramental channels composed of shrines, saints, and indulgences, all of which were essential to the popes of the sixteenth century. In so doing, Luther would formally challenge the Church's system of ritual in its entirety.[24]

---

19. For a review of the vast literature on the Reformation see Steven Ozment, "Trends in Reformation Research," in his *The Reformation in the Cities: The Appeal of Protestantism to Sixteenth-Century Germany and Switzerland*, New Haven and London: Yale University Press (1975:1-15) and his appendix in *Protestant* (1993:218-20).

20. Carlos M.N. Eire, *War against the Idols: The Reformation of Worship from Erasmus to Calvin*, Cambridge and London: Cambridge University Press (1986:6).

21. Roland Bainton, *Reformation of the Sixteenth Century*, Boston: Beacon Press (1985:30).

22. David Chidester, *Christianity: A Global History* (2000:312).

23. Roland Bainton, *Reformation* (1985:30).

24. "Peace comes in the word of Christ through faith. He who does not have this is lost even though he be absolved a million times by the pope, and he who does have it may not wish to be released from purgatory, for true contrition seeks penalty" (Martin Luther quoted in Roland Bainton, *Here I Stand: A Life of Martin Luther*, New York: Meridian Press [1995:63]).

The manner by which Luther directed his attack made him an unusual figure, differentiating him from those who previously had held very similar critiques of the Church. His condemnation assumed a clearly particularistic tone that represented not Christendom, as it had thus far been traditionally articulated, but the German princes and their interests. Nowhere is this more plainly stated than in his 1520 piece entitled, *To the Christian Nobility of the German Nation Concerning the Reform of the Christian Estate*:

> Since the pope with his Romanist practices...usurps for himself all the German foundations without authority and right, and gives and sells them to foreigners at Rome who do nothing for Germany in return, and since he robs the local bishops of their rights and makes mere ciphers and dummies of them, and thereby acts contrary to his own canon law, common sense, and reason, it has finally reached the point where the livings and benefices are sold to coarse, unlittered asses and ignorant knaves at Rome out of sheer greed....Consequently the poor *German people* must go without competent and learned prelates and go from bad to worse.[25]

These were revolutionary words. Beyond its polemical nature, this document displayed a unique call for the freedom of the German people from an incompetent and unholy Church of Rome. As it emerged in the context of a changing political environment, it would resonate forcefully and have a significant effect upon the history of Europe. The princes and monarchs had, by then, acquired great enough authority by which to make their own claims for freedom from Charles V and the Holy Roman Empire. Clearly, Luther's dispute with the Church was perceived and courted in light of this struggle. Indeed, in many instances, Luther's own writings addressed the nobility directly, as in the following entreaty:

> I intend the writing for the consideration of Christians belonging to the ruling classes in Germany....The Romanists have very cleverly surrounded themselves with three walls, which have protected them till now in such a

---

25. Quoted in Denys R. Janz, *A Reformation Reader: Primary Texts with Introductions*, Minneapolis: Fortress Press (1999:95-96), emphasis added.

way that no one could reform them....Let us begin by attacking the...wall.[26]

Other reformers would soon join Luther's campaign, while northern nobility and the Calvinists in France began to pursue policies aimed at disengaging from Rome and opposing southern Spain as well as the Habsburg Empire. In response, southern Europe united at Rome's side in defense of the Vatican. As the Protestant Reformation had developed in opposition to both Spain and the Vatican within the context of a growing cultural and national awareness, Martin Luther quickly assumed a myth-like status and was given such titles as the "German Hercules." Having begun merely as a tirade against traditional Roman hegemony, his protest, by the 1520s, backed by Ulrich von Hutten, the German nationalist knight, would evolve to assume the form of a well-established renewal movement on a national and religious scale, giving rise to such revolutionary notions as a German national monarch possessing the title of Holy Roman Emperor.[27] Further, as Carlos Eire adds:

> To the iconoclasts, the idols were not only false gods, but the gods of the Church of Rome, as represented by the priests. Protestants knew that to rid a city of "idols" was to rid it of Rome, that in destroying the images and abolishing the Mass they were also destroying the priests.[28]

Such sentiments could be found throughout Europe. In England, which had a policy of limiting Papal intervention, John Wycliffe waged a strong protest against the Church, contributing to further the union of nationalism with religious reform through his support of an English translation of Scripture, which would soon be followed by the immensely popular King James Version.[29] Sweden, in a similar spirit, represented the strongest expression of Scandinavia's embracing the Reformation as a religious affirmation of national independence. Across the continent, Rome's association with sovereignty was being diminished and Chris-

---

26. Quoted in John Dillenberger, *Martin Luther: Selections from His Writings* (1962:404-7).
27. Michael Mullet, *Radical Religious Movements in Early Modern Europe,* London: Allen and Unwin (1980:3).
28. Carlos Eire, *War against Idols* (1986:6-7).
29. Michael Mullet, *Radical Religious Movements* (1980:3).

tendom, as the Catholic Church had for centuries articulated it, slowly began to erode.

Thus, in his struggle with the Papacy and with Charles V, who had sentenced him to death for the sake of preserving Christian unity, Luther unsurprisingly had found protection in the form of the German prince of Saxony, Frederick the Wise. Having denounced Papal taxes and refused to permit agents of the church to offer indulgences in his territory even before Luther's posting of his *Ninety-Five Thesis*, Frederick, like many German princes, had already been seeking independence from the political authority of Rome. In this sense, the Reformation had been something of a grassroots movement, spreading across localities on the shoulders of magistrates who were seeking political authority over resources within their provinces.[30] Henri Pirenne summarizes this process well:

> [The] princes...were allowed, without protest, to put themselves in the place of the bishops, appoint superintendents of the clergy, suppress the ecclesiastical foundations, close the monasteries, secularize their properties, and organize the schools: in short *each of them, in his own principality, replaced the universal Church, subject to the Pope, by a territorial Church subject to the secular power*.[31]

The Church had long exercised authority over many aspects of social life, often presiding over institutional forms and practices within the jurisdiction of rising monarchies. The church calendar, for example, regulated the daily life of the city and roughly one third of the year in sum was set apart for some kind of religious observance or celebration. Throughout Europe, the most prominent families placed their offspring within monasteries and nunneries.[32] Local aristocrats, Steven Ozment explains, "closely identify[ied] with particular churches and chapels, whose walls record[ed] their lineage and proclaim[ed] their generosity." In the churches "the Mass and other liturgies are read in Latin." Images of saints are "regularly displayed and on certain holidays their relics are

---

30. See Steven Ozment, *Reformation in Cities* (1975).

31. Henri Pirenne, *A History of Europe*, Vol. 2 (1958a:288), emphasis added.

32. For an expansion on this theme see the work of the anthropologist Talal Asad, *Genealogies of Religion: Discipline and Reasons of Power in Islam and Christianity*, Baltimore, Maryland: Johns Hopkins University Press (1993).

paraded about and venerated."[33] State officials could not avoid the prominence of church life and perceived it as an obstacle to supreme power over their localities. It thus became essential for the objectives of state-building to nationalize this predominant aspect of religious life.

Nevertheless, the most effective forms of resistance to Rome's supremacy would come in the Reformation's negation of sacred space. Martin Luther had not only rejected Rome's sacramental channels of confession, acts of penance, pilgrimage to holy shrines, miracles of saints, and indulgences, but, perhaps more importantly, he had dislocated Rome's position in the sacred mapping of the world. For Luther, a faithful Christian was first and foremost one who directly *hears* the Word of God, rather than one who *sees* its imagery. A true Christian did not proclaim his faith through the powers of artificial statues and symbols or by visiting sacred sites. These were mere demonstrations of the mundane and material world. Christian worship, Luther contended, did not require the use of such material things as lights, candles, paintings, images, or altars, as were found in Rome, "for these are all human inventions and ornaments which God does not heed, and which obscure the correct worship, with their glitter."[34]

Other reformers would push this idea even further by urging Christians to destroy idols and to destroy statues, paintings, and altars. According to radical reformers, such as Andreas Karlstadt (1480-1541) and Ulrich Zwingli (1481-1531), for instance, "no other than Christ alone can mediate between God and us." Henceforth, they argued, no aspect of the material plane, as Rome represented with its relics, its preservation of antiquity, and its production of saints, could possibly hold sacredness within it. Such reformers sought to undermine the belief that any space could be demarcated as more holy than another space. David Chidester explains further:

> Protestants introduced a new space of homogeneity into urban sacred space. Since they assumed that any building could in principle be consecrated for worship, Protestants ignored the Catholic sensitivity to the subtle and complex differences among sacred sites, each with its own relics, saints, and traditions.[35]

---

33. Steven Ozment, *Protestant* (1993:25).
34. Luther cited in David Chidester, *Christianity: A Global History* (2000:312-31).
35. David Chidester, *Christianity: A Global History* (2000:330).

In this manner, Rome came to be viewed as a farce, a human production not unlike any other urban center unworthy of special recognition. It held no place in God's Kingdom, as advertised, and therefore sanctification of its boundaries in the effort to maintain its purity and protection seemed, at very best, disingenuous. This disrespect for Rome's claim to spiritual hegemony was especially apparent in the Sack of Rome of 1527 when "those uplandish Lutherans" (as Thomas More described them in his *Dialogue concernynge Heresyes*, published in 1528),[36] entered forcibly into the city's heart, harnessing their horses at St. Peter's and the Sistine Chapel, marking up walls with Martin Luther's name and scribbling over major "paintings in the Vatican Stanze." Some of the invading troops purporting to belong to a Lutherian army "assembled under the pope's window at the Castel San' Angelo, insisting that they were going to eat him." Luckily for the pope, he had fled the complex shortly before the invasion had begun, but Cardinal del Monte, the Pope Julius III to be, fared less well and "was hung by his hair."[37] Wandering the streets of Rome during this time, one could find a poster equating the great city of the pope to that of a whore:

> *She has fallen, fallen that great city*
> *In which the Red Whore long resided*
> *With her cup of abomination*[38]

Rome responded to this affront on many levels. Most effective was its ambitious revisiting of heavenly city imagery and its deepening contention of saintly origins, which greatly emphasized its essential link with the most important of saints, Peter and Paul.[39] The Papal Counter-Reformation included yet another restructuring of Rome, which dramatized the Church's collection of relics even further than had been done in the past and saw its basilica rebuilt in order to capture the attention of Europe. As Barbara Abou-El-Haj describes:

---

36. The citation of Thomas More is from Andre Chastel, *The Sack of Rome, 1527*, Princeton, New Jersey: Princeton University Press (1983:37).

37. The last three citations are from Eamon Duffy, *Saints and Sinners: A History of the Popes*, New Haven, Connecticut: Yale University Press (1997:158).

38. This poem, found on a poster, is cited in Andre Chastel, *Sack of Rome* (1983:24).

39. See Rudolph Wittkower, *Art and Architecture in Italy: 1600 to 1750*, Baltimore: Johns Hopkins University Press (1964:1-3).

As the commercial north freed itself from Rome and its surrogates, particularly the Spanish regency in the Low Countries, Protestant reformers particularly attacked priestly hierarchy, sacraments, and the veneration of saints with all its paraphernalia. In this constellation, St. Peter's was a catalyst for Reformation and a centerpiece for the papal response. Rather than adapt itself to the call for an apostolic-like church stripped of its hierarchy and luxury, the Counter-Reformation church affirmed its apostolic succession by enlarging every traditional Catholic practice and ceremony under attack, using Constantine's prototypical church and Catholicism's prototypical saint.[40]

Pope Paul III's insistence on embracing with renewed zeal the tradition of indulgence and lavishing more relics and paraphernalia upon Rome does not appear to have been an irrational response, as some Reformation historians conclude. The pope seems to have clearly understood that instead of reforming the Church to meet this new challenge, his best plan of attack would be to press even further "ahead with the reconstruction of Rome, to reflect both the spiritual and the temporal glory of the Church and papacy."[41] Following Pope Paul III's lead in commissioning Michelangelo to work on St. Peter, post-Reformation popes would continue to enshrine the city with an abundance of artwork as they continued to resist reforms, particularly those of an administrative and moral nature, that might increase the power of potential competitors and challenge their privilege.[42] The most serious of such rivals, as we will see below, would transcend spiritual and doctrinal themes to include those of a nationalist and temporal slant in their condemnations.

Thus, when Rome was sacked yet again in 1870 by the Italian nationalists, Protestant countries were unsurprisingly the least likely to protest the sequestering of Papal territories. If they even expressed any concerns at all, such countries did so in a manner that can be described as *real politik* (for statesman), or simply for aesthetic value, containing little

---

40. Barbara Abou-El Haj, *The Medieval Cult of Saints* (1997:4).

41. Eamon Duffy, *Saints and Sinners: A History of the Popes* (1997:166).

42. Steven Ozment, *The Age of Reform (1250-1550): An Intellectual and Religious History of Late Medieval and Reformation Europe*, New Haven and London: Yale University Press (1980:399).

religious themes, if any at all.[43] By this time, Rome had been reduced to an archaic and anomalous nuisance on the stage of the European political scene. Soon, it would face still greater hurdles.

NATIONALISM AND ROME

The most serious threat to Rome's political integrity would come in nationalist garb, knocking at the Vatican's door in the mid-nineteenth century. The movement for Italian unification, known as the *Risorgimento*, followed in the footsteps of its French and English predecessors, challenging the Church's control of key social and religious institutions throughout the peninsula. However, this assault, surpassing the break in Papal channels of authority that had occurred in France and England, extended directly into the very center of Western Christendom. The Italian nationalist thus came to embody Martin Luther's call upon his German nobility to finally tear down the walls that protected Rome and, in time, they would come to enter and occupy the Eternal City.

Before the nineteenth century, Italian unification had been a blurry ideal at best, as the peninsula had been composed of numerous city-states, each having been parceled out for centuries between foreign powerful dynasties that had shared a vested interest in preserving the balance of power. Moreover, since the Middle Ages, each of these cities had developed its own miniature version of nationalism. The Neapolitan historian, Lughi Blanch, writing in 1850, illustrates this theme:

> The patriotism of the Italians is like that of the ancient
> Greeks, and is love of a single town, not of a country; it
> is the feeling of a tribe, not a nation. Only by foreign

---

43. Take, for instance, this plea by a writer trying to persuade readers to look "beyond" the religious character of Rome: "Not everyone is terribly excited by the idea of Rome, perhaps because of its close association with the Christian religion. To non-Catholics, the long succession of popes does easily arouse boredom, and the concept of the pilgrimage now seems somewhat anachronistic...I had to persuade the potential reader that Rome too has its artistic attraction, and that *a journey to Rome could be something more than a pilgrimage*" (emphasis added), Brian Barefoot, *The English Road to Rome*, Upton-upon-Severn, U.K.: Images Publishing (1993:10).

conquest have they ever been united. Leave them to themselves and they split to fragments.[44]

According to Owen Chadwick, "(f)ew thought about Italy. They thought of Lombardy, Venezia, the Papal States, Naples, Sicily, the duchies..."[45] To further illustrate this, by the mid-nineteenth century, only a meager 3 percent of Italy's population spoke Italian, while the rest spoke "fourteen major variations that were not so much dialects as distinct languages."[46]

Linked as they were to the trade routes of the Mediterranean, these city-states would have found national unity disastrous to their merchant classes, whose loyalties to Christendom came second to those toward the city.[47] Even as the commercial center had been shifting from the Mediterranean to the Atlantic in the sixteenth century, the Italian city-states had been perceived as significant territories and were protected by the powerful states of the time, especially by the Spanish overlords.[48] France, Austria, and Spain all zealously guarded their independence and had not looked favorably upon any movement inside or outside of the peninsula that attempted to alter the status quo. Rome's Papacy had continued to maintain this status quo right into the nineteenth century and, consequently, had found itself drawn into an offensive alliance with these external state powers, at times even inviting them into the internal affairs of the peninsula with the intent of protecting itself from the encroaching reach of the *Risorgimento*.

It is within this context that "the Question of Rome" would emerge. The Papacy, struggling over its rule of the Papal States, had found itself on the side of the most reactionary forces of the modern period, beginning with Spain in the sixteenth century and followed by France, Austria, and the Habsburg Empire. At no time would Rome consider these alliances more essential than in the nineteenth century, particularly following the Restoration period after 1815, for as long as these powerful states would continue to oppose the rising forces of nationalism throughout the

---

44. Quoted in Dennis Mack Smith, *Modern Italy: A Political History,* Ann Arbor: University of Michigan Press (1997:6-7).

45. Owen Chadwick, *The Popes and European Revolution*, New York: Oxford University Press (1981:90) cited in John Lie, *Modern Peoplehood*, Cambridge, Massachusetts: Harvard University Press (2004:112).

46. John Lie, *Modern Peoplehood* (2004:16).

47. Dennis Smith, *Modern Italy* (1997:7).

48. See Giovanni Arrighi, *The Long Twentieth Century* (1994:36-47).

better part of the nineteenth century, Rome could safely expect continuity as champion of the old social order.

Couched in this unique political environment, "the Roman Question" posed a special situation in European diplomacy with far-reaching implications.[49] Since its conception, the notion of Papal power had always envisioned an essential link between the possession and full sovereignty over a territorial claim and the pope's successful embodiment of spiritual function. By the time modernity had been fully ushered onto the political stage, the pope had long presided over its segment of Italy. Besides the fact that the majority of Italians were Catholic, millions as well were scattered across the globe and many inhabited neighboring states. Further, numbers of Catholic forces within Germany, France, Spain, and Austria had developed an interest in the maintenance of Papal authority, believing that an operative international Church was the most effective form of support for local bishops under fire by their respective governments. Within this camp, such bishops, particularly those who withstood adversarial movements, would have the option of petitioning the Papacy itself for aid in maintaining order. A stronger, more authoritarian Rome would further be capable of assisting such local churches and bishops against revolutionary and independence movements and was therefore welcome.[50]

Pope Pius IX (1846-1878), presiding over the Vatican during those trying and difficult times, insisted upon the necessity of Church sovereignty for the spiritual independence of Rome, viewing a compromised hold over the Papal States as a disastrous and unacceptable outcome. As the landscape had become one of national statehood, Pius understood such sovereignty to serve as a guarantee of the Church's independence from any other worldly power, thus authorizing its sustained freedom to act in matters pertaining to spiritual issues.[51] Hence, while nationalism would soon become the greatest threat to its continued existence, the concept of territorial sovereignty appeared as the Church's most profound justification for retaining the Papal States.

---

49. For the significance of the "Roman Question" in the diplomacy of Europe see Rene Albrecht-Carrie, *A Diplomatic History of Europe: Since the Congress of Vienna*, New York: Harper and Row (1973:94-106).

50. See Owen Chadwick, *A History of the Popes: 1830-1914*, New York: Oxford University Press (1998:95-131).

51. Joseph Moody, "The New Forces and the Papacy," in his (ed.), *Church and Society; Catholic social and political thought and movements, 1789-1950*, New York, Arts (1953:33).

Aside from its diplomatic aspects, a more fundamental underpinning defined "the Roman Question." The issue evoked emotional and deeply religious sentiments that could not be captured in diplomatic statements. Henry Edward Manning, an Anglican who converted to Catholicism in the mid-nineteenth century, for instance, defended Rome's sovereignty in a style common to those who supported the Papal States. He declared that the temporal power of the pope signified "the freedom, the independence, the sovereignty of the kingdom of God upon earth," and he justified this position on the theological grounds that the Papal States were "the only spot of ground on which the Vicar of Christ can set the sole of his foot in freedom" so that "they who would drive the Incarnation off the face of the earth hover about it to wrest it from its hands."[52] Manning was of the widespread opinion that the Church was a universal and supranational body whose head could not be subject to an earthly power. Even the conscious acceptance of external temporal rule could not be mirrored in the heavens. Such notions led Pius IX to plainly summarize Papal resolve in his declaration that he would not serve under the House of Savoy.[53] Since he viewed himself as the trustee of a sacred spot on earth that God had entrusted to him, Pius IX could presume subservience to no force other than that of Divinity.[54]

Such claims made Rome's position a unique one upon the stage of European diplomacy. As nineteenth-century Italy had hosted two competing ideologies that advanced different principles for the organization of society, Rome highlighted those differences more clearly than could have any other region, certainly in Italy, and perhaps throughout the whole of Europe. While proponents of national statehood had to overcome and, at times, do battle with local, particularistic, as well as universalistic forces in other areas of Europe, in Italy such clashes were inflated by the fact that Rome, the supranational territory of an ecclesiastical community, resided at the center of the proposed new state.

Shortly before the occupation of Rome in 1870, a middle ground between the nationalist and the pope had developed in which "the Roman Question" could be resolved through a scheme of federation. A priest named Vincent Gioberti, having written of Italy's luminous history from

---

52. Quoted in Eamon Duffy, *Saints and Sinners* (1997:225).
53. Joseph Moody, "New Forces" (1953:29).
54. On the pope's reaction to the invasion of Rome at the hands of the *Risorgimento*, see Lillian Parker Wallace, "The Occupation of Rome," in her *The Papacy and European Diplomacy: 1869-78*, Chapel Hill: University of North Carolina Press (1948:116-50).

the perspective that its Catholic flavor exemplified the highest ideals of European civilization, had most clearly articulated such a solution in his *On the Moral and Civil Primacy of the Italian People*, published in 1843. He had proposed that the pope, because of his special position within the Catholic community, would preside over the whole of Italy as the head of a federation under which the Italian states would be united. But this suggestion would soon fall on deaf ears. Opposition to it came from both the Papacy and the nationalist factions; the former arguing that it could not be nationalized, while the latter insisted that such a proposition would not lead to any significant constitutional reforms.[55]

The fundamental dilemma facing the new state had thus remained unchanged. The Italian nationalists, confronted with the issue of a strip of territory that many saw as belonging to the world Catholic community, asserted that Italy as a unified state could not exist without Rome. However, they failed to appreciate the power of Catholic as well as non-Catholic sentiments that would not accept the city's incorporation by the *Risorgimento*, based on the notion that Rome stood above and beyond all nations. This view contended that reducing Rome to another province of Italy, even if it was to be the state's capital, would diminish the city's supranational quality and contradict its mission to serve the world for all. The Church, of course, facing resignation of authority over the Papal States, had been the most expressive representative of this view, but it was by no means the lone voice on this matter, as evidenced by the wide display of international interest at the time.[56]

These conflicting visions greatly dramatized "the Question of Rome" and "made it a thorny question in international politics."[57] The idea that the state was supreme within its territories could not be reconciled with the well-established and transnational notion of a city under divine authority. Many feared that subservience to the will of an exclusive community in the form of state sovereignty would jeopardize Rome's universalistic appeal, ending its spiritual resonance throughout the Catholic world. As Lillian Wallace observes:

---

55. On this movement see Owen Chadwick, *History of Popes* (1998:53-56).
56. A sense of this can be observed by browsing the newspapers published in 1870 on the issue in the United States, Great Britain, France, Ecuador, and other countries. As Lillian Wallace claims, "The question was one of vital concern to all states, Catholic and Protestants alike." Lillian Wallace, "The Occupation of Rome," in her *The Papacy and European Diplomacy: 1869-78*, Chapel Hill: University of North Carolina Press (1948:123).
57. Joseph Moody, "New Forces" (1953:33).

That it was considered a matter of grave importance by all states had been amply demonstrated since 1861 when the loss of a part of the papal possessions had dragged the question into the foreground of European politics. Manning, the head of the Catholic Church in England, had proclaimed at that time, "The civil order of all Christendom is the offspring of the Temporal Power." Even earlier, when the Pope's possessions were attacked in the revolutionary uprising of 1849, a debate had occurred in the British Parliament on the question of the necessity of the maintenance of the Temporal Power. The question, then, was one of vital concern to all states, Catholic and Protestant alike.[58]

What is most interesting and telling regarding the magnitude of this debate for the international community is the fact that there were Protestants who supported the Papacy, viewing a nationalist appropriation of Rome with a sincere sense of regret. The German Protestant historian Gregorovius, for example, had dedicated his life to studying Rome. He had cultivated a great fondness for the city, not for the reasons that Catholics had adored it, to be sure, but because he had perceived it to be "the moral capital of the world," a cosmopolitan city that had now, with its fate in the hands of the *Risorgimento*, been "reduced to the capital of just one of the kingdoms of the world."[59] His sense of dismay is clearly evident in his writing:

> The greatness of Rome is not suited to a young aspiring kingdom....The King of Italy will cut a figure here only such as that of one of the Dacian prisoners of war on the triumphal arch of Trajan....Rome will forfeit the cosmopolitan atmosphere which I have breathed here for eighteen years. She will sink into becoming the capital of the Italians, who are too weak for the great position in which [she stands]....The Middle Ages have been blown away by a tramontana, with all the historic spirit of the past; yes, Rome has completely lost its charm.[60]

---

58. Lillian Wallace, "Occupation of Rome" (1948:122-23).
59. Quoted in Owen Chadwick, *History of Popes* (1998:225-26).
60. Quoted in Ibid. (1998:226).

When the Italian nationalists finally occupied Rome in 1870, they were thus forced to be cautious in their handling of the city. Indeed, Giuseppe Mazzini had understood, some three decades before Victor Emmanuelle entered the city, what was at stake in this endeavor to take Rome. Upon reaching Rome, he had written to his fellow nationalists these cautionary words:

> You have in your hands the fate of Italy, and the fate of Italy is that of the world. You do not know, O ye forgetful people, the power exercised by the conjunction of four letters which form the name of your city; you do not know that that which is merely a word elsewhere when coming from Rome is a fact, an imperious decree—*Urbi et Orbi. Perdio!* Do not the monuments, the historical memories, put a single inspiration into the minds of men?[61]

The Italian nationalists were well aware that it was in their interest "to prove to the world—and to half-Catholic Italy—that the Pope would be treated with maximum honour."[62] With great concern for the sacred precincts of the city, particularly the Papal palace, the great churches, and other religious locations, they quickly demarcated a few acres that would remain free, appointed a secret service officer to protect the pope, and established a line of guards around the walls of the Vatican.[63] Visconti-Venosta, speaking on behalf of the nationalists, gave assurances that the new Italy would honor the spiritual sovereignty of the Papacy: "Italy naturally desires that His Holiness remain at Rome, for nowhere will the Pope be surrounded with more respect and regard and nowhere will he have a greater liberty for the exercise of his spiritual functions."[64]

Despite the gesture of good will toward the world Catholic community and the acknowledgment of the Vatican as an internationally recognized sacred site, the Italian nationalists anxiously anticipated a response from the international community, fearing, with good reason, that the Catholic European states and even Protestant Britain might insist upon

---

61. Quoted in E.E.Y. Hales, *The Catholic Church in the Modern World: A Survey from the French Revolution to the Present*, Garden City, New York: Doubleday Image Books (1960:104).
62. Owen Chadwick, *History of Popes* (1998:228).
63. Ibid. (1998:226-28).
64. Quoted in Lillian Wallace, "Occupation of Rome" (1948:129).

the restoration of Rome to the Papacy.[65] Indeed, shortly following the seizure of Rome, the French Parliament had debated a proposal to reinstate by force the entire city of Rome to the Catholic Church. A French warship, the *Orenoque*, still sat ready off the coast near Rome in case the pope needed it.[66] In Germany, petitions abounded calling for an intervention on behalf of the pope.[67] And even Protestant Britain had sent a representative to Rome to inform the pope that "the ship, *The Defense*, would have to go to Naples for safe anchorage but could be brought back whenever he [the Pope] wished it."[68]

Nevertheless, Pius IX who saw his city dwindle from seventeen thousand square miles to a mere few acres never seriously considered such military options.[69] Instead, from the moment of seizure in 1870, he would, in protest, stay within the confines of the Vatican and the Holy See for the remainder of his days, inspiring the dramatic characterization of this period as the "imprisonment years." French Catholics invoked the imagery of martyrdom, praising his implementation of Papal infallibility in the face of such lowly temporal fortune.[70]

During this time, a German ambassador, Arnim, insisted that the pope should accept his proposal of asylum in the historic Benedictine town of Fulda in the heart of Germany, but both the pope and Bismarck would refuse—the latter on grounds that Fulda was not a site adequate to contain the grandeur of the Papacy.[71] Pius IX further understood, from the disastrous lessons of Avignon centuries earlier, that no matter how dire the situation should become, without the Roman Church and the direct link with St. Peter, the Papacy would become an empty institution, void of any religious legitimacy. From the conversion of Constantine in 312 until approximately 1870, Rome had been a distinct part of the Holy Roman Empire's sociopolitical order and the Church's own international

---

65. Owen Chadwick, *History of Popes* (1998:227).

66. Frank Coppa, *The Modern Papacy since 1789*, London and New York: Longman (1998:112).

67. Lillian Wallace, "Occupation of Rome" (1948:147).

68. Ibid. (1948:131).

69. Francis Sugree, *Popes in the Modern World* (1961:1-2)

70. Ruth Harris, *Lourdes: Body and Spirit in the Secular Age*, New York: Penguin Press (2000:16). Indeed, Harris suggests that the French, in their horror at seeing Rome overrun, organized a new national pilgrimage to Lourdes as a "way for Catholics across the country to show their solidarity and strength with Rome" (2000:17).

71. Lillian Wallace, "Occupation of Rome" (1948:131).

standing had come to depend upon its association with Rome. Pius IX understood that under no circumstances would the essential quality of this link be altered.

Ironically, this bitter loss would in time come to serve as an asset. Freed from its temporal and geo-political interests, the Papacy was able to shed its worldly cloak and concern itself once again with religious issues. As Gene Burns argues in his careful study, *The Frontiers of Catholicism*, in shifting its interests, "the papacy actually had more latitude over internal Church affairs and doctrine, given the decline of state meddling."[72] Indeed, this trend became so pronounced in the century to come that by the time of the Second Vatican Council under Paul VI (1963-1978), the Church was forbidden to take an active role in temporal government whatsoever.[73]

Meanwhile, the new nationalist elites had grown greatly in their influence over Rome and within decades, the fascist Mussolini would fulfill the *Risorgimento* objective of further consolidating Rome within the nationalist orbit. Considering the *Risorgimento* movement to be lacking in its will to nationalize Rome, Mussolini made the completion of this task one of his administration's highest priorities. Indeed, the creation of the "New Rome," as he liked to refer to it, with the wide and attractive streets that characterize it today, is directly the result of this fascist past. Its sanitized, modern look and its statues of great Roman, "Italian" military and historical figures came only with the complete dismantling of many neighborhoods, many of which included working-class and ethnic minority neighborhoods, including those of Jews, all in the effort to make Rome the symbol of a new and modern Italian nation. Such an endeavor assumed the age-old and time-tested logic of purification, as evidenced in the exhuming of bodies from a local Jewish cemetery in order to transfer them elsewhere, to Campo Verano, and to erect a monument on the site in honor of Giuseppe Mazzini, a hero of the "Italian" nationalist movement.[74] As Borden Painter, Jr., explains further in his *Mussolini's Rome*, this transformative process displayed "the values of the regime and its goal to change Italy through producing a new generation of Italians," and showcased Mussolini's hunger to rebuild the city "as the

---

72. Gene Burns, *The Frontiers of Catholicism: The Politics of Ideology in a Liberal World*, Berkeley: University of California Press (1992:17).
73. Ibid. (1992:23).
74. Borden W. Painter, Jr., *Mussolini's Rome: Rebuilding the Eternal City*, New York: Palgrave Macmillan (2005:33).

centerpiece of his 'fascist revolution.'"[75] Resembling the Arab national-ists in their objectives over Mecca, as we will see in the following sec-tion, Mussolini also attempted to negate the Christian period of the popes in favor of that earlier age of the great "Italian" Roman emperors.

Today, Rome's split personality is impossible to miss with one cor-ner dominated by its Christian history, showing little trace of Italy's na-tional flavor, while the other is unmistakably Italian and hardly Christian in character. Current travel guidebooks to Rome and Italy capture this divide well, as some begin with the Vatican, while others favor the Pi-azza Venezia. Rome thus has come to embody a peaceful, but mutually exclusive compromise between the universalistic aspirations of Christen-dom and the particularistic foundations of nationalism.

II
Mecca: The Pan-Islamic City and the Withering of the Ottoman Empire

We are Arabs before being Muslim, and Muhammad
is an Arab before being a prophet.... We were Arabs even before the
time of Moses, Muhammad, Jesus, and Abraham.[76]

King Faisal

While Rome-centered Christendom experienced a paradigmatic shift in landscape at the hands of modernity, Islam and Mecca faced a similar crisis. In Europe, as we have seen, the union of nationalism with the Ref-ormation had cornered the Papacy into a collision course over the issue of temporal power, causing it to take refuge in the spiritual realm. The Papacy had survived the onslaught of modernity having lost an emperor, but having retained its spiritual head. In the case of Mecca, the power of these new European states would come thundering into the *Abode of Is-lam*, fracturing it into pieces and severing it from its Ottoman Caliphate, ultimately leaving the *umma* headless and disembodied. In losing the Caliphate, Islam would be without *both* its spiritual and its imperial head.

---

75. Ibid. (2005:xv); for more on Mussolini's Rome, Borden Painter provides a detailed inventory and analysis of this period.
76. Quoted in Sylvia G. Haim, *Arab Nationalism: An Anthology*, Berkeley: Uni-versity of California Press (1974:35).

Nevertheless, Mecca would continue to grow in its international appeal, attracting a growing number of pilgrims yearly and becoming the world's most annually visited sacred site, as though having survived the death of a body that had once been given life by it only to have been reincarnated as an entity that modernity has yet to identify.

During the Crusades, long before the age of modern colonialism, Western Europe had dominated much of the Muslim territories, including the strongholds of Sicily and Spain. Reduced to a primarily extra-European empire, Islam's greatest threat prior to the modern period had come in the form of the Mongols from the east, who had succeeded in toppling the enduring Abbasid Caliphate. The Mongols had left Baghdad, its capital, in ruins and had managed to disturb eastern trade routes, but such difficult episodes would not sufficiently prepare Islam for its slow decline during the modern era at the hands of a Europe transformed. While the old invaders had taken slices of the Islamic Empire, leaving it otherwise intact, modernity would attack its core and spread throughout its span like a dramatically malignant cancer, leaving no organ untouched. Modernity thus restructured every aspect of the empire, from its class makeup and trade patterns to its formal political structure. As evidenced by this process, a new and unique set of rules had been introduced, in which invasion was no longer limited to acquisition and redistribution of territories, but came to include complete domination over internal elements as well.

The most enduring impact of modernity upon Islam to date has been the imposition of its formal political structures. Prior to the modern period, under the Islamic Empire, territorial boundaries *within the empire* had been either non-existent or constantly shifting. Under the modern paradigm, territorial regions had become clearly defined and frozen solid, with armies and checkpoints separating one region from another. Wherever they established their colonies during this emerging period, Europeans demarcated territorial jurisdictions, insisting upon the observance of these permanent boundaries. Subject to such treatment, the Islamic Empire quickly vanished, hacked to unrecognizable pieces in the form of multiple territorial states with which Muslims would come to identify.

Modernity therefore negated organizational principles of the Ottoman Empire, shattering its political superstructure and radically transforming the old political, social, economic, and religious social networks that resided within it. Although the empire had not integrated its territories very effectively, it had managed to join the interests of such elite groups within its jurisdiction as Janisaries, bureaucrats, tax farmers, and

prebend holders under a translocal system of acquisition that had functioned efficiently until the mid-nineteenth century. During its reign, the
Ottoman Empire had further been able to curtail ethnic and national dis-
cord by emphasizing an inclusive configuration of varied religious and
political ties. Its institution of the *millet* system, for example, loosely
modeled upon the Islamic notion of *dhimmi* (through which Jews and
Christians—"People of the Book"—were accorded the privilege of maintaining their communities under Muslim rule, albeit with varying degrees
of lower status and imposed laws) had linked, within an elaborate inter-
active network, a diverse set of religious communities with the center.[77]
Thus, the empire administratively secured communal rights and some
sense of belonging for its religious communities, providing the template
for a solid structure composed of designated tribal, familial, and communal leaders "directly responsible to the central government."[78]

In the nineteenth century, modernity would dismantle this symbiotic
world by redirecting linkages that had served to maintain relationships
between local elites and the imperial center. Despite Istanbul's resolve to
address the divisions that were occurring during the *Tanzimat* period
(state centralization and modernization, mid-ninetenth-century), new as-
sociations with emerging European powers and resources encouraged
prominent locals to sever their ties with the imperial center. As the merchant classes grew in strength through increased trade with Europe, particularly those of the empire's Christian population, which was accorded
various privileges by European powers, the *millet* system began to un-
ravel at its seams. This decline in the effectiveness of central authority
further allowed local ethnic communities to increasingly thrive apart
from the empire and embrace particularistic qualities with greater assur-
ance.[79] Ultimately, the Islamic *umma* would become disjointed, both ma-

---

77. Studies on the *dhimmi* and the *millet* are extensive, most of which are politically charged to either demonstrate hatred of Jews at the hands of Muslims, or to
argue for a symbiotic Islamic-Jewish "golden age." For a fair treatment of this
topic, see Mark R. Cohen, *Under Crescent and Cross: The Jews in the Middle
Ages*, Princeton, New Jersey: Princeton University Press (1994).
78. Albert Hourani, *Arabic Thought in the Liberal Age: 1798-1939*, London and
New York: Oxford University Press (1967:31).
79. See Caglar Keyder, *State and Class in Turkey: A Study in Capitalist Development*, London and New York: Verso Press (1987); Kemal Karpat, *An Inquiry
into the Social Foundations of Nationalism in the Ottoman State: From Social
Estates to Classes, from Millets to Nations*, Princeton, New Jersey: Princeton
University Center of International Studies, Research Monograph no. 39 (1973).

terially and politically, causing "a drastic transformation in the structure, philosophy, and identity of the non-Muslim *millets*...who broke up into smaller groups in which ethnic and religious affinity became outwardly the basis of identity."[80]

This process of fragmentation was first rooted in the Greek revolt of 1821 and would continue throughout the nineteenth century with the subsequent emergence of Arab nationalism, coming into maturity only after World War I. For the first time in its history, Islam's universalism faced the threat of disintegration as Greek, Arab, Turkish, Kurdish, Armenian, and other regional nationalists made restorative claims over "lost" remnants of cultural identity. Similar in character to the process that Luther and the *Risorgimento* had introduced in Europe, this would entail a re-mapping of sacred space.

As sociologists and anthropologists have repeatedly demonstrated, religious institutions seem to be an essential element in the formation of social identities and thus affect all forms of social and political life.[81] Their symbols, festivals, and rituals have accordingly proven to be sticky points for the modern nation-state. Quite conscious of this dynamic at their inception, states would seek to nationalize religious institutions. Within the Islamic world, as was generally the case elsewhere, developing states introduced new symbols and rituals in order to give particularistic expression to an otherwise universalistic ethos. "These colonial States," as one Islamic writer complains, "now called nation-States, are replete with national flags, national anthems, national days...national dresses, national cultures, and national histories....Every new nation is defined in exclusivist terms."[82] The methodical division of the Ottoman Empire into discrete states under British and French mandates and other so-called "Protectorate" policies was carried out in such a way as to suggest and provoke the existence of nationalist struggles within those

---

80. Kemal Karpat, "The Ottoman Ethnic and Confessional Legacy in the Middle East," in Milton J. Esman and Itamar Rabinovich, *Ethnicity, Pluralism, and the State in the Middle East*, Ithaca and London: Cornell University Press (1988:46).

81. For an interesting discussion of how "religion" interweaves into the politics of the modern state see Talal Asad, *Genealogies of Religion: Discipline and Reasons of Power in Christianity and Islam*, Baltimore, Maryland: Johns Hopkins University Press (1993).

82. Kalim Siddiqui, "Nation-States as Obstacles to the Total Transformation of the *Ummah*," in M. Ghayasuddin, *The Impact of Nationalism on the Muslim World*, London: Open Press (1986:3).

newly formed state boundaries. History was thus employed so as "to instill patriotism in Egyptians, Iraqis, Jordanians, Lebanese, and Syrians."[83]

While much of the *umma* was being sliced to pieces in the late nineteenth and early twentieth century, many intellectuals, including Jamal al-Din al-Afghani and Muhammad Abduh, responded that the *umma* was greater than the countries, nations, and languages that composed it. In the words of Abduh, the "religion of Islam is the one bond which unites Muslims of all countries and obliterates all traces of race or nationality."[84] Indeed, some have gone so far as to argue that Afghani and Abduh understood nationalism "as a divisive rather than a unifying spirit—a cover, in fact, for tyranny and injustice."[85]

The question that would naturally emerge out of the conflict between nationalism and the *umma* would challenge the Muslim world to revisit how its "community" was to be defined. The disintegration of the Ottoman Empire eventually led even its Muslim inhabitants to search for alternative forms of identity. The Arab nationalist response was composed of Arab elites who substituted the concept of *watan* (the nation) for that of the *umma*, opening up debate as to questions regarding which historical memories and narratives the "nation" and its "people" should retain. Suddenly, for example, the notion of identity being inextricably linked with Mecca and Muhammad as symbols of origin was not a given, as new national borders implied ownership of such older legacies as those of the Pharaohs, the Hittites, and the Phoenicians. Whether or not the *umma* could be retained under this new system of states was also difficult to answer, mainly because the unified political structure of the world empire was no more, which made references to Mecca, a singular place and time, as the foundation of identity tenuous. Such new states would instead look for alternative time-space markers to define their "nation."

Thus, the concept of the Arab nation would break radically with the old narrative of time and space embodied by the *umma*, having an effect upon the centrality of Mecca in the imagination of the peoples that popu-

---

83. Eugene Rogan and Avi Shlaim (eds.), *The War for Palestine: Rewriting the History of 1948*, Cambridge, U.K.: University of Cambridge Press (2001:5).

84. Citation of Abduh is from Charles C. Adams, *Islam and Modernism in Egypt: A Study of the Modern Reform Movement Inaugurated by Muhammad 'Abduh*, London: Oxford University Press (1933:59).

85. Malcolm H. Kerr, *Islamic Reform: The Political and Legal Theories of Muhammad 'Abduh and Rashid Rida*, Berkeley: University of California Press (1966:138-39). Citation is from Adeed Dawisha, *Arab Nationalism in the Twentieth Century*, Princeton and Oxford: Princeton University Press (2003:20).

lated the region. According to the old, imperial conception, temporal meaning began with Muhammad's revelation and the events occurring around Mecca and Medina. Everything preceding this time and place was relegated as prehistory, a period defined as "the age of ignorance" (*Jahiliyya*). Identifying as a Muslim entailed a historical memory that recalled Muhammad's engagement with the Archangel Gabriel, the purification of the Prophet's heart, his great pilgrimage to Mecca, and his cleansing of its Ka'ba, in which he dismantled all the old pagan deities from the Sacred House. All of these memories created a unified notion of time. Space, likewise, flowed from this very center and resonated outward through the Islamic expansions, with Mecca retaining its centrality even in the peripheral regions of Islam.

Arab nationalists would shatter the *umma's* time-space paradigm by going on a quest for a new "golden age." In some instances this nationalist model would entail a reappraisal of the *Jahiliyya* period by highlighting the glorious past of pre-Islamic civilizations found in Babylonia and Assyria, and in the periods of the Pharaohs, the Phoenicians, the Hittites, and the Canaanites. Sami Shawkat, for instance, an Iraqi director-general of education, wrote in his speech of 1939:

> The Arabs existed before Islam and before Christianity.... We have up to now neglected a most vital aspect of our glorious history; we have made it start at the prophetic message, and this is a period of less than fourteen centuries. In reality, however, the history of our illustrious Arab nation extends over thousands of year....This took place before the Torah, the Gospels, or the Koran. [A particularistic play on Muhammad's universalistic insistence that Abraham was a Muslim before the Torah or Gospel?]....The Chaldean, the Assyrian, the African, the Pharaonic, or the Carthaginian, all these [are] our ancestors. These...are all our property; they are of us and for us; we have the right to glory in them and to honor their exploits, just as we have the right to cherish and exalt the glories of Nebuchadnezzar, Hammurabi, Sargon, Rameses, Tutankhamen.[86]

---

86. Quoted in Sylvia G. Haim, *Arab Nationalism: An Anthology*, Berkeley: University of California Press (1974:36-37).

Shawkat was but one of a group of many nationalists that discovered the lure of this pre-Islamic past and worked aggressively to collect antiquities, many of which they had to acquire from the French and from other European countries, for their newfound museums and storehouses.[87]

As the nationalist conception of space was inherently narrower in scope than that of the *umma*, derived notions of sacred space would tend to be limited within regional borders, effectively undermining the centrality of Mecca and Medina virtually across the whole of the Islamic world. In order for a nation to successfully inspire a sense of identity specific to the peoples within its borders, it had to articulate imagined origins also contained exclusively within its territorial reach. Consequently, each new nation-state would carefully re-frame social perceptions of time and space to form new historical narratives that could engender a novel sense of peoplehood.

Alongside this concerted effort there existed numbers of Pan-Arabist nationalists who spoke of a grander Arab nation that extended well beyond any particular state and included all regions sharing the linguistic and cultural characteristics of the much larger *watan*. These nationalists, unlike their territorialist counterparts, insisted upon the continued centrality of Mecca, but in doing so, they would give it a nationalist twist, appropriating its time-space specificities to fit their own conception of the Arab nation. As Israel Gershoni argues, they nationalized Islam "so as to make it comport with the postreligious nature of Arab nationalism" and, in effect, "stripped away its universal transcendental and legal dimensions, undermining its status as the supreme arbiter of communal identity." For these Pan-Arabists, Mecca would become a vehicle, a symbol, "a tool, another 'component' to erect the edifice of Arab national identity."[88]

Moreover, when many from this camp discussed Islam or Mecca, they placed it within the context of its Arabness and spoke of it as the property of a "Chosen People" in a manner not unlike that found in the Old Testament. Implicitly denying Muslim identity, they argued that *Ar-*

---

87. Indeed, most of the Arab intellectuals who would come to theorize and develop the concept of the Arab nation were educated in Europe and attained much of their knowledge and admiration of ancient civilizations through the collections provided to them by the great European Orientalists of their time. See Albert Hourani, *Arabic Thought in the Liberal Age* (1967).

88. Israel Gershoni in James Jankowski and Israel Gershoni (eds.), *Rethinking Nationalism in the Arab Middle East*, New York: Columbia University Press (1997:8).

abs were chosen by God, through the *Arab* Prophet Muhammad, to spread the glorious message of the Qur'an. Rashid Rida, a prominent proponent of this idea, writing in 1900, in his influential essay "The Turks and the Arabs" remarks:

> I want to say that the greatest glory in the Muslim con- quests goes to the Arabs, and that religion grew, and be- came great through them; their foundation is the strong- est; their light is the brightest, and they are indeed the best *umma* brought forth into the world....A little knowledge of past and present history shows that most of the countries where Islam was established were con- quered by the Arabs who were the active agents of the propagation of Islam.[89]

The Qur'an and Sunna, he continues, are their cultural property, for "both are in Arabic. No one can understand them unless he understands their noble language."[90]

Not all Arab nationalists spoke of Islam in this way. Some, on the other end of the spectrum, actually chose to narrate and construct the na- tion by completely denying Islam its Meccan heritage. This was espe- cially the case for Christian Arab intellectuals who almost completely ignored the topic in their speeches and treatises. References to the Hijaz, if made at all, were rare, and their descriptions of forthcoming Arab states would envision its "natural frontiers" to include "the valley of the Euphrates and the Tigris, the Suez Canal, the Mediterranean, and the In- dian Ocean."[91] This group would even at times go so far as a complete erasure of the Hijaz, including its two cities of Mecca and Medina, from their maps of the Arab world. Much like Luther's attempt to filter into obscurity Rome's sacred place within the imagination of European

---

89. Quoted in Sylvia Haim, *Arab Nationalism* (1974:23).
90. Ibid. (1974:23). But as Adeed Dawisha and others have recently argued, Rashid Rida and many other intellectuals of his time were not necessarily na- tionalists and in fact saw nationalism "as a Western-inspired assault against the solidarity of the Islamic *Umma.*" Adeed Dawisha, *Arab Nationalism* (2003:22).
91. Sylvia Haim, *Arab Nationalism* (1974:27).

Christians, some Arab nationalists would likewise attempt to eradicate Mecca as the spiritual centrality of the Arab world.[92]

Unlike Luther, however, this view would remain in the minority as most Arab nationalists would include Mecca and the Hijaz within their vision of the Arab state, albeit as a national symbol alluding to the historical greatness of the Arab spirit. Thus, the old narrative that had long endured, presenting Mecca as the spiritual capital of the entire Islamic *umma*, was transformed into a symbol of Arab greatness that non-Arab Muslims would be obliged to recognize and accept. As Abd al-Rahman al-Kawakibi states in his "The Excellences of the Arabs":

> The peninsula is the place from which the light of Islam originated. It contains the Exalted Ka'aba. In it is found the Prophet's Mosque and the holy ground of his house, pulpit and grave....The Arabs of the Peninsula have Islamic unity because religion has become ingrained in them because religion is more compatible with their social customs than with those of others....The Arabs of the peninsula are the most zealous of all Muslims in preserving religion, in supporting it, especially as that zeal for the Prophet's cause is still alive among them in the Hijaz.[93]

The Pan-Arabists who led the efforts to include Mecca within the nationalist framework inducted it into the emerging vision of an Arab commonwealth that had already generated its own flag and anthem. By this time, many nationalists began to debate whether or not to Arabize the Caliphate as well, disliking that a Turk should be given such distinction in place of an Arab, without which neither Prophet and Qur'an, nor Islam and its expansion would exist. Such logic reasoned that the spiritual head, as represented in the Caliphate, ought to emulate God's own Choice in designating an Arab to be His Prophet. Moreover, the framing

---

92. This does not mean that they sought to eradicate all physical sacred space by insisting upon the necessity of faith in place of seeing, as Luther had done earlier. Indeed, Jerusalem was very important to these Arab Christians (as well as to the Muslims), partly because they identified it with their faith, but also because it was a universally sacred site to all Arabs, which made it very attractive as a nationalist symbol.

93. Quoted in Sylvia Haim, *Arab Nationalism* (1974:78-79); originally published in Cairo in the influential periodical *al-Manar* in 1901-1902.

of this argument would also support the renewal of Mecca as an Arab
national theme of centrality, as God's Choice of an Arab land would be
emphasized alongside His Choice of an Arab people. Such particularistic
language would lead to a notion that the Caliph should be of Arab
"stock" and residing in the Arab land of Mecca itself. Al-Kawakibi articulates this idea most clearly:

> Because of the Arab's special place in the history of Is-
> lam, regeneration of the Islamic world should be the
> work of the Arabs who could simply be a caliph, resid-
> ing in Mecca, and acting as a spiritual head of the Is-
> lamic union. He would be a religious authority, a kind of
> Islamic pope, an ultimate authority in matters of religion,
> and a symbol of Islamic unity.[94]

Further, the Caliph was to be an Arab, because "of all nations [he is] the
most suitable to be an authority in religion and an example to the Muslims; the other nations have followed their guidance at the start and will
not refuse to follow them now."[95]

The belief that non-Arab Muslims as well as Shiites would accept
this Arab and Sunni nationalization of Mecca, Medina, and the Hijaz
proved, however, to be a flawed one, as we will see shortly. As this became apparent to the Arab nationalists, they grew defensive and even
more arrogant, further amplifying their nationalist position. This account
by Abd al-Rahman al-Bazzaz demonstrates to what length they would
push the argument:

> These *shu'ubis* (non-Arab Muslims) confined their inter-
> est, their consideration and their appreciation to the
> Prophet in a forced manner and separated him from oth-
> ers before him, from his contemporaries and his compa-
> triots, *converting him into a universal being snatched
> from his land and sky, freed from his history and people.*
> These *shu'ubis* pictured Muhammad as a prosperous
> plant growing in an empty desert, no one having helped
> him, and himself indebted to anyone's help.[96]

---

94. Quoted in Sylvia Haim, *Arab Nationalism* (1974:26-27).
95. Ibid. (1974:27).
96. Quoted in Nissim Rejwan, *Israel in Search of Identity*, Gainesville and Tallahassee: University Press of Florida (1999:128-29). Emphasis added.

Such a framework would be explicitly used to compare the Arab's role in the Islamic world with that of the Russian in the Communist world, suggesting that just as Communism had been birthed by a national, Russian population and then passed onto other nations, so too had Islam been born of Arabs who had only later made it available to others: "If we may take an instance of contemporary history, we can say that the positions of the Arabs in Islam is like that of the Russians in the Communist order."[97] Nationalists would use no imagery more frequently than that of the Arab in their efforts to rub out the universalistic tone of the *umma* and promote the particularism of the *watan*. Faisal positioned himself to be king of Greater Syria prior to his expulsion by the French in 1920: "We are Arabs before being Muslim, and Muhammad is an Arab before being a prophet....We were Arabs even before the time of Moses, Muhammad, Jesus, and Abraham."[98]

Eventually, a compromise was proposed that would integrate the universalistic theme of the old narrative with this chauvinistic nationalism: an Arab Caliphate was to reside within the Hijaz with a guarantee from nationalists of its independence, so that it might properly serve the entire Islamic world. This position bore great resemblance to that of the neo-Guelfs in Italy, in which they proposed that the pope would lead the Christian world from within the confines of his home in the new Italian kingdom, which had also been reduced to a strict territorial interpretation of the religion's spiritual and historical center. Indeed, the similarity between the two solutions is baffling, as is evident in Negib Azour's 1905 statement entitled, "Program of the League of the Arab Fatherland":

> The Arab fatherland offers the universal religious caliphate over the whole of Islam to that sherif (descendant of the Prophet) who will sincerely embrace its cause and devote himself to this work. The religious caliph will have as a completely independent political state the whole of the actual vilayet of the Hijaz, with the town and the territory of Medina, as far as Agaba. He will enjoy honors of a sovereign and will hold a real moral authority over all the Muslims of the world....The successor of the Prophet of Allah must enjoy an incontestable moral prestige; his whole life must be of unblemished honor, *his authority suffering no diminution, his majesty*

---

97. Quoted in Ibid. (1999:29).
98. Quoted in Sylvia Haim, *Arab Nationalism* (1974:35).

independent of anything other than itself. His power will
be universal; from his residence he will rule morally
over all the Muslims of the universe who will hurry in
pilgrimage to the sanctuaries of Muhammad....There is
indeed no country more Islamic than the Hijaz, and there
are no towns more suitable than Medina and Mecca to
receive the Supreme Head of the believers.[99]

But this compromise would meet the same fate as that of the neo-Guelfs,
falling upon deaf ears and becoming lost to history. Arab nationalists
would reign supreme and find a home among the most influential sectors
of Arab society.

The Arab nationalist, however, was not the only force seeking to nationalize Mecca. Events surrounding World War I, along with its baggage of political turmoil, would catapult the holy region onto center stage
in the Middle East, eventually capturing Great Britain's attention. The
British understood as well as did the nationalists and Ottoman officials,
that the Hajj, the most central event in the Islamic calendar, could be appropriated as a political tool, becoming in the process more than a purely
religious festival. As Malise Ruthven remarks, "with so many Muslims
gathered together from different parts of the world, it contains a political
message and the potential for political action."[100] The question of
Mecca's centrality to the Islamic world was especially delicate for Britain in 1914, as it had, by then, colonized more than half of the global
Muslim population. Many British officials feared that the political implications of being too closely involved might provoke Istanbul, to which
the Hijaz belonged, causing the sultan to rally the entirety of its Muslim
population against the British and its allies under the rubric of Jihad. This
fear of a Holy War would hound the British for the duration of the
war.[101] A British operative, for example, stationed in Cairo in 1916
would report having overheard the following scheme discussed by some
Egyptian *ulema* (Qur'anic sholars):

---

99. Quoted in Sylvia Haim, *Arab Nationalism* (1974:81-82), emphasis added.
100. Malise Ruthven, *Islam in the World*, New York: Oxford University Press
(1984:29).
101. David Fromkin, *A Peace to End All Peace: The Fall of the Ottoman Empire
and the Creation of the Modern Middle East*, New York: Avon Books (1990:97-
98).

They were maintaining that the movement of the Sherif [Husayn of Mecca] is a political device arranged between the Sherif and the Turkish Government to deceive the British, by an apparent loyalty....The Allies were to be deceived, and the pilgrims were to arrive from Egypt, India and elsewhere. Mecca would then be made a meeting place of a Muslim congress, which would arrange a general union of Islam and a declaration of a Holy War in all Christian-controlled countries.[102]

British, as well as French fears of a massive, Pan-Islamic movement targeting Allied interests was no new development, as many Europeans had held a notion that the Ottoman sultan "sat at the centre of an intricate web of intrigue and conspiracy with tentacles all over the world of Islam."[103] The Germans, having formed amicable relations with the Ottoman Empire, in contrast to the British, entertained the same themes with a sense of optimism, possibly even fanning the flames when, for example, the foreign minister foresaw "that the sultan would 'awaken the fanaticism of Islam' and might lead to a large scale revolution in India."[104]

As Britain constantly dreaded the possibility of upheaval, not only within its colonies, but also near strategic sea routes, it pondered closely the possibility of a strong involvement in the development of a nationalized Mecca. Despite a clear understanding of the dangers involved, many British officials who were aware of various Arab nationalist sentiments, particularly of the strong efforts to disengage from Ottoman rule, began to favor the institution of an Arab Caliphate in Mecca, which would draw authority away from Istanbul. In fact, this position had already been advocated long ago, when in 1878, for example, a servant of the British consul, named James Zohrab, had relished the possibility of a centralized Mecca within the orbit of British influence. Zohrab had even gone so far "as to advocate the separation of the Hijaz from the Ottoman Empire, and its affiliation with Great Britain, which would then be in an enviable position to influence Muslims in India and elsewhere."[105] However, he

---

102. Quoted in Martin Kramer, *Islam Assembled: The Advent of the Muslim Congress*, New York: Columbia University Press (1986:57).
103. Elie Kedouri, *Islam in the Modern World and Other Studies*, London: Mansell Publishing (1980:54-55).
104. Quoted in David Fromkin, *Peace to End All Peace* (1990:109).
105. Martin Kramer, *Islam Assembled* (1986:13-14).

would also caution that a failure in developing strong commitments with Mecca could profoundly injure British colonial designs:

> The Province of the Hedjaz is the centre to which the ideas, opinions, sentiments and aspirations of the Mussalman world are brought for discussion. The annual meeting at a fixed time ostensibly for the performance of the Pilgrimage of Representatives from every Mussalman community affords a means, without creating suspicion, to exchange opinions, to discuss plans, to criticise the actions of the European Governments and to form combinations to resist supremacy of the Christian Powers.[106]

By the time the Great War was in full swing, Britain would begin to set its wheels in motion. In Cairo, the notion of a counter-Caliphate of Meccan and Quraishi origin was revived by British representatives and intelligence officials in an attempt to attract Muslim support for a confrontation with the Ottoman Empire. Sir Mark Sykes, who would propose a few years later to divide the Middle East between Britain and France into "Protectorates," wished "if possible to stimulate an Arab demand for the Caliphate of the Sherif" as part of a policy "to back the Arabic speaking peoples against the Turkish Government on one consistent and logical plane." Ronald Storrs took the same position, arguing that "it will presumably be not disagreeable to Great Britain to have the strongest spiritual head in the hands of the weakest temporal power," and he urged "that nothing remotely resembling an obstacle should be placed between the Sherif and his ambition." Lord Kitchener agreed with the sentiments of this view and had actually written a memo to Sherif Hussein to that effect: "[I]t may be that an Arab of true race will assume the khalifate at Mecca or Medina and so good may come by the help of God out of all the evil that is now occurring."[107] As the British had expected, Istanbul did attempt to invoke Jihad in an effort to bring the Islamic

---

106. Quoted in ibid. (1986:14).

107. All of the citations in this paragraph are quoted in Kramer, *Islam Assembled* (1986:62-63). Sherif Hussein was also in regular contact with the British, requesting support in his endeavors to create an Arab state. In one memo, for instance, he asks "England to approve of the proclamation of an Arab Khalifate of Islam," and for "England to acknowledge the independence of the Arab countries...." Quoted in Sylvia Haim, *Arab Nationalism* (1974:90).

world together in opposition to Europe, but upon its failure to do so, British officials eagerly took credit for having effectively intervened to nurture a split between Mecca and the Ottoman Sultan.[108]

It would be quite a stretch to propose that the British officials most closely involved in this matter had masterminded the so-called Great Arab Revolt against the Ottoman Empire, or even that they had initially supported the idea of Arab nationalism. Arab nationalists had been entertaining the advancement of a Meccan Caliphate for a few decades prior to the outset of the Great War. The British simply recognized that such a movement existed and when the time was ripe, it provided incentives for some Arab nationalists to continue down that path. However, they aided the nationalists only insofar as it helped the British war effort. Once that reason had expired, the British and French cooled down their rhetoric and worked not only to dismember the old Ottoman Empire, but also to extinguish the Pan-Arab dream they had once seemed to have supported. Mecca and the Hijaz had only been of interest to the Allied Forces in that they had provided a key to limiting Istanbul's leverage over the Islamic world. The Allies had thus used the holy city only as a neutralizing device upon Ottoman efforts to stir Islamic sentiment.[109] In short, the Sherif of Mecca and his Arab nationalists had been duped and, to this day, the Arab world would be reminded of it at every crossing of a border checkpoint from Lebanon to Syria, Iraq to Jordan, Jordan to Israel, and so on, and perhaps most vividly so in making the Hajj and crossing into Saudi Arabia.

The Ottoman Empire, however, would not give up so easily. In response to the British and French backing of Arab nationalists and their discourse of Mecca, Istanbul launched its own propagandist reprisal, exploiting an alternate Pan-Islamicist message that the holy cities belonged to the *umma* and could not serve as a prized possession of any one group. Under this pretense, it advanced an alternative to nationalism in the form of Ottomanism, a thinly veiled and perhaps not so cleverly modernized version of the old empire. "By the very need to emphasize Ottomanism," writes William Cleveland, the sultan was "prevented from employing the political vocabulary of nationalism."[110] The Ottomans, who appreciated,

---

108. David Fromkin, *Peace to End All Peace* (1990:109).

109. Elie Kedouri, *Islam in the Modern World* (1980:53).

110. William Cleveland, "The Role of Islam as Political Ideology in the First World War," in Edward Ingram (ed.), *National and International Politics in the Middle East: Essays in Honor of Elie Kedourie*, London, England: Frank Cass Press (1986:96).

as did the nationalists, Mecca's great potency within the Muslim imagination, felt confident that its symbolic character held far more familiarity, through its historic association, with the empire than it did with political notions of nationalism.[111] Arab nationalists, pushing a highly particularistic agenda, needed to somehow reconcile their vision with the Muslim belief that had evolved of Muhammad having received Islam from above for the sake of all peoples. A famous *hadith* (recorded sayings of the prophet Muhammad) illustrates this: "Other prophets before me were sent only to their peoples, I have been sent to all humanity." The Ottomans thus believed that the Arab nationalist insistence that Mecca was to be regarded as first and foremost an Arab city went against the grain of thirteen centuries of Islamic history. In deploying a refurbished universalistic discourse, the Ottoman Sultan regularly advertised his full title as "Servant of the Holy Places" and commander of the faithful.[112] In this way, "the Ottoman ruler was elevated beyond nationality, and the Turkishness of the Ottoman house was subsumed by its dedication to the larger cause of Islam."[113]

Moreover, the Ottomans made the argument that Arab nationalists had broken solidarity with the Muslims and that the Sherif of Mecca had "agreed with the enemy of the Hejaz to place the blessed house of Allah, the *qibla* of Islam, and the resting place of the Prophet under the protection of a Christian state." Further dramatizing the dispute, the Sultan continued to harangue the Sherif, Hussein, claiming that he did "not serve the faith of Allah, of the messenger, or of the Islamic community," and that he had "broken the bond," having become "a traitor who sought to separate brother Muslims from one another and to aid the victory of the *kafir* [unbeliever] over the believer."[114] Such language was predominantly aimed at the empire's Arab subjects with the intention of crafting the message that non-Arab Muslims across the empire supported the Pan-Islamic cause:

> The Muslims of India say that the Ottoman Empire can
> be proud of its defense of the faith and that its sultans
> can be proud of their service to the two holy cities and
> their defense of them; and they say that the Ottoman

---

111. Sylvia Haim, *Arab Nationalism* (1974:40).
112. Suraiya Faroghi, *Pilgrims and Sultans: The Hajj under the Ottomans, 1517-1683*, London: I.B. Taurus & Co. (1994:10).
113. William Cleveland, "Role of Islam" (1986:94).
114. Ibid. (1986:95, 97).

Empire is today the main prop of the *sharia*....Those
who secede are *kafir*, especially at a time when the empire is engaged in a general war for the liberation of Islamic communities.[115]

This tug-of-war between the proponents of Arab nationalism and
those in favor of Pan-Islam would continue long after the Great War,
even surviving the abolition of the Caliphate in 1924. It would persist
throughout the short Sherifian period, extending into the establishment of
the kingdom of Saudi Arabia, and still remains evident in our contemporary period, in which the struggle is most vividly displayed within the
conflict between the Saudi-supported Wahabi creed of Islam and the Shiites of Iran.

Originating in the eighteenth century, the Wahabis followed Muhammad ibn Abd al-Wahab (1703-1787), a Hanbali spiritual reformer
who had called for the restoration of a "pure" Islam, as existed in
Mecca's and Medina's seventh-century era of prophecy. Al-Wahab, having formed a military alliance with the Saud tribe and its network of allies, embarked with them upon a conquest of the entire Arabian peninsula and managed by 1926 to have crowned the successful effort with a
hold over the Hijaz in its entirety.[116]

The Wahabi movement zealously identified customs and rituals derived from historical Islam, such as its perception of an "excessive cult of
Muhammad" and "the worship of saints and reverence for their
shrines,"[117] as polytheistic innovations completely unrelated to the message contained within the Qur'an. Using such rhetoric, the Wahabis
railed against "impure idolatry," demolishing tomb sites attributed to
saints and Imams. Most remembered for their actions of 1802, the Wahabis, on this occasion, ravaged the tomb of the venerated Imam Hussein
in Karbala, massacring thousands of Shiites, "not sparing the infirm,
women and children who took refuge in the mosque."[118] In a report sympathetic to the Wahabi assault, the incident is described as follows:

Sa'ud set out his divinely supported army and cavalry....
He made for Karbala and began hostilities against the

---

115. Quoted in William Cleveland, "Role of Islam" (1986:94).
116. Malise Ruthven, *Islam in the World* (1984:26-27).
117. Quoted in Albert Hourani, *Arabic Thought in the Liberal Age* (1967:37).
118. John Sabini, *Armies in the Sand: The Struggle for Mecca and Medina*, New York: Thames and Hudson (1981:68).

> people of the city of al-Husayn....The [Wahabis] scaled
> the walls, entered the city by force, and killed the major-
> ity of its people in the markets and in their homes. Then
> they destroyed the dome placed over the grave of al-
> Husayn by those who believe in such things.[119]

The wider Muslim world, particularly Iranian and Indian Shiites, responded with great fury and often with violence to Wahabi hostilities
that had culminated in 1806 with the destruction of an important Shiite
cemetery in the Hijaz, later to be followed by a greater attack on the al-
Baqi tomb, which held the bodies of Fatima, Muhammad's daughter, and
of four of the original Imams.

Standard accounts of this Shiite-Wahabi conflict tend to describe it
as an eternal sectarian conflict between the two major sects of Islam,
emanating from the original disagreement in seventh-century Arabia over
the controversy of the Caliphate. Martin Kramer, for example, following
this line of reasoning, argues that the nineteenth- and twentieth-century
struggles over the shrines in the Hijaz are a product of the "Sunni-Shiite
animosities that had their origins in the seventh century, at the very dawn
of Islam."[120] While such depictions of derivative divergence offer an interesting and speculative perspective, it is astounding that modernity and
the grand transformative project of state building do not seem to figure
into the equation of these characterizations. After all, it is within the context of Arab nationalism and its aspirations toward a rigid sense of state
boundaries that radical shifts in Muslim identity begin to take shape, giving rise to newly inspired notions of a polluted "other," in this case, the
Shiites.

For the Saudis, therefore, Wahabism seemed to embody a religious
ideology that could be used to fuse its young notions of statehood with
society. As this alliance came to possess the most significant sacred sites
of the Muslim world in its effort to build a huge state, national unity was
taking form in religious themes of purity and eternity alongside a modern
atmosphere in all areas of daily life except for attire. Further, Saudi notions of purity were being developed within a context of defining territoriality. As Joseph Kostiner remarks, "Ibn Saud had to forego his concept
of flexible, undemarcated frontiers...and adopt the European concept of

---

119. Citation from Hamid Algar, *Wahhabism: A Critical Essay*, Oneonta, New
York: Islamic Publications International (2002:24).
120. Martin Kramer, *Islam Assembled* (1986:162).

a border line,"[121] when, coming into contact "with the British-dominated Transjordan and Iraq in the north," he was approached by the British high commissioner for Iraq, Sir Percy Cox, who educated him on the spot, through a carefully drawn line, as to what constituted a more "civilized" form of boundary.[122] As Wahabism, from the perspective of religious cultural identity, predominantly informed the emerging nationalism of the infant Saudi Arabia, sacred sites contained within the territory were subject to Wahabi notions of purity. Hence, those sites that were considered abominations were either eliminated, or remained within an atmosphere of growing cultural animosity. Clearly then, this modern nationalist project exploited religious notions of purity that referenced early imagery and notions of Islam and redefined them to serve *nationalist*, rather than religious initiatives. In this respect, the radical negation of Shiites within Saudi-dominated territories is more meaningfully understood as a repercussion of nationalist aspirations to build a modern state.

The newness of this conflict can be satisfactorily appreciated by comparing the status of Shiites in the age of Islamic Empires to that of our own. In the older narrative of empire, the Shiites, even though their religious law was not recognized under Sunni *sharia*, were visible members of the larger community of Muslims, forming a regional, religious *millet*. As Hourani explains, the Shiites formed a *millet* in which "their residence in distant places, in mountain valleys or on the edge of the desert, secured them a certain tolerance, and they lived as communities grouped around their holy cities and with their great families of scholars."[123] While it is true that under the rule of the Sunni Ottoman Empire, Shiites were at times "denied entry" to the holy cities on account of their religious practices,[124] violence toward them was rare. Indeed, Ibn Saud's famous remark in 1918 ("I would raise no objection if you demolished the whole lot of them, and I would demolish them myself if I had a chance")[125] would have made little sense in prior periods. As we will see in the next chapter, such nationalist discourse is not unlike certain ex-

---

121. Joseph Kostiner, "Transforming Dualities: Tribe and State Formation in Saudi Arabia," in Philip S. Khoury and Joseph Kostiner (eds.), *Tribes and State Formation in the Middle East*, Berkeley: University of California Press (1990:234).
122. Ibid. (1990:234).
123. Albert Hourani, *Arabic Thought in the Liberal Age* (1967:29).
124. Martin Kramer, *Islam Assembled* (1986:164).
125. Quoted in ibid. (1986:164).

tremist strains of present-day Zionism looking to demolish all traces of Palestinian existence in Jerusalem and Palestine.

Under the nationalist agenda and its implicit negation of universalistic notions of Islam, the clash between Saudis and Shiites would pose conflicting visions of Mecca. Each made claims of authenticity regarding how Mecca and the Hajj were to be maintained in the changing Muslim world. Indeed, this dispute had begun to play out immediately following Ibn Saud's assault upon the Hijaz, as a considerable segment of the Muslim world called for the formation of a general assembly in order "to regulate the holy cities." Moreover, Iranian and Indian diplomats strongly implored "all Muslims to use every possible means to expel Ibn Saud from the Hijaz."[126]

Such requests would continue throughout the period of Saudi rule in a manner reminiscent of the struggle that had earlier taken place between the Ottomans and the Arab nationalists. The Shiites, predominantly those residing in Iran, would appeal to the Muslim world community employing the universalistic discourse of the *umma* in opposition of Saudi claims of sovereignty over the Hijaz. Such strife is evident even as recently as 1987, when Saudi police killed more than four hundred rioting Iranian pilgrims, mostly Shiites, in Mecca. In response, the Ayatollah Khomeini, emphasizing the universality of Mecca, made the following charge against the Saudis:

> How is it that the Saudi police attack Muslims with jackboots and weapons, beat them, and send them to prisons from inside the holy mosque, a place which according to the teaching of God and the text of the Qur'an is refuge for all, even deviants?[127]

The message is clear: the Saudis had betrayed the will of God, having denied the privilege of *all* Muslims to congregate in His holy Mosque, where even the most estranged and downtrodden is welcome. They had acted arrogantly, as though claiming ownership of God's domain. Further, the Iranians insisted that the dispute did not stem from Sunni and Shiite differences, but from discordant conceptions that pitted a true vision of Islam against a false one: "They [Saudis] are now propagandizing and claiming that the incident was a war between Shiites and Sunnis," claimed Khomeini after the 1987 violence. "This is a lie! Of

---

126. Quoted in ibid. (1986:164-65).
127. Quoted in ibid. (1986:169).

course there is a war, but a war between the American perception of Islam and true revolutionary Islam."[128] Even prior to the Iranian revolution, the *sunni* and founder of the Muslim Brotherhood of Egypt had reached similar conclusions, claiming that the current struggle had been between those rightly guided, the Islamists, and those wrongly so, the nationalists:

> The point of contention between us and them is that we define the limits of patriotism in terms of creed, while they define it according to territorial borders and geographical boundaries. For every region in which there is a Muslim who says "there is no God but God, and Muhammad is his prophet" is a homeland for us, having its own inviolability and sanctity, and demanding love, sincerity, and striving for the sake of its welfare. All Muslims in these geographical regions are our people and our brothers; we are concerned about them, and we share their feelings and their sensibilities. The advocates of patriotism alone [*al-wataniya faqat*] are not like this, since nothing matters to them except the affairs of that specific, narrowly delimited region of the earth.[129]

Clearly, Mecca has remained a powerful symbol, having been preserved within a sharply delineated and divided Muslim world as the clearest expression of resistance to the particularistic character of modern statehood that has been superimposed over the universalistic vision of Islam. This is evident in the Iranian response of 1987 to the increase of U.S. troops placed in the Gulf, as the Hajj and traditional notions of Mecca were mobilized to display opposition, which sadly triggered the Saudi response.

Presently, the Saudis, as the largest U.S. ally in the Muslim world, cautiously assume guardianship of the Hijaz. While its holy cities of Mecca and Medina can serve to legitimize this role, displaying the grandeur of Saudi financial investment in their majestic appeal, they also have been a source of condemnation and conflict with the greater Muslim world regarding notions of ownership. The *umma* has managed to survive modernity, continuing to watch over its prized source that it can under no circumstances neglect, and the gaze that composes this com-

---

128. Quoted in ibid. (1986:162).
129. Quoted in Israel Gershoni and James Jankowski, *Redefining the Egyptian Nation, 1930-1945*, Cambridge, U.K.: Cambridge University Press (1995:82).

munity "is more outside the state boundaries of Saudi Arabia than inside it."[130] A sacred world city whose reach is too wide to be domesticated by any one state, Mecca continues to be a symbol of unity for a community dispersed over multiple states that often disrupt its sense of identity. In this manner, Mecca, as do its sister sacred world cities, invokes an imagined community that exists outside the scope of nationalism and cannot seem to be wholly appropriated by it.

---

130. Joseph Nevo, "Religion and National Identity in Saudi Arabia," in *Middle Eastern Studies*, vol. 34, no. 3, July (1998:35).

4

MODERNITY AND THE UNRAVELING OF JERUSALEM

But when the chosen people grew more strong,
The rightful cause at length became the wrong.

John Dryden, 1668

The border is not a spatial fact with sociological effects,
but a sociological fact which takes a spatial form.

Georg Simmel,[1]

Recent events clearly illustrate that the historic city of Jerusalem has hosted one of the world's most enduring and violent expressions of nationalism to date. Zionists and Palestinians alike have seen Jerusalem as an essential symbol of their sovereignty and, consequently, it has proven to be one of the final stumbling blocks in a peace process that has unfolded with tremendous difficulty, thus far unsuccessfully. Yet, in complete contradistinction with this virulent nationalism, the city has proven to be one of the most anti-nationalist sites in the world, for it is here, perhaps more than anywhere else, that a nationalist representation of geography has failed to concentrate the complex multidimensional identities that communities display on the ground. In this sense, Jerusalem has in recent times evolved a polar quality, in which fierce and chauvinistic nationalist identities exist in sharp contrast and highly at odds with universalistic, intertwined, and symbiotic ones that remain inextricably linked with the city's sacred character.

---

1. Georg Simmel quoted in Michel Warschawski, *On the Border*, Cambridge, Massachusetts: South End Press (2005:xvi).

It has long been fashionable among a wide range of scholarship to assume a time-immemorial origin for present-day conflicts that surround Jerusalem, in which the dispute between Jews and Arabs is colored with a primordial quality extending for thousands of years. While such illustrations, often veiled as factual and historical observations, may be meaningful on a mythological level, their underlying perspective falls exceedingly short in terms of analysis. Indeed, as Immanuel Wallerstein has argued generally about ethnic conflicts, the problem with claims of "ancient quarrels" is that they "are often inventions of contemporary imagination," a product of very recent developments, stemming from the institutional requirements of a modern world system.[2] From this perspective, any meaningful understanding of the Palestinian-Israeli conflict must begin with the recent process in which each began to perceive the other as a separate nation with distinct national identities and an imagined need for separate territorial spaces. Such a process, by definition of the term "nationalism," could not have been conceived in any historical period other than that of modernity, and more precisely, the nineteenth century, when ethnic particularism merged with nationalism in dramatic fashion. Although Israel would not be formed until several decades later, the seeds from which it would sprout can be understood to have been planted then.

Nevertheless, this picture becomes far more complicated when taking into account the fact that three sacred sites representative of the three great monotheistic religions in the West—the al-Aqsa Mosque, the Holy Sepulcher, and the Temple Mount—all continue to stand triumphantly, as though immune to such earthly disasters as nationalist territorial claims. While the world around these sites fragments and shatters into particularistic identities, they stand together, oddly unified. As witnesses to the rise and fall of world empires over the many centuries that they have endured, they have thoroughly blended into one another, forming, in effect, one intertwined and inseparable structure containing multiple layers of identity. As such a unit, these sites have managed to continually inspire a facet of the human imagination that has kept at bay nationalist forces that attempt to appropriate them and separate the communities they represent from one another.

---

2. Immanuel Wallerstein, *Utopistics: Or, Historical Choices of the Twenty-first Century*, New York: New Press (1998:55). As the French philosopher Ernest Renan has said, "A nation is a group of people united by a mistaken view about the past and a hatred of their neighbors," cited in Avi Shlaim: *The Iron Wall: Israel and the Arab World*, New York: W.W. Norton & Company (2001:xiii).

A predominant quality that distinguishes the nationalist intrusion of Jerusalem is that it has invoked a vision of the world that is divisible as an assembly of distinct individualities; in the present case, as two physically separate nations making essentialist claims on a shared territory. This notion is problematic in that it inspires conflict through a communal sense of otherness, as no territorial ground has yet proven capable of peacefully containing more than one nationalist notion of a "people," in its broadest and most reductive sense. In parts of the modern world, differing communities have existed side by side, to be sure, but nationally identified peoples have, to a large degree, only tolerated one another so far as they have agreed upon some established dividing line, not to be crossed under any circumstances without giving up prior allegiances, if such a transfer is even permitted. The question of nationality in the case of Jerusalem is particularly complicated in that its sacred spaces, invoking millennia of differing allegiances, have inspired distinct historical narratives that, over a long period of time, have become intertwined. The modern vision of a neatly divided world thus becomes extremely difficult to realize, as not only local communities, but world civilizations identified with different sacred sites diverge drastically in their claims upon the city, while almost paradoxically acknowledging the foundation they share in common. The spectrum of imagined community regarding Jerusalem ranges widely as it does in no other part of the Western world from a radical universalism that is inclusive of all faiths, even to the extent of non-faith-based secular beliefs, to several equally radical particularist notions that are sharply fundamentalist, nationalist, and bitterly divisive. Jerusalem is thus a place in which no clear demarcations can be drawn without threatening the entire foundation and relative sense of equilibrium that holds each and every group identified with the city. Stacked one upon the other, the removal or limiting of access to any one of the sacred sites would potentially lead to the collapse of Jerusalem's entire sacred structure. In this sense, as we will explore in conclusion, Jerusalem holds a unique place in the world for exploring the resolution of differences.

Here, however, we will limit the inquiry to an exploration of how a once symbiotic sacred landscape has deteriorated into levels of conflict that have not been seen since the horrific period of the Christian Crusades. Specifically, we will focus on locating the precise social roots regarding how the Palestinian/Arab has come to be seen as distinct from the Jew of the Middle East, to the contemporary conclusion that each now requires its own separate homeland. We will further analyze the repercussions of Jerusalem's partitioning upon Jewish, Arab, and Christian relations, examining the nationalist tug-of-war that has emerged out of an earlier age of world empires interested in unifying multiple identities. In doing so, we will trace the process by which the city's symbiotic culture was shattered, splintering into various particularistic identities, in a manner reminiscent, to some degree, of the radical impact that an encroaching Eurocentric capitalist system had only recently imposed upon the Ottoman *millet* system. Finally, as a contemporary example of conflict between nationalist and civilizational identities, we will consider the consequences of such dramatic social change that Jerusalem and its inhabitants have experienced to this day.

I
From Porous Frontiers to Policed Borders: Palestine and the Coming of Modernity

They're going to build the wall through my neighborhood.
My family and I, we are going to be on the wrong side of the wall.
I am in shock. I don't know what to do.[3]

The Palestinian author, Sami Hadawi, in his book *Bitter Harvest: A Modern History of Palestine*, tells of his childhood in Jerusalem before the coming of World War I and of the Balfour Declaration's proposal for a Jewish "home" in Palestine. His recollections reveal much about how radically Arab-Jewish relations have changed in such a short period of time. He remembers, for example, how children eagerly anticipated the springtime festivities in which "Moslem, Christian and Jew alike took part in the Moslem pilgrimage to the tomb of the prophet Moses." During the summer, he recalls, they all "flocked to the Valley to take part in the Jewish celebrations at the tomb of Sadik Shameon." And in other parts of the year, members of the three faiths "picnicked in the gardens around the tomb of the Holy Virgin Mary, near Gethsemane, where the Christian community spent a day and a night rejoicing." Savoring such memories, Hadawi concludes:

---

3. A female Palestinian resident of Jerusalem, cited in "Jerusalem Wall Will Cut Life in Two": http://www.oxfam.org.uk/what_we_do/where_we_work/israel_palterr/jerusalem_wall.htm.

Ours was indeed a Holy City, a city of peace, love and brotherhood, where the stranger could find shelter, the pilgrim loving care and the faithful salvation.[4]

Yet, by the time Hadawi had entered his youth, a change was already brewing in Palestine. At the turn of the twentieth century, as a young movement on the nationalist scene, Zionism had begun to turn its focus upon Palestine as a place ripe for the creation of a Jewish state. As Zionists, recognizing that the land was predominantly populated by Arabs, began to articulate an objective of replacing its indigenous non-Jewish population with a Jewish one, specifically showing preference for European Jewry, relations between Jews and Arabs in Palestine began to erode. Indeed, in Jaffa, for example, despite the fact that local elites from each community formed close personal bonds in many instances, Jewish sources reported a fear in the Arab population "that 'the Jews came to impose a foreign Government upon [them].'"[5] In 1905, Negib Azouri, an Arab journalist writing in Paris, had already predicted in a pamphlet the coming of a conflict between Jews and Arabs. Azouri called attention to an emerging effort by Jews "to reconstitute [themselves] on a very large scale the ancient kingdom of Israel," and he forecasted that such a movement would trigger the "awakening of the Arab nation." Further, he concluded that the confrontation between the two movements was a continuous function of destiny that could have implications for that of the entire world.[6]

Such reports would transform notions of "Arab" and "Jew" as separate peoples, posing the two "in a kind of permanent, irreconcilable opposition to each other, representing two entirely different cultures, ways of life, temperaments, mentalities, sets of values, and aspirations."[7] As Zionists proposed and generated exclusively Jewish settlements throughout Palestine, a nationalized mentality began to take clear form, in which "Jews would no longer want to live among Arabs, even in 'nice'

---

4. Sami Hadawi cited in Baruch Kimmerling and Joel Migdal, *The Palestinian People: A History*, Cambridge, Massachusetts: Harvard University Press (2003:77).

5. Mark LeVine, *Overthrowing Geography: Jaffa, Tel Aviv, and the Struggle for Palestine, 1880-1948*, Berkeley: University of California Press (2005:41).

6. Negib Azouri cited in Baruch Kimmerling and Joel Migdal, *Palestinian People* (2003:79).

7. Nissim Rejwan, *Israel's Place in the Middle East: A Pluralist Perspective*, Gainesville and Tallahassee: University Press of Florida (1999:4).

neighborhoods."[8] Today, such nationalist views have crystallized to the point that some Israelis even maintain the impossibility of loyal citizenry on behalf of Arabs residing in Israel. This view extends to essentialist notions that Arabs form a separate nationality that would be better served if they were "somehow able to find their way out of the country and settle in neighboring Arab states 'among their own people and in the midst of their Arab brethren.'"[9] In fact, such a position is not novel to the current state of affairs, as many of Israel's founding fathers, including the nation's first prime minister, David Ben-Gurion, went so far as to argue that since Arab Palestinians "did not constitute a distinct, separate nation, and were not an integral part of the country," they should be expelled from Israel and "transferred to other Arab countries."[10]

Many critics of Israel blame this change in social relations on the demographic transformation of Palestine. They emphasize, for instance, that at the time of Hadawi's childhood years, immediately preceding the very large expansion of Jewish immigration into Palestine under British control, the population of Jews was fewer than ten percent of the total Palestinian population, comprising 56,000 Jews as compared to 600,000 Arabs.[11] These numbers would be radically altered after the Zionist movement, verging upon the realization of an internationally recognized Jewish state, would provoke some 750,000 to 1 million Arab Palestinians, in fear of Jewish attacks on their villages, to abandon their homes in 1948, only to be denied the right of return by the new Israeli government. Many such families remain scattered even today in refugee camps throughout the occupied territories and other regions of the Middle East.[12]

---

8. Mark LeVine, *Overthrowing Geography* (2005:63-64).

9. Nissim Rejwan, *Israel's Place* (1999:4-5).

10. Nur Masalha, *The Politics of Denial: Israel and the Palestinian Refugee Problem*, London: Pluto Press (2003:16).

11. Avi Shlaim, *Iron Wall: Israel and the Arab World* (2001:7). Jewish numbers in Palestine were initially even smaller. In the 1880s there were only about 25,000 Jews in Palestine. See Rhoda Kanaaneh, *Birthing the Nation: Strategies of Palestinian Women in Israel*, Berkeley: University of California Press (2002:29).

12. Today, after the "Israeli state [has] carried out an active immigration policy," the majority of the inhabitants living in traditional Palestine are Jews, numbering approximately 4 million. Rhoda Kanaaneh, *Birthing the Nation* (2002:29).

While such numerical details obviously contribute to an understanding of the eventual conflict that would emerge, a deeper explanation lies in the manner by which Zionists distinguished Jews from Arabs, not only in nationalist terms, but along racial lines as well. As leading Zionists rejected the idea of sharing Palestine for the long term with its native population, embracing instead notions of transforming it into a "mono-religious" Jewish state, "its success," as Edward Said et al. argue, "required it to be as intent on the destruction of the indigenous Arab society as it was on the construction of a Jewish life in Palestine."[13] Consequently, the Zionist movement, following an agenda of complete segregation from its inception, created a "dual society" with an economic development policy devised to construct territorial partition and an employment program designed to refuse Palestinians jobs and create exclusively Jewish kibbutzim.[14] As Theodor Herzl, the founding father of Zionism, proclaimed:

> We shall try to spirit the penniless population across the border by procuring employment for it in the transit countries while denying it employment in our own country....Both the process of expropriation and the removal of the poor must be carried out discreetly and circumspectly.[15]

---

13. Edward Said et al., "A Profile of the Palestinian People," in Edward Said and Christopher Hitchens (eds.), *Blaming the Victim: Spurious Scholarship and the Palestinian Question*, London: Verso Press (1989:238). Former Prime Minister Yitzhak Rabin believed in minimizing the Palestinian population: "The red line for Arabs is 20% of the population, that must not be gone over," with the belief that the state of Israel must act aggressively to "preserve the Jewish character of the state of Israel not by name only, but also in action, values, language, and culture....This does not mean that no one lives in it except the Jews. But today [1993] there are 4.4 million Jews versus 2.8 or 3 million Arabs and this cannot continue." Yitzak Rabin cited in Rhoda Kanaaneh, *Birthing the Nation* (2002:50); original in *'Ittaihad*, Nov. 1, 1995.
14. For an extended discussion of this see the fine work of Gershon Shafir, *Land, Labor, and the Origins of the Israeli-Palestinian Conflict, 1882-1914*, Berkeley: University of California Press (1996).
15. Theodor Herzl, in Raphael Patai (ed.), *The Complete Diaries of Theodor Herzl*, New York: Herzl Press (1960: 87-88), cited in Michael Prior, *The Bible and Colonialism: A Moral Critique*, Sheffield, Eng.: Sheffield Academic Press (1997:113).

This combination, therefore, of demographic change with novel racialized and nationalized representations of peoplehood served to provide quite sufficient fuel for an inevitable and dramatic shift in social relations between Jews and Arabs. Zionist terminology would further fan flames as the movement enacted a "Judaization" project, while simultaneously "de-Arabizing" the land. Such language would concretize Arab otherness in the popular Jewish imagination, posing the Jew as a superior, more developed race that performed its duty by conquering, developing, and modernizing a Palestine that Arabs had neglected. In creating such a discourse, Zionism introduced a new notion of peoplehood into traditional Palestine, through which a border could be seen as a natural result of difference, hiding intentions to "negate the identity of those on the other side."[16] As John Rose has recently argued, this is how Zionism had introduced a divide between Arabs and Jews that was contrary to imperial Islamic Arab legacy.[17]

In order to appreciate the gravity of such change, particularly in light of time-immemorialist scholarship, it is important to emphasize that before the late nineteenth century, with few exceptions, the inhabitants of traditional Palestine, especially its Muslim, Christian, and Jewish communities, not only intermingled in the streets, but lived, played, and prayed in a neighborly fashion far more closely than can be imagined today;[18] and in no place was this more evident than in Jerusalem, where, as S.D. Goiten among others note, homes and other residential compounds were often shared to the extent that Muslims and Jews occupied different rooms under the same roof.[19]

Current formations of identity permit such familiarities precious little room. Even contemporary temples of knowledge house library stacks that are shelved in different sections, according to Jewish or Arab affiliation, "studied by different scholars, and are taught by different departments even though in some cases they come from the same place and time."[20] Indeed, in complete contradiction to modern notions of progress that champion tolerance, exchange, and inclusive societies, the nearer to

---

16. Michel Warschawski, *On the Border* (2005:xvii).
17. John Rose, *The Myths of Zionism*, London: Pluto Press (2004:63).
18. Ibid. (2004:74).
19. S.D. Goiten's comment is found in ibid. (2004:74); Mark Cohen, *Under Crescent and Cross: The Jews in the Middle Ages*, Princeton, New Jersey: Princeton University Press (1994:126).
20. Maria Rosa Menocal, *The Arabic Role in Medieval Literary History: A Forgotten Heritage*, Philadelphia: University of Pennsylvania Press (2004:21).

the present the lens is focused, the sharper the view of exclusivity becomes. As if obsessed with a newfound skill, nations are more efficient
than ever at policing their borders, always choosing to reinforce them at
any sign of tension or breach. In Israel, this has translated into an ever-
maturing image of Jews and Arabs as of two chemical compounds that
may combust if mixed together. This insistence upon separateness that
has engulfed Jew and Arab alike has served to implicitly suggest a sense
of ideological, social, and political volatility.[21]

Thus, turning to the post-WWI period, after three decades of British
colonial rule followed by the creation of the state of Israel in 1948, not
only has a demographic distortion of Palestine and the city of Jerusalem
emerged, but a completely new understanding of religion, ethnicity, and
nationality has as well. If thirteen centuries of Muslim/Arab rule, with its
complex, yet relatively effective system of inter-communal relations,
existed prior to modern times, "the present campaign by Israel and the
Zionist movement," as Naseer Aruri observes, "is geared towards a Jewish ascendancy and an erosion of Christian and Muslim influence."[22]

These changes are clearly visible when journeying through the region between Jordan, the Occupied Territories, and Israel, where one
must travel through many checkpoints, exclusively Jewish settlements,
and highways. Lacking proper papers and a properly colored license
plate, crossing from the Jordanian border into Jerusalem may take longer
than would a similar journey during the time of the Apostle Paul. For a
Palestinian, the journey is virtually impossible. G.W. Bowersock, a historian of the Middle East, captures this well:

> I have made the journey from the old Roman city of
> Philadelphia, which is the modern Jordanian capital of
> Amman, across the new Allenby Bridge to Jerusalem,
> but only with my papers in good order. There is no more
> instructive experience for a student of the Middle
> East...than this journey....For an ancient historian each

---

21. Ammiel Alcalay, *After Jews and Arabs: Remaking Levantine Culture*, Minneapolis: University of Minnesota Press (1993:8).
22. Naseer H. Aruri, "Misrepresenting Jerusalem," in Munir Akash (ed.), *The
Open Veins of Jerusalem*, Syracuse, New York: Jusoor Book distributed by
Syracuse University (2005:124).

barrier is a constant reminder that there was nothing comparable in former times.[23]

Those who posit an inherent conflict between Jews and Arabs rooted in ancient claims would be well served to compare the recent experience with the Muslim/Arab period, during which indigenous Jews and Christians were, with rare exception, accorded sufficient privileges with which to flourish as an essential element within a large international body despite having been placed in rank below Muslims.[24] Indeed, as Mark Cohen adds, "the Jewish and Christian *dhimmis* occupied a recognized, fixed, safeguarded niche within the hierarchy of the Islamic social order."[25]

The ghetto-like existence under which most Palestinians live today in both the Occupied Territories and Israel proper reveals just how utterly bankrupt the present circumstances have become. In his analysis of the Islamic period, Cohen observes further that "the topography of residence in a Muslim town lent the Jew an aura of inclusion, of normalcy" to the extent that "in most cities of the Islamic Mediterranean...Jewish quarters, in the sense of exclusive Jewish districts, hardly existed."[26] Such a description is in sharp contrast with the present period in which Jewish settlements have created a Swiss-cheese-like topography of Palestine, enclosing Arab inhabitants into Bantustans and ghettos. In the words of S.D. Goiten, most Jews under Muslim/Arab rule "lived in their towns in noncontiguous clusters, such that 'there were many neighborhoods predominantly Jewish, but hardly any that were exclusively so.'"[27] Indeed, it would appear that moving forward in time, at least in Palestine under nationalist rubric, severe regression has occurred rather than progress, as the common modern mythology would advertise.

Further examining the comparison, Moses Maimonides, a Jew living in twelfth-century Cordoba under Muslim-ruled Spain, exemplifies the notion of successful integration, while fully retaining cultural and religious roots. As Leon Roth explains, Maimonides did not entertain "the conception [that]...Judaism for him is...a product of 'race' or an inheritance of 'blood,' nor is it bound up exclusively with any one people or

---

23. G.W. Bowersock, "Palestine: Ancient History and Modern Politics," in Edward Said and Christopher Hitchens (eds.), *Blaming the Victim* (1989:185).
24. Ibid. (1989:187).
25. Mark Cohen, *Under Crescent and Cross* (1994:112).
26. Ibid. (1994:126).
27. S.D. Goitein cited in Ibid. (1994:126).

any one soil."[28] Living, as he did, within an imperial context that allowed for relatively healthy relationships between Jews and Christians and their Arab Muslim neighbors, naturally influenced his views.[29] Throughout his life, as he spoke and wrote in Arabic, dressed and behaved in Arabic fashion, and developed styles, patterns of thought, and worldviews that were Arab in flavor, Maimonides appreciated his existence as an Arab, while never once questioning his Jewish identity. The mere notion of friction and discontinuity between these two aspects of his identity seems never to have entered his thinking, to the extent that even the conception of his Arab surroundings as a contaminant would have been inconceivable.

Maimonides does not represent an isolated example, but rather the general state of affairs, at least in the fruitful Middle Ages of Islamic rule, if not throughout its entirety, with few exceptions. The manner, therefore, in which Zionists in the contemporary world would come to identify a notion of "influences" as the source of racial and national contamination requires further inquiry. Many of those who have subscribed to Zionist views have often used such language in fear that allowing Palestinian refugees to return would "undermine the Jewish state," or dreading mention of the one-state solution that would invite a radical shift in demography, in which Arabs and Jews would live as equal citizens. The policies pursued as a result of such language have been, under any standard, racist in flavor, and are only upheld due to the lack of public concern in both Israel and the United States, which continue to provide a green light.

As the Zionist movement developed its objective of transferring a largely Arab owned land into Jewish possession in the late nineteenth century and, by 1917, under the tutelage of imperial Britain, began to implement such goals, it would work extensively toward revising Arab notions of Jewish status under the Muslim social order.[30] As Charles Smith argues:

> Zionists and Zionist claims changed completely the traditional Muslim conception of Jews as occupying *dhimmi* status, protected by, but subordinate to, Mus-

---

28. Leon Roth, *The Guide for the Perplexed: Moses Maimonides* cited in Nissim Rejwan, *Israel's Place in the Middle East* ((1999:114).
29. Ibid. (1999:114).
30. Charles D. Smith, *Palestine and the Arab-Israeli Conflict*, New York: St. Martin's Press (1996:32-34).

lims....Zionism, as a European movement, came to be
seen initially as another attempt by Western imperialism
to subordinate Muslims to Europeans, and became even
more threatening once it was realized that the Zionists
wished to take part of what had been Arab lands for centuries and remake it into a Jewish homeland. Arab opposition emerged before World War I in response to Zionist immigration and land purchases...[31]

Such recent political realities, as opposed to claims of ancient and
destined quarrels that are almost genetic in character, provide a clear
context for understanding the origins of current conflict between Jews
and Arabs. With the final demise of the Ottoman Empire at the end of
World War I, a sense of "communal solidarity" that had predominantly
characterized relations between Jews and Arabs continued to exist under
the British mandate period, albeit subject to French and British manipulation and influence along sectarian lines.[32] Indeed, the status of the *millet* system that had existed in the nineteenth century under the Ottoman
Empire, which protected Christian and Jewish minorities, was quickly
being undermined by the early twentieth century, under the influence of
Britain and the Zionist movement. As Europe had recently risen in power
and had incorporated the Middle East into a Euro-centered modern
global system, the old confessional structure of the *millet* had given way
to a new system of special privileges for Christians. Such privileges
would come to extend to Jews as well.

The increase in hostilities that began to emerge between Palestinians
and Jews, as between Christians and Muslims in other parts of the Middle East, thus embodied an immediate response to changes that were occurring in the material and ideological realm of *modern* Palestine, quite
in contrast to biased and racialized characterizations that would describe
Arabs and Muslims as having an inherent cultural and religious incapacity to adjust to modernity. Typifying such a view, many Orientalists have
long produced studies of the "Orient" from the perspective of otherness,
presuming that some cultural and religious essence or worldview has
been the cause of regional hostilities and of failure to adjust to the tolerant and pluralistic standards of the modern West.[33]

---

31. Ibid. (1996:32-34).
32. Rhoda Kanaaneh, *Birthing the Nation* (2002:139).
33. In addition, as Rhoda Kanaaneh extended this argument to understanding
other inter-communal conflicts in the Middle East, "It is misleading to think of

Further examining the collusion between Britain and Zionists, it is worthy to note that Zionist Jews were active in the military administration of the British colony in Palestine throughout the entire period of British mandate, to the extent that an exclusively Jewish military force existed. Zionist Jewish experts were also important members of the British colonial land authority. Such realities help to portray the precise manner in which European intervention in Palestine strengthened the position of Zionist settlers at the expense of native Palestinians.[34] Economically, Britain facilitated Jewish land acquisition and provided for Jewish enterprises in a clearly recognizable protectionist policy of preferential tariffs that included the free importation of raw materials already produced in Palestine. Native Palestinians, by contrast, were treated as just another colonized nation and naturally resented such policy as a double standard. As British authority supported Jewish industry, while simultaneously weakening the Palestinian economic sector, it created in the process a dual economy with a discriminatory labor policy that introduced separate wage systems, which further alienated the indigenous population and encouraged the emergence of an exclusively Jewish industrial sector fully independent of the Palestinian Arab population and its economy.[35] Furthermore, as the British worked to weaken Palestinian resistance to their occupation, Jewish settlers benefited economically and politically as they continued to form massive and exclusive Jewish settlements on once Palestinian lands, while the British did the dirty work of actively subduing an indigenous Palestinian anti-colonial and anti-Zionist movement.[36]

---

so-called communal or sectarian divisions as inherent, ancient ones. They have been created at particular moments in specific ways. After the British and not unlike them, Israel attempted to consolidate its power by 'feeding and reinforcing confessional loyalties until they eclipsed national feelings' [Jiryis 1976:197]. Hence 'the government's preferences with regard to the maintenance of separate Druze, Christian, Moslem, Bedouin and Circassian identities, as opposed to the emergence among the non-Jewish minority of an overarching Arab or Palestinian sentiment' [Lustick 1980:135]." Both authors cited in Kanaaneh, *Birthing the Nation* (2002:140).

34. Samih Farsoun, *Palestine and the Palestinians*, Boulder, Colorado: Westview Press (1997:70).

35. Ibid. (1997:82-85).

36. See Gershon Shafir, *Land, Labor, and the Origins of the Israeli-Palestinian Conflict* (1996); Tom Segev, *One Palestine Complete: Jews and Arabs under the British Mandate*, New York: Metropolitan Books (2000).

Michel Warschawski, an Israeli activist, recently argues in his book *On the Border*, "it is a great historical irony that Zionism, which wanted to tear down the walls of the ghettoes, has created the biggest ghetto in Jewish history, a super-armed ghetto, capable of continually expanding its confines, but a ghetto nonetheless, turned inward upon itself."[37] In producing these ghettos, Jewish settlements today are placed strategically around largely Arab villages with the intent of fragmenting territorial access and blocking physical expansion.[38] The goal has been clearly articulated time and again: to produce a Jewish homeland at the expense of an indigenous population; to keep Arab and Jew completely separate, allowing little, if any space for mingling. Abba Eban has stated this most clearly: "We do not want Israelis to become Arab. We are duty bound to fight against the spirit of the Levant, which corrupts individuals and societies."[39]

II
Zionism's Devastating Impact on Jerusalem

In my work at the Ministry of Education I feel [the Palestinian] absence all the time. Not only are we educated to forget that Palestinians lived here and were deported when the state was established, but those Palestinians who did stay and became a minority among us are seen mainly as a threat to the Jewishness of the state. [40]

Daphna Golan-Agnon

THE RACIALIZATION OF JERUSALEM

Although early Zionists are well known for having depicted Palestine as "a land without a people for a people without a land," it is evident that upon their initial visits Zionists recognized conversely that the land was, in fact, well populated. However, they did not like what they found: numbers of Arab and "Oriental" Jews who had lived there for many cen-

---

37. Michel Warschawski, *On the Border* (2005:x).
38. Ghazi Falah (1989) cited in Kanaaneh, *Birthing the Nation* (2002:52).
39. Abba Eban cited in Ammiel Alcalay, *After Jews and Arabs* (1993:31).
40. Daphna Golan-Agnon, *Next Year in Jerusalem*, New York and London: New Press (2005:19).

turies. Indeed, with the exception of one century during the Crusades, Jerusalem had been fully integrated into the Arab Muslim world since the seventh century and its Jewish communities illustrated this fact well. During the 1,300 years of Muslim rule over Jerusalem, Muslims had comprised the majority of its population, while Jews had traditionally remained a small, but significant minority. In 1800, about a century before Zionism became an active force in Palestine, the Jewish population of Jerusalem was estimated to be about 2,000. Alexander Scholch, a scholar of Middle East studies, indicates that the Jewish presence in the city only began to significantly rise under the heavy pressure of the Zionist movement, which by 1880 had successfully increased the Jewish population to 17,000, and by 1922 had doubled that number to 34,400.[41]

In fact, the highly influential Israel Zangwill, who invented the slogan "a land without a people for a people without a land," soon discovered, upon visiting Jerusalem in 1905, "that Palestine proper had already its inhabitants. The province of Jerusalem is already twice as thickly populated as the United States, having fifty-two souls to the square mile, and not 25 per cent of them Jews."[42] Based on such unexpected observations, Zangwill summed up: "[We] must be prepared either to drive out by the sword the [Arab] tribes in possession as our forefathers did or to grapple with the problem of a large alien population, mostly Mohammedan and accustomed for centuries to despise us."[43]

The situation was further complicated by the fact that many of the Jews who had long been living in Palestine and had become part of its Arab social fabric were not initially attracted to Zionism.[44] Despite limited numbers, Jews were well represented in the everyday life of Jerusalem and formed part of the city's mosaic. Many of the old Sephardic quarters, such as Nahlaot, built by Jews from Yemen and Kurdistan, or the Moroccan Jewish Boukhara district, "still resemble the Moroccan Mellahs or the Jewish quarter of Damascus":

> Givat Mordechai was a village of young religious couples who lived in modest homes with red tile roofs surrounded by orchards. In Machane Yehuda, the Pinto, Gabai and Eliashar—those who are called "native

---

41. Alexander Scholch's population figure was taking from Naseer H. Aruri, "Misrepresenting Jerusalem" (2005:121).
42. Israel Zangwill cited in Masalha, *Politics of Denial* (2003:16).
43. Zangwill cited in ibid. (2003:15).
44. Michel Warschawski, *On the Border* (2005:14).

Sephardim"—were a true local aristocracy before the
seizure of the community by the Zionists. They still
spoke Ladino in the cafes where they played backgam-
mon while drinking arak to the sound of songs by Farid
el-Astrashe.[45]

Upon witnessing the existence of such Arab Jews, an utterly alien reality
to them, Zionists, who had already begun to characterize the Arab world
with racial terminology, did not even consider forming strong relationships with the existing Jewish population.[46] They had already begun to
envision a modern, European-inspired Jewish state.

In fact, many of the early Zionists, such as Theodor Herzl, Chaim
Weizmann, Ahad Ha'am, Vladmir Jabotinsky, and David Ben-Gurion,
all shared little respect for the Old City as it stood. Herzl, quite secular in
his outlook, never having circumcised his only son, looked to Haifa, with
its access to Europe and the Mediterranean Sea, rather than Jerusalem,
which he felt, "was redolent with fanaticism and superstition, the musty
deposit of 'two thousand years of inhumanity and intolerance....The
amiable dreamer of Nazareth has only contributed to increasing the hatred.'"[47] In his futurist novel, *Old New Land*, Herzl would carry this
theme in a more racist direction: two Germans, a Jew, and a Christian
visit Palestine before and after the establishment of the state of Israel,
witnessing how the Zionist movement has effectively exchanged the Oriental impurities of the past for the more modern and Europeanized society the new Israel has become.[48]

Herzl's racist discourse toward Palestinian Arabs and Oriental-Jews
was quite typical of the Zionist movement. Chaim Weizmann followed
similar themes. After his visit to Jerusalem in 1910, he wrote of his dis-
pleasure with its Oriental character, adding that "I remained prejudiced
against the city for many years and even now I still feel ill at ease in it,

---

45. Ibid. (2005:14)
46. Arthur Hertzberg, "Jerusalem and Zionism," in Nitza Rosovsky (ed.), *City of
the Great King: Jerusalem from David to the Present*, Cambridge and London:
Harvard University Press (1996:150).
47. Theodor Herzl cited in Amos Elon, "The Deadlocked City," in *The New
York Review of Books* (October 18, 2001).
48. Theodor Herzl, *Old New Land*, Lotta Levensohn (trans.), Princeton, New
Jersey: Markus Wiener ([1902] 1997:61).

preferring Rehovoth to the capital."[49] Weizmann further was "revolted by rabbis imposing themselves on politics and by politicians playing with religious fires"[50] and he complained that he would not even take the Old City "as a gift," for it presented "too many complications and difficulties."[51]

Even those early Zionists who were critical of such views as their comrades held did not have many good things to say about Jerusalem. As Arthur Hertzberg recounts, in 1891 Ahad Ha'am, a writer who was highly critical of the Herzl camp, watched a great many Jews praying out loud as they stood in front of the Western Wall in Jerusalem. Ha'am's remarks reveal much about how Zionists viewed the Arab Jewish community in Palestine. As these Jews formed part of the Old Yishuv, Ahad Ha'am was not pleased with what he saw:

> As I stand and look at them, a single thought fills my mind. These stones bear witness to the destruction of our land, and these men to the destruction of our people. Which of the two catastrophes is the worse? Which gives greater cause for mourning?[52]

Early Zionists were heavily influenced by European anti-Semitic ideas, and they believed themselves to be on a mission to remake the Jew as a modern, European-like subject. The old Jewish communities of Jerusalem represented what these new Zionist settlers wanted to negate. As a result, Zionists would aggressively denounce these Arab Jews as "parasitical": "He was to be replaced by a 'new Jew' who would achieve the settlement of Palestine by means of productive agricultural work."[53] Even European non-Zionist Jews, such as Sigmund Freud, soon joined the discussion. After the militant Zionist group, Betar, had begun to clash with Palestinians not far from the Wailing Wall in 1936, Freud, in his remarks to Einstein, complained that he had no sympathy "for the mis-

---

49. Chaim Weizmann cited in Naseer H. Aruri, "Misrepresenting Jerusalem" (2005:111).
50. Amos Elon, "Deadlocked City" (October 18, 2001).
51. Chaim Weizmann cited in ibid.
52. Ahad Ha'am cited in Arthur Hertzberg, "Jerusalem and Zionism" (1996: 157).
53. Joseph Croitoru cited in Joachim Schlor, *Tel Aviv: From Dream to City*, London: Reaktion Books (1999:31).

guided piety that makes a national religion out of a piece of the wall of Herod..."[54]

Many of the early settlers consciously stayed away from Jerusalem.[55] A good number of them worked and lived in the emerging and completely new Tel Aviv, which quickly became the center of the movement. Tel Aviv was a "modern" and "Western" city, which settlers preferred to other urban centers that many perceived as infested with Oriental-like inhabitants. While they loved the modernity of Tel Aviv, they equally despised Jerusalem: "With its synagogues, ghetto-like neighborhoods and its Oriental market, its Jews in kaftans and fur hats, it reminded them too much of the Diaspora they hated."[56] Such imagery represented an old world to the European settlers that seemed to belong to earlier times. Further, the city, having been under Arab/Muslim rule for many centuries, was profoundly marked by its centrality to Arab and Muslim civilization, and its more mundane Arab characteristics, such as its cafes and "their nargilah pipes, gramophones and parrots,"[57] seemed to epitomize everything they wanted to negate in creating a new Jewish state. Such sentiments extended to other Arab cities, such as Jaffa, for example, which "was not the right place 'for new people with new thoughts to live in.'"[58]

Conversely, by such measures, Tel Aviv, built by "modern" Jews and completely new to the twentieth century, was not tainted by a long history of Arab/Muslim influences. It represented the most recent and modern urban planning ever to enter the Orient, becoming a city where one "might easily imagine himself in some Italian port."[59] Indeed, even the name, Tel Aviv, says much about this desire to overcome the Orient, as it symbolizes the birth of the new out of the old, much in the same way that Herzl envisioned in his *Old New Land*: "'Tel' is an excavated mound, and so signifies the remains of old settlements, while 'aviv' means the first shoot of the new wheat harvest, and also springtime, the sign of a new beginning."[60] In this spirit, the establishment of Tel Aviv provided the newcomers with a space that could represent the new Israel

---

54. Sigmund Freud cited in Amos Elon, "Deadlocked City" (October 18, 2001).
55. Avishai Margalit, "The Myth of Jerusalem," in *The New York Review of Books* (December 19, 1991).
56. Michel Warschawski, *On the Border* (2005:11-12).
57. Joachim Schlor, *Tel Aviv* (1999:39).
58. Ibid. (1999:40).
59. Theodor Herzl, *Old New Land* ([1902] 1997:61).
60. Joachim Schlor, *Tel Aviv* (1999:44).

as the first exclusively Jewish city to have been established for countless generations, while containing and articulating their contemporary brand of Jewishness.[61] James Morris, one of Tel Aviv's earliest settlers, expresses this sentiment succinctly: "I do not feel altogether abroad in Tel Aviv....If you feel yourself to be a Western man, you will always be half at home in this...city."[62]

THE CREATION OF ISRAEL AND THE REMOVAL OF ARAB/MUSLIM JERUSALEM

The Zionist dichotomy between a modern Jewish Tel Aviv and a hopelessly Oriental Jerusalem would soon change form, as the movement, gaining acceptance by colonial powers, found new avenues through which to unleash their nationalist project upon Jerusalem. In 1948, with the creation of the state of Israel, Zionists would attempt to eradicate Jerusalem's unique Muslim, Jewish, and Christian mosaic. As the new state was accorded international legitimacy, it immediately embarked upon a policy that moved to consolidate settlements throughout West Jerusalem and pursued aggressive claims upon many of the Palestinian neighborhoods that had been temporarily abandoned by Arabs who hoped to return soon after the conflict subsided. Taking advantage of the mass evacuation, Israel moved quickly toward a Judaization of Jerusalem, transforming it in such a way as to make it Jewish politically, nationally, and racially.

Many of West Jerusalem's once Arab villages, such as Deir Yasin, al-Maliha, Lifta, and Ein Kirma were quickly annexed to the new state. Ninety percent of these village populations had been Arab,[63] but upon their departure after the 1948 war, Israel immediately confiscated their homes, granting the most lavish ones to the generals of the Israeli army and eventually demolishing those that were less appealing in order to create space for the housing of incoming Jewish settlers. Today, all of these villages have been Judaized and are now occupied by many of Israel's ministries, including the Knesset and the prime minister's office.[64] This territory includes Deir Yasin, a village that was once the home of Palestinian women and children who were gunned down by Menachem

---

61. Arthur Hertzberg, "Jerusalem and Zionism" (1996:157).
62. Cited in Joachim Schlor, *Tel Aviv* (1999:29).
63. Naseer H. Aruri, "Misrepresenting Jerusalem" (2005:125-26).
64. Ibid. (2005:125-26).

Begin's Irgun, and is now used as a Jewish industrial zone.[65] Of the Palestinians that have remained in Jerusalem, many continue to be denied building permits, and if they leave the country for longer than 12 months, they would find themselves stamped with the status of refugee and not permitted to return, with "their resident permits arbitrarily canceled."[66]

The Judaization of Jerusalem would escalate further with the 1967 war, when Israel expanded to include all of traditional Palestine, including East Jerusalem, which was overwhelmingly Palestinian. Israel's victory further induced Jewish nationalism in Israel, giving many Israeli Jews an enhanced sense of triumph.[67] With renewed confidence, Israel used its victory to integrate more Palestinian territory into the state of Israel, even though such action was contrary to international law. This was especially the case in East Jerusalem, where Israel quickly moved to extend its boundaries by annexing numbers of Arab communities and territories into Israel proper.[68] As in its 1948 treatment of West Jerusalem, Israel would follow the same policy in 1967, attempting to make East Jerusalem "Jewish physically, ethnically, and politically."[69] Towards that end, it strategically enlarged the city through land seizures, while minimizing Palestinian presence in the new zones.[70] Although Israel claimed to guarantee the right of Palestinians to access Jerusalem, to this day many of the Palestinian Muslims and Christians that became refugees in 1967 have found that this is not the case, as the Israeli occupation authorities imposed a permit-only policy upon Palestinians living within the Occupied Territories, thus criminalizing those who enter the city without permit in hand.[71]

As Israel occupied Jerusalem entirely in 1967, it planted some 200,000 Jewish settlers in East Jerusalem with the objective of consoli-

---

65. Ibid. (2005:126). To be more precise, some "30,000 of the inhabitants of the Arab villages and urban centers around Jerusalem were driven out by force or fled the outbreak of violence....The residence of the Israeli President stands today on Palestinian-owned land in Talbiya. The nearby Muslim cemetery of Mamilla [Ma'man Allah] was converted to the Israeli Independence Park with lawns, playgrounds and restrooms" (2005:126).
66. Amos Elon, "Deadlocked City" (October 18, 2001).
67. Avishai Margalit, "The Myth of Jerusalem" (December 19, 1991).
68. Naseer H. Aruri, "Misrepresenting Jerusalem" (2005:127).
69. Naseer H. Aruri, *The Obstruction of Peace: The United States, Israel, and the Palestinians*, Monroe, Maine: Common Courage Press (1995:331).
70. Naseer H. Aruri, "Misrepresenting Jerusalem" (2005:128).
71. Naseer H. Aruri, *The Obstruction of Peace* (1995:329).

dating its hold over the city and making it very difficult for Palestinians to claim any portion of it in future negotiations.[72] Moreover, it dismantled an entire Muslim quarter near the Wailing Wall, expelling all of its inhabitants without compensation and demolishing their houses in order to build an extensive plaza.[73] Today, the plaza has been turned into a nationalist site where Israelis, just below the sacred Muslim site, hold nationalist rallies and swear in army recruits.[74]

MAKING PALESTINIANS INVISIBLE

After the 1967 occupation of Jerusalem, Israeli policy for its east sector aimed explicitly to "create facts on the ground" by enlarging the Jewish population demographically, while restricting Arab resettlement from the West Bank.[75] This dual character of Israeli occupation engendered a "process of dispossession, displacement, dismemberment, disenfranchisement and dispersal" of East Jerusalem's Palestinian population.[76] Further exacerbating tensions, many Orthodox Jewish families were encouraged to move into largely Arab neighborhoods in the congested Muslim Quarter of the Old City. As some social scientists have suggested, these settlements had little interest in creating diverse neighborhoods where Arabs and Jews would live together. On the contrary, the objective behind such strategy was based in "a religious-nationalist ideology,"[77] consistent with the tenets of Zionist discourse: to Judaize Jerusalem by implanting "ethnically pure" Jewish settlements.

Moreover, the Israeli authorities made it very difficult for the reverse to occur. To this day, very few Arabs have been allowed to move into West Jerusalem, including those who continue to hold the keys to their homes, hoping to return to the now largely Jewish sector of the city. Similarly, no known cases exist in East Jerusalem of Arabs being permit-

---

72. Amos Elon, "Deadlocked City" (October 18, 2001). According to Elon, "200,000 more were settled elsewhere in the West Bank and Gaza Strip."
73. Ibid. (October 18, 2001).
74. Ibid. (October 18, 2001).
75. Michael Romann and Alex Weingrod, *Living Together Separately: Arabs and Jews in Contemporary Jerusalem*, Princeton, New Jersey: Princeton University Press (1991:21).
76. Naseer H. Aruri, "Misrepresenting Jerusalem" (2005:131).
77. Michael Romann and Alex Weingrod, *Living Together Separately* (1991:38).

ted to settle within recently established Jewish neighborhoods.[78] In one case, for example, Arab families seeking to reside in a Jewish neighborhood were met with strong opposition and "were forced to leave their homes in order to permit the reestablishment of a totally homogeneous Jewish residential zone."[79]

This policy has aimed to make it as difficult as possible for future generations to propose a shared Jerusalem in which Palestinians and Jews alike can claim the city as their capital. Clearly stated in 1981 by Beni Ricardo, an activist of the Jewish fundamentalist movement, Gush Enumim, the intention of Israeli policy in East Jerusalem is "to change the idea of dividing the city into something that is utterly ridiculous, as is the idea of returning the Arabs to Cordoba or Andalusia today— ridiculous."[80] Ricardo understood this strategy as "one way to prevent the separation of Israel from expanded East Jerusalem."[81] Such nationalist assaults on East Jerusalem have created the political context in which Palestinians, nearly 30 percent of the city's population today, are largely treated as a "demographic" hazard threatening the city's Jewish majority.[82]

In their efforts to create racial segregation, Israeli officials have instituted differential access to public resources and services, favoring Jerusalem's Jewish population far over its Arab inhabitants.[83] Even as activist Jews and Palestinians have repeatedly warned of the implicit dangers surrounding such discrimination, Israel continues to spend dramatically less on the education, health, housing, and other social services of Palestinian Arabs than it does for its Jewish inhabitants.[84] As Amos Elon elucidates:

> It was not a "mosaic," as [the former mayor of Jerusalem] Kollek often called it; mosaics have a certain harmony of design; here the division reflected only discrimination and a deepening chasm. There was an enor-

---

78. Ibid. (1991:38).

79. Ibid. (1991:38).

80. Beni Ricardo quoted in Ian Lustick, "Reinventing Jerusalem," *Foreign Policy*, no. 93, Winter (1994:44-45).

81. Ibid. (1994:44-45).

82. Daphna Golan-Agnon, *Next Year in Jerusalem* (2005:28).

83. Michael Romann and Alex Weingrod, *Living Together Separately* (1991: 21).

84. Amos Elon, "The Deadlocked City" (October 18, 2001).

mous disparity between the public funds allocated respectively to the Israeli and Palestinian quarters.[85]

The policies that have stemmed from the events of 1967 not only represent an administrative occupation of Jerusalem, but a linguistic Judaization as well. As Daphna Golan-Agnon has recently argued, Jerusalem is "a city closed to almost all Palestinians, a city where the municipal parking lot has no signs in Arabic, the language spoken by 30 percent of its inhabitants," producing, in effect, an apartheid-like situation comparable to that of South Africa, in which "the Arab inhabitants of Jerusalem live as foreigners in their own city."[86] Further, the most psychologically damaging aspect of Israeli policy has taken form in its attempt to obliterate any traces of Palestinian village life, as Israelis continue to be inundated with a historical revisionism that ignores the Palestinian cultural heritage and demographic presence in recent times, as well as its subsequent deportation upon the establishment of Israel's statehood.[87] This objective has been accomplished so thoroughly that today, many Israelis are unaware of the fact that the streets they walk, the kibbutzim they visit, and the art communes they enjoy were only quite recently inhabited by Arab Muslim and Arab Christian families. Despite a continued Palestinian presence, all traces of numbers of families that were expelled in 1948 and again in 1967 have been removed or forgotten.[88] Precious little recognition abounds of the historical existence of the many men, women, and children who once lived and shared the same land, having anchored their roots and heritage to it.[89]

As Edward Said explains, such Zionist objectives have aimed to deny

> ...the existence of the Palestinian people, and by dehumanizing them, Zionists meant to hide from the world the intended victims of their colonization. They paraded before world public opinion as the national liberation

---

85. Ibid. (October 18, 2001).

86. Daphna Golan-Agnon, *Next Year in Jerusalem* (2005:26-28).

87. Ibid. (2005:19).

88. Edward Said, "Introduction," in Edward Said and Christopher Hitchens, *Blaming the Victim* (1989:4-5).

89. See the fine work of Walid Khalidi, *All That Remains: The Palestinian Villages Occupied and Depopulated by Israel in 1948*, Washington, D.C.: Institute of Palestine Studies (1992).

movement of the Jewish people, but they could not do so
if the fact were known that they were destroying an indigenous Asian community struggling to be free.[90]

Said further characterizes popular Israeli sentiment as one in which "the
Arabs are a nuisance and their presence is a fly in the ointment."[91] In Tel
Aviv, Haifa, and Hertzlia, for example, Israeli Jews are oblivious to the
existence of Arabs. Such Israeli cities are segregated, while Jewish settlements in East Jerusalem and the Occupied Territories have their own
road system, guarded by checkpoints and armored Israeli troops:

> They're protected from them, just as whites were pro-
> tected from blacks during apartheid...because the roads
> went around in such a way as to avoid the sight, in that
> case, of blacks.[92]

Israeli Jews thus rarely have had contact with Palestinians, who remain distant, visible to them only through ideologically mediated depictions of suicide bombers, or of Palestinians chanting, "Death to Israel."
Consequently, they remain insulated and largely incapable of witnessing
the effect that their government has had on Palestinians. As Meron Benvenisti, the former deputy mayor of Jerusalem, remarks:

> I recall the first time I felt the tragedy of the Palestinians
> penetrate my Zionist shield....I remembered the place
> from a trip with my father, and the desolation—the
> empty houses still standing, the ghost of a village once
> bustling with life—stunned me. I sat with my back
> against an old water trough and wondered where the vil-
> lagers were and what they were feeling.[93]

As a young man in 1948, Meron Benvenisti witnessed firsthand how
the existence of the new state affected the indigenous inhabitants of Pal-

---

90. Edward Said et al., "A Profile of the Palestinian People," in Said and
Hitchens, *Blaming the Victim* (1989:241).
91. Edward Said in David Barsamian and Edward W. Said, *Culture and Resistance: Conversations with Edward W. Said*, Cambridge: Massachusetts
(2003:73).
92. Ibid. (2003:73).
93. Meron Benvenisti, *Sacred Landscape: The Buried History of the Holy Land
since 1948*, Berkeley: University of California Press (2000:3).

estine. Suddenly, he recalls in his writing, a Muslim family disappeared on Gaza Road; the memory of Palestinians from the village of Deir Yasin was "paraded through the main streets of Jewish Jerusalem by their [Zionist] captors"; abandoned Arab neighborhoods were looted and kibbutzniks, upon seizing the land, "harvest[ed] the ripe barley left by the Arab farmers of Hittin in the lower Galilee."[94] Upon such difficult reflection, he asked himself: "Have we transformed a struggle for survival into an ethnic cleansing operation, sending people into exile because we wanted to plunder their land?"[95]

Still more unsettling than the scarcity of such Israeli voices as that of Benvenisti is the reality that this loss of historical memory now extends also to the Palestinian refugees themselves. In the account of his trip back to Palestine after many years of exile, the Palestinian author Mourid Barghouti writes that he has "completely forgotten what the road to Deir Ghassanah looks like":

> I no longer remember the names of the villages on both sides of the twenty-seven kilometers that separate it from Ramallah. Embarrassment taught me to lie. Each time Husam asked me about a house, a landmark, a road, an event, I quickly replied "I know." The truth is I did not know. I no longer knew....The long Occupation that created Israeli generations born in Israel and not knowing another "homeland" created at the same time generations of Palestinians strange to Palestine; born in exile and knowing nothing of the homeland except stories....[96]

Such discontinuity of personal and cultural memory is the direct result of an Israeli nationalist policy designed to silence the Palestinian experience, while simultaneously promoting a Jewish historical narrative. One example of how this has been accomplished was in the immediate development of archeological excavations following the capture of Jerusalem's Old City in 1967 with the attempt to promote the legitimacy of a Jewish nation's "return" to its original homeland.[97] These digs natu-

---

94. Ibid. (2000:2).
95. Ibid. (2000:3).
96. Mourid Barghouti, *I Saw Ramallah*, New York: Anchor Books (2000:61).
97. Nadia Abu el-Hajj, "Translating Truths: Nationalism, the Practice of Archeology, and the Remaking of Past and Present in Contemporary Jerusalem," in *American Ethnologist*, vol. 25, no. 2 (May 1998:168).

rally emphasized, not the city's many centuries of Muslim history, but rather the era of the Israelite Temples that represented an ancient Jewish national claim.[98] In this manner, Israel pursued a narrative suggesting its revival of an original community that has always been linked with the land of Palestine.[99] Abu el-Hajj articulates this clearly, asserting that such historical accounts were

> ...used to bolster the nationalist mythology of ancient destruction righted by modern rebirth....These excavators sought and produced what they regarded as evidence of national ascendance and prosperity in antiquity, in relation to which the legitimacy of Israeli control over the Old City in the present would be fashioned.[100]

The significance of this strategy to accentuate a biblical past at the expense of the more recent Islamic period should not be underestimated, for as the historian Michel-Rolph Trouillot argues in his *Silencing the Past*, the production of a historical narrative between competing groups is always biased toward the groups that have greater access to the means of such production, and the consequences of this power, although not as visible as gunfire or political crusades, are equally as effective.[101] Even today, the overwhelming majority of "research" digs are those perceived to be of national significance to the state of Israel,[102] despite the fact that such efforts only represent a window to one chapter of the great Palestine saga.[103] Bulldozers are regularly used in Israel to dig through many layers, casting aside or perhaps destroying significant Christian and Islamic archeological treasures in favor of the Iron Age, as they search particularly for remnants of the First and Second Temples that are at once recognized as important "national" artifacts.

As I visited the museum of Jerusalem a few years ago, I was stunned to discover how small was its showcase of the Islamic period in comparison to the Jewish showcases. Trouillot succinctly captures the sentiments

---

98. Ibid. (May 1998:169).
99. Ibid. (May 1998:169).
100. Ibid. (May 1998:169).
101. Michel-Rolph Trouillot, *Silencing the Past: Power and the Production of History*, Boston, Massachusetts: Beacon Press (1995:xix).
102. Nadia Abu el-Hajj, "Translating Truths" (May 1998:171-72).
103. Keith W. Whitelam, *The Invention of Ancient Israel: The Silencing of Palestinian History*, London and New York: Routledge (2001:3).

I felt at the time: "[a]t best, history is a story about power, a story about those who won."[104] While archeologists continue to gain funding, prestige, and media coverage as they focus "on eras of 'national ascendance' and 'glory' in the ancient or medieval pasts," the historical memory of Islamic and Palestinian history will continue to be marginalized and silenced.[105]

Indeed, nationalist manipulation or production of historical memory is not only intended for the victors, but also functions to remind those on the other side of the fence that they have forever lost. As Mourid Bargouti once remarked upon reaching a checkpoint in Palestine:

> My eyes stopped at a poster of Massada. Their myth recounts that they had held fast in the fortress of Massada until they were all killed—but they did not surrender. Is this their message to us, they hang it on the gate to remind us that they will stay here forever? Was this a deliberate choice, or just a poster?[106]

The persistence of such narratives have yielded an almost commonsensical Israeli discourse regarding Jerusalem as the eternal capital of the Jews, as evidenced in a remark that Yitzak Rabin made during a speech to the Knessett in 1993: "Jerusalem will not be open to negotiation. It has been and will forever be the capital of the Jewish people, under Israeli sovereignty, a focus of dreams and longings of every Jew."[107] Many other Israeli officials have gone on record negating Palestinian, Muslim, and Christian claims to Jerusalem, while stating that the city was and will eternally continue to be a Jewish capital. Teddy Kollek, the mayor of Jerusalem for 28 years until 1993, for instance, arrogantly distorted history when he commented to former President Clinton that the Jewish claim to Jerusalem is much more authentic than any other: "In another few years we in Jerusalem will celebrate 3000 years since the construction of the city by King David, whereas the Palestinian claim is less than one generation old."[108] Similarly, Ehud Olmert recently remarked "that there was no Arab Jerusalem. There was only a 'Jewish Jerusalem',"

---

104. Michel-Rolph Trouillot, *Silencing the Past* (1995:5).
105. Nadia Abu el-Hajj, "Translating Truths" (May 1998:167).
106. Mourid Barghouti, *I Saw Ramallah* (2000:14).
107. Yitzak Rabin cited in Naseer H. Aruri, *The Obstruction of Peace: The United States, Israel, and the Palestinians*, Common Courage Press (1995:330).
108. Naseer H. Aruri, "Misrepresenting Jerusalem" (2005:133).

only to be outdone by Ariel Sharon who has insisted that Jerusalem is "Israel's Capital, united for all eternity."[109] Arthur Hertzberg sums up well this exclusionary nature of Zionist discourse regarding the city: "In the mind of [Zionists], Jerusalem had been fashioned by long history as the Jewish capital. Jerusalem could no more be taken away from the Jews than Rome could be kept from the Italians."[110]

III
Religious Fundamentalist Zionism:
Strange Bedfellows

I'm going to tell the Prime Minister, the Defense Minister, the Chief of Staff you are part of our army, of our power, of our defense. [111]

Ehud Olmert

The Jewish national ideal has always particularly appealed to English feeling.

Nahum Sokolow, 1919

THE WESTERN APPEAL OF ZIONISM

From its earliest days, the Zionist movement recognized that its successful creation of a Jewish state in a territory populated by others depended upon the sanction of current imperial powers that were colonizing the region. Such forefathers as Herzl, Weizmann, and Ben-Gurion, for example, regularly appealed to Great Britain and the United States, quickly concretizing the discourse they chose to employ into two forms. First, they suggested that a new Jewish state could contribute to colonial efforts, as Moses Hess, an early advocate explained, by opening the roads, "that lead to India and China—those unknown regions which must

---

109. Ehud Olmert and Ariel Sharon cited in Amos Elon, "The Deadlocked City" (October 18, 2001).

110. Arthur Hertzberg, "Jerusalem and Zionism" (1996:163).

111. Ehud Olmert, then mayor of Jerusalem, giving a speech to an audience containing the American-based group "Christian Friends of Israeli Communities" in 1998.

ultimately be thrown open to civilization."[112] Herzl's political project can be understood as the type of colonialist discourse in search of an imperial sponsor for a new Jewish state intended to "form a portion of a rampart of Europe against Asia, an outpost of civilization as opposed to barbarism."[113] A second approach, which also proved to be politically effective for gaining the attention of Western powers, appealed to sentiments of Christian obsession with the Holy Land.

During the fledgling years of the Zionist movement, many European and American leaders had, for some time, already been showing enthusiasm for the creation of a Jewish homeland in the ancient Middle East. Indeed, as Donald Akenson argues, the appeal for a Jewish state up until the late nineteenth century, "was more widespread among Bible-reading Protestants—especially those of the British Isles—than among diaspora Jewry."[114] By the twentieth century, the Holy Land had become a largely recognized element of popular European and American self-perception. While the typical imperial ambitions of cheap labor, new markets, and natural resources had played a part in the colonization of Palestine, the emergence of a national and religious identification with the region, particularly with Jerusalem, that many Western Christians felt, formed a unique factor that set it apart from other colonized territories. In this sense, Palestine had formed an unusual part of the colonial imagination, principally because it was not perceived as an ordinary colonial outpost of Western powers. As Edward Said explains, Palestine embodied "an almost mythological territory saturated with religious ideology and endowed with overwhelming cultural significance...weighed down with historical as well as political meanings for many generations, peoples, and traditions."[115]

The 1917 Balfour Declaration and subsequent British/American support for the creation of the state of Israel thus cannot be adequately understood in light of geopolitical considerations alone without acknowledging the significant role that religious identities of major diplomatic figures and key religious constituents have played in advancing the trans-

---

112. Moses Hess cited in L.S. Stavrianos, *Global Rift: The Third World Comes of Age*, New York: William Morrow and Company (1981:542).
113. Theodor Herzl, *The Jewish State*, New York: Dover Publications (1988:96).
114. Donald Harman Akenson, *God's People: Covenant and Land in South Africa, Israel, and Ulster*, Ithaca, New York: Cornell University Press (1992:152).
115. Edward Said, "Introduction," in Edward Said and Christopher Hitchens, *Blaming the Victim* (1989:1).

formation of Palestine. To this day, Holy Land symbolism has comprised an essential part of the Western conception of self, in which Hebraic and Christian Scriptural axioms, visual representations, and the tremendous production of pilgrimage literature have contributed to a vibrant and living historical memory of the Holy Land. Consequently, Western sentiments of owning such memory have culminated in a consensus many Westerners share that it is essential to their own sense of national identity.

It is within this context that Zionists began, during the early years of the twentieth century, to explore the possibility of a coalition with Christian evangelicals, first in Great Britain and soon thereafter in America, in their efforts to establish a Jewish state.[116] Christian Zionists—embodying a tradition older than its Jewish counterpart—thus became essential to the Zionist movement. Today, evangelical traditions of biblical prophecy still form one of the key supportive discourses regarding Israel's occupation of Palestinian territories, specifically East Jerusalem and the West Bank.[117] As we will see, both Christian and Jewish Zionists have long shared a desire to remove native populations from the Holy Land in such a manner that "Israel's offending non-Jewish population is 'excluded from the world of concern' and thus denied equal right with Jews."[118]

PROTESTANTS AND THE CHOSEN PEOPLE

Upon Constantine's successful conquest of Jerusalem in the fourth century, the Holy Roman Empire restructured the sacred topography of the city by strategically enshrining it in a manner that negated Jewish topography. The Church of the Holy Sepulcher, for example, was positioned to project a Christian reading onto the city at the expense of a Jewish one. Following this theme for many centuries to come, the Catholic Church would nurture the traditional position that God had exiled the Jews from their homeland based upon their sins, consequently affording them no rightful claims to their beloved forfeited territories. The medieval Crusades would later represent a more aggressive continuation of this

---

116. Michael Prior, *Zionism and the State of Israel*, London and New York: Routledge (1999:140).

117. Barbara R. Rossing, *The Rapture Exposed: The Message of Hope in the Book of Revelation*, New York: Basic Books (2004:49).

118. Edward Said, "On Michael Walzer," in Edward Said and Christopher Hitchens (eds.), *Blaming the Victim* (1988:167).

theme, as legions of Crusaders would identify all Jews living in cities and villages along their sweep toward Palestine as "infidels" subject to pogroms, or unbridled massacres.[119] By the onset of modernity, as conceived in the Reformation of the sixteenth century, the Christian vision of the Holy City that was based upon the total negation of Jewish heritage would be radically transformed, making it theologically possible to emphasize the Jewish character of Palestine.

This revision of Christian attitudes toward Palestine, coupled with the growing influence of Europe, particularly Protestant Britain, over the affairs of the Middle East, represents a significant paradigmatic shift that would in time make it possible for a small sector of European Jews in the nineteenth century to invent Jewish Zionism, while it provided fertile soil for a sympathetic attitude within Europe regarding the movement's proposal for a Jewish homeland in Palestine. Without such a shift, any notion of a physical return to the Holy Land would have been very unlikely. As the Old Testament was adored by Protestants who had memorized prophetic writings describing struggles and triumphs in Palestine, Zionists would find in them a useful ally in their goals of building and establishing a Jewish state.

Within this modernist context, Christian Zionism, as it evolved, was not a traditional Christian reading of Scripture, but had its origins in the Protestant Reformation, gaining momentum with the European colonization of the Middle East, particularly Palestine. As nation-states emerged in Europe, the notion of a universal Christian community gave way to new nationalist and particularistic identities. Rosemary Ruether and Herman Ruether explain further that "the idea of the 'New Israel' was shifted from a universal religious community, the Christian church, to the nation as an 'elect people,' commissioned by God to defend the true faith and evangelize the 'heathen.'"[120] They state:

> This nationalization of the New Israel as elect nation was aided by the new biblical scholarship of the Renaissance and Reformation. Allegorical interpretation was rejected in favor of literal, historical interpretation. Bible reading in the vernacular, among Protestants, created a new identification with the people of Hebrew Scripture.

---

119. Rosemary Ruether and Herman Ruether, *The Wrath of Jonah: The Crisis of Religious Nationalism in the Israeli-Palestinian Conflict*, Minneapolis: Fortress Press (2002:70).
120. Ibid. (2002:70).

The prophets and heroes of Hebrew Scripture replaced
the Catholic saints as the figures of Christian story and
self-identification. The Promised Land of the Hebrew
Bible was understood as the actual historical land of Palestine, not as an allegory for a transcendent realm.[121]

As such views developed, Jews came to be seen as a central part of
the renewed Chosen People narrative. This modernist Christian reading,
resting on a belief that Scriptural claims alone prove that God has promised the land to the Hebrews, clearly demonstrates the political innovations contained within Christian Zionism, as its rhetoric came to be
couched within modern nationalist notions. Scholars such as Hector
Avalos contend that current notions of Zionism are not predominantly a
political dilemma,[122] but are rather a religious issue derived within a
time-immemorial context. Contrary to such contentions the historical
convergence of modern nationalism with the development of Christian
Zionism suggests that Zionism, as it exists today, could not have even
become a political reality without a modern political framework, and the
idea of a "Jewish return" to Palestine, if it could even have been conceived, would surely have been no more than a marginal concept of
Western Christianity.

As the Protestant Reformation highlighted Old Testament notions of
God's covenant with the Chosen People, an idea that would be essential
in linking Jews with Palestine, a modern Christian doctrine of the Second
Coming of Christ began to develop alongside it, suggesting a powerful
moral and symbolic justification for the Jewish "return" to Palestine,
which was understood as a necessary prerequisite for Christ's return.
Unimaginable prior to the modern nationalist period, by the time Jewish
Zionist sentiments arrived in Europe such a discourse was easily de-
ployed in support of the new movement's political aims toward the crea-

---

121. Ibid. (2002:70).
122. Hector Avalos, *Fighting Words: The Origins of Religious Violence*, Amherst, New York: Prometheus Books (2005:130-31). Avalos explains further:
"Whatever one thinks of who owns what specific piece of land in Israel, it is fair
to say that this conflict would not exist if it were not for the belief that God had
given the land to Israel....In sum, it is untenable to see the conflict between Palestinians and Jews as simply a secular or political fight for land. The main argument for Palestine as a Jewish homeland is inspired by religious claims from
the Bible" (2005:136-37).

tion of a Jewish state.[123] Rosemary Reuther and Herman Reuther explain further:

> In the countries influenced by the Protestant Reformation, particularly among Calvinists, the new identification with the Hebrew Bible created a more positive relationship between the biblical Israel and the Christian national New Israel. Jews fleeing from Spain and Portugal were welcomed in the Protestant commercial cities of Amsterdam and Hamburg. Such Protestants came to look on such Jews as living descendants of the ancient biblical heroes, rather than as despised members of a superseded covenant.[124]

Traditional Christian biblical discourse had always filtered notions of nationalism through the Bible. As Conor Cruise O'Brien notes, "[i]f everything in the Old Testament had to be taken as an allegorical prelude to the New, then nationalism was out, since it is either nonexistent or implicitly rejected in the New Testament." However, as modern nationalist ideology began to sprout a new language of discourse, such Protestants as Luther and Calvin "deallegorized the Bible" in a manner that "tended to reactivate the nationalism of the Old Testament."[125] The consequent emergence of innovative nationalist readings of the Old Testament by Puritans in the seventeenth century[126] would prefigure Jewish nationalism by at least two centuries.

This shift in Christian discourse was a tremendously useful tool for Zionists to appropriate toward their goals of building and establishing a Jewish state. Long before the arrival of Theodor Herzl and other prominent Jewish nationalists, as Regina Sharif has so persuasively argued, there had already existed a significant non-Jewish Zionist movement within Europe.[127] Had such a historical context not been available in the nineteenth century, Jewish nationalism and its vision of the Holy Land would surely have taken a very different form. The fact that a modern

123. Michael Prior, *Zionism and the State of Israel* (1999:138).
124. Rosemary Ruether and Herman Ruether, *Wrath of Jonah* (2002:71).
125. Conor Cruise O'Brien, *God Land: Reflections on Religion and Nationalism*, Cambridge, Massachusetts: Harvard University Press (1988:26).
126. Ibid. (1988:26).
127. Regina Sharif, *Non-Jewish Zionism: Its Roots in Western History*, London: Zed Press (1983).

Zionist template had been developed and nourished by Bible-reading Protestants is highly significant, for when the time was ripe for the Jewish proposal of a Jewish state, amid a fully deflated Ottoman Empire in the grips of Europe, the idea of Israel had already seemed "obvious." The memory of a Land called Holy and the intrigue it inspired in the European imagination played a major role in the development of Jewish Zionism. As Walter Eytan announced in 1958, "the very name 'Israel' is so much part of the Christian heritage" that "when the Jewish State was established and called Israel, it did not have to explain itself."[128] In order to understand the development of Zionism, therefore, it is pertinent to locate its discursive property as emanating from and latching onto the religious changes taking place within imperial Europe.

PROTESTANT PALESTINE

The founding fathers of the Zionist movement were aware of the potential appeal their ideas would hold for Christian fundamentalists and many often consciously appropriated European Protestant notions as they developed a mythology of the land of Israel. In this manner, they employed a script with which the British could identify and sympathize. As Jewish settlements and Zionist ideas flourished within the context of British colonial maneuvers in the Holy Land, the success of the Zionist movement would come to depend greatly upon its alliance with Christian Zionists, as well as upon British commitment regarding the Jewish "return" to Palestine.

By 1900, it had already been made evident in a speech Herzl delivered in London that a clear recognition of the alliance between Jewish and Christian Zionists was fully in play. During the fourth Zionist Congress, he addressed the assembly acknowledging with full confidence the role of Great Britain:

> From this place the Zionist movement will take a higher and higher flight....England the great, England the free, England with her eyes fixed on the seven seas, will understand us.[129]

---

128. Walter Eytan, *The First Ten Years, A Diplomatic History of Israel,* New York: Simon and Schuster (1958:181).
129. Regina Sharif, *Non-Jewish Zionism* (1983:74).

Herzl had been made well aware of Christian Zionist wishes a decade earlier when an influential American evangelist named William E. Blackstone learned upon his visit to Palestine in 1889 that Herzl had been considering Uganda and Argentina as possible sites for the Jewish homeland. Immediately, he sent Herzl a Bible, "marking every passage which referred to Palestine, with instructions that it alone was to be the site of the Jewish State."[130]

In 1916, David Lloyd George became Great Britain's prime minister. Fascinated with the Old Testament, he had been strongly attracted to Zionism and he quickly appointed Arthur James Balfour, who had shared his passion for Hebraic tradition and for the notion of reconstructing a Jewish homeland in Palestine, as foreign secretary.[131] Balfour's familiarity with Zionist claims and his identification with them ran so deeply that it afforded an evident insensitivity to the rights of indigenous Arabs. He had been raised in a thoroughly Protestant environment that regularly emphasized biblical stories and events within its educational system, while it virtually ignored the history of Palestine as it had unfolded after the time of Jesus. Balfour's ideas regarding Palestine as the rightful Jewish homeland were consistent with what he had been taught, but his blindness to historical facts on the ground led him to the troubling conclusion that Arab inhabitants had no real claim to Palestine. In his memorandum entitled, *Respecting Syria, Palestine and Mesopotamia*, he proclaimed:

> For in Palestine we do not propose even to go through the form of consulting the wishes of the present inhabitants of the country, though the American commission has been going through the form of asking what they are. The Four Great Powers are committed to Zionism. And Zionism, be it right or wrong, good or bad, is rooted in age-long traditions, in present needs, in future hopes, of far profounder import than the desires and prejudices of the 700,000 Arabs who now inhabit that ancient land.[132]

---

130. See Don Wagner, "Beyond Armegeddon," in *The Link*, vol. 25, no. 4 (1992:1-13); Michael Prior, *Zionism and the State of Israel* (1999:140).
131. Donald Harman Akenson, *God's People* (1992:162).
132. Regina Sharif, *Non-Jewish Zionism* (1983:78).

Balfour would regard the notion of a Jewish homeland as "an instrument for carrying out a Divine purpose,"[133] and such sentiments would be used to justify negating the rights of the indigenous Palestinian population.

Today, this Christian form of Zionism is nowhere stronger than in the United States, where its influence can be felt even at the very highest offices. For decades, American politicians and religious leaders have made statements suggesting that the Holy Land is a great part of their American identity. In 1948, for instance, after Congressional and Senate hearings about the issue of Palestine had emerged shortly before the state of Israel was created, Henry Cabot Lodge, a senator from Massachusetts, declared:

> You may smile when I tell you that, as a child I read my Bible, both the Old and New Testaments, I got my first idea of the present condition in Palestine and the Mohammedan possession from two of Scott's novels....I had of course intense sympathy with the Crusaders, and it seemed to me a great wrong that Jerusalem should be beneath the Muslim rule....That Jerusalem and Palestine, sacred to the Jews, who had fought through the centuries to hold their city and their temple, a land profoundly holy to all the great Christian nations of the West should remain permanently in the hands of the Turks has seemed to me for many years one of the great blots on the face of civilization that ought to be erased.[134]

Such strong affiliations with the Holy Land, in which childhood memories of Bible lessons play an essential role in the formation of belief systems, have engendered a sense of entitlement that has played out in both Great Britain and the United States. The following early account by an American Episcopalian bishop of his trip to Palestine in 1874 exemplifies this further:

> This is the first country where I have felt at home....As I try to clear away the mists, bring forward the distant, and make present what seems prehistoric, I find myself at my mother's side and my early childhood renewed. Now I see why this strange country seems natural. Its customs,

---

133. Balfour cited in Regina Sharif, *Non-Jewish Zionism* (1983:78).
134. Hector Avalos, *Fighting Words* (2005:133-34).

sights, sounds, and localities were those I lived among in that early time, as shown to me by pictures, explained by word, and funded as part of my undying property.[135]

This American Evangelical reading of the Bible preceded the formation of a dispensationalist discourse postulating that the Second Coming of Christ could only occur once all Jews were returned to the Promised Land. Even more troubling, such reasoning further envisioned a third Jewish temple built in place of a demolished Dome of the Rock as an essential setting for the return of the Messiah. Nowhere is this view more clearly expressed than in Hal Lindsey's best-selling book, *The Late Great Planet Earth*, in which he claims that biblical prophecy necessitates not only the establishment of a Jewish state, but Jewish control over all of Jerusalem.[136] Lindsey writes:

> There remains but one more event to completely set the stage for Israel's part in the last great act of their historical drama. This is to rebuild the ancient temple of worship on its old site.[137]

In Lindsey's American Evangelical view, only the Dome of the Rock stands in the way of preparing for a Messianic age. He explains in his account that the sacred Mosque atop the Temple Mount plays no role in the Messiah's return and must be removed or relocated to another site: "Obstacle or no obstacle, it is certain that the temple will be rebuilt. Prophecy demands it."[138] Some American Evangelist groups have adopted such biblical prophecies, making preparatory arrangements for the future Third Temple with a small group of messianic Jews, known as the Temple Institute, unabashedly located in the heart of the Arab district of Old Jerusalem—a group that has been producing such ritualistic items

---

135. Melani McAlister, *Epic Encounters: Culture, Media, and U.S. Interest in the Middle East, 1945-2000*, Berkeley: University of California Press (2001:13-14).

136. Hal Lindsey, *The Late Great Planet Earth*, Grand Rapids, Michigan: Zondervan (1970).

137. Hal Lindsey, *The Late Great Planet Earth* (1970:55-56) cited in Barbara R. Rossing, *The Rapture Exposed* (2004:56-57).

138. Original in Hal Lindsey, *The Late Great Planet Earth* (1970:3-4), cited in Barbara R. Rossing, *The Rapture Exposed* (2004:59).

as "incense shovels, temple vessels and special priestly garments in preparation for the day they can be used in a rebuilt temple."[139]

Since the 1967 and 1973 Arab-Israeli wars, the Israeli government has deepened its relationship with extreme Evangelical groups, having recognized them as a valuable political ally.[140] As did the founders of Zionism, Israeli officials today regularly court such groups, accepting countless offers of Christian Zionist support from around the world, even though they are quite aware of the fact that such Christians hold anti-Semitic beliefs in which Jews, with the Second Coming of Christ, are destined to choose between conversion to Christianity and a death of eternal damnation. As Gershom Gorenberg cautions, "People who see Israel through the lens of Endtimes prophecy are questionable allies."[141] Gorenberg further observes in a *Sixty Minutes* interview:

> They don't love real Jewish people. They love us as characters in their story, in their play, and that's not who we are....If you listen to the drama that they are describing, essentially, it's a five-act play in which Jews disappear in the fourth act.[142]

THE CONSEQUENCE FOR THE PALESTINIANS

The Evangelical form of Zionism has often been more fanatical than those of the Israeli right, as its routine insensitivity to Arab inhabitants is such a given that it makes the most extremist elements of the Likud Party look like doves. Just as Balfour had been incapable of a real engagement with Palestinians, because his deep commitment to a distant biblical his-

---

139. Barbara R. Rossing, *The Rapture Exposed* (2004:60-61).

140. Melani McAlister, *Epic Encounters* (2001:174-75).

141. Gershom Gorenberg, *The End of Days: Fundamentalism and the Struggle for the Temple Mount*, New York: Oxford University Press (2000:240), cited in Barbara R. Rossing, *The Rapture Exposed* (2004:62).

142. "Zion's Christian Soldiers," *Sixty Minutes*, October 6, 2002; http://cbsnews.com/stories/2002/10/03/60minutes/main524268.html, cited in Barbara R. Rossing, *The Rapture Exposed* (2004:62). The Jewish American writer Roberta Feuerlicht notes, "In Jewish history, when fundamentalists came, Cossacks were not far behind." Roberta Feuerlicht, *The Fate of the Jews: A People Torn between Israeli Power and Jewish Ethics*, New York: New York Times Book Co. (1983:166), cited in Anatol Lieven, *America Right or Wrong: An Anatomy of American Nationalism*, New York: Oxford University Press (2004:178).

tory clouded his understanding of twentieth-century realities, extremist Evangelicals likewise view the region through a biblical lens, rarely taking the time to visit Muslim sites if they happen to visit, or to intermingle with Palestinians. When I visited Jerusalem not long ago, I joined a few Christian Fundamentalist tours and was shocked to learn how Palestinian reality seemed invisible during such tours, an effort that appeared at times to be quite intentional.[143]

Of course, such inattentiveness as is found in the evangelically inspired tourist industry is but a mild example in comparison to the funding of Jewish settlements in Palestinian territories, the call to expel Arabs from Jerusalem, and the intention to see the Dome of the Rock destroyed. As Barbara Rossing contends, the consequence of Evangelical practice is that "Palestinians in the West Bank, Gaza, and East Jerusalem—many who have been refugees with their families since 1948—feel the crushing weight of this triumphalistic understanding of biblical prophecies."[144] According to Prior, this form of Christian Zionism is "insensitive to the human rights of the Palestinians, demonises Islam, and assists in the immigration of Jews to Israel."[145]

Evangelical Zionists adopt one of the earliest tenets of Zionism, maintaining that the indigenous Arab population has no rightful claim of nationhood and ought to be transferred to Jordan, but they add the variant that the Bible promises Israel's right to all of East Jerusalem and the Occupied Territories.[146] In this biblical narrative, the entire history and existence of a people is suppressed so as to create a political project that favors one imagined national community at the expense of another. Father Michael Prior echoes this sentiment in his examination of Zionism: "With the controlling voice exercised by them the wider history of the region was effectively silenced."[147] Just as Israeli archeology marginalizes other histories for the sake of bringing forth a Jewish nationalist narrative, Evangelical Zionists render Palestinians invisible in order to invoke their Christian Endtimes narrative, in which Muslims do not make the stage.

---

143. In one instance, however, the tour leaders left the group with a Palestinian bus operator, and unbeknownst to them, the driver diverged from the official route and visited Palestinian restaurants and cafes in Hebron (Khalil in Arabic).
144. Barbara R. Rossing, *The Rapture Exposed* (2004:51).
145. Michael Prior, *Zionism and the State of Israel* (1999:136).
146. Barbara R. Rossing, *The Rapture Exposed* (2004:65).
147. Michael Prior, *Zionism and the State of Israel* (1999:138).

While such views may have once been popularly understood as mar-
ginally belonging to fanatical American Christians, they are now openly
operative within the U.S. government, articulated by Congressmen,
Senators, and White House staff. Oklahoma Senator James Inhofe, for
example, made the following remarks on the floor of the Senate in 2002:

> I believe very strongly that we ought to support Israel;
> that it has a right to the land....Because God said so. As
> I said a minute ago, look it up in the book of Genesis. It
> is right up there on the desk.
>
> In Genesis 13:14-17, the Bible says: "The Lord said
> to Abram, 'Lift up now your eyes, and look from the
> place where you are northward, and southward, and
> eastward: for all the land which you see, to you will I
> give it, and to your seed forever....Arise, walk through
> the land in the length of it and in the breadth of it; for I
> will give it to thee.'"
>
> That is God talking.
>
> The Bible says that Abram removed his tent and
> came and dwelt in the plain of Mamre, which is in Heb-
> ron, and built there an altar before the Lord. Hebron is in
> the West Bank. It is this place where God appeared to
> Abram and said, "I give you this land," the West Bank.
>
> This is not a political battle at all. It is a contest over
> whether or not the word of God is true.[148]

This type of discourse is designed to arouse anti-Arab sentiments
while it inspires a noble sense of enthusiasm for the existence of Israel.
The narrative that Christian Zionists employ thus merges with the political project of Israel in its push to free the Holy Land of its multicultural
quality with the intention of realizing an exclusively Jewish nation. As
we shall see, the induction of religious messianic interpretation into the
Zionist political project over the course of its evolution has effectively
served to shift an imposed Palestinian/Arab identity from inconsequen-
tiality into a demonized status.

---

148. James Inhofe, "Seven Reasons Why Israel Is Entitled to the Land,"
http://cbn.org/cbnnews/news/020308c.html, accessed March 4, 2002, cited in
Barbara R. Rossing, *The Rapture Exposed* (2004:52-53) and Anatol Lieven,
America Right or Wrong (2004:181).

ZIONISM FOR RELIGIOUS JEWS

While numerous Jewish Zionists legitimately fear a Christian Messianic project that ultimately culminates in a fairly well camouflaged finale of Jewish extermination through conversion or death, there have also been a great many who have been unable to resist adopting as their own the aspect of this script that accords Jews the political discourse of explicit supremacy in the Promised Land, prior to the Second Coming of Christ. Much like their secular counterparts, who have attempted to extract Eastern qualities from Palestine in order to produce a Westernized modern Jewish state, religious Zionists have incorporated Western notions of Zionism into their visions of a mono-religious state, which has produced a new form of religious identity that is highly nationalistic and rarely sympathetic to the complex religio-cultural symbioses that have traditionally existed in Palestine.

Prior to 1948, the Zionist movement had been almost exclusively secular, despite having courted some aspects of religious identity, and it predominantly viewed Orthodox Jews with disdain. Religious Jews looking to join the Zionist movement felt obliged "to take off the skullcap, lose one's accent and choose Western and secular modernity."[149] Early Zionists thus found it extremely difficult to convince an already extant community to accept the idea of establishing a Jewish state in its midst, as pious Jews living in Palestine, many of whom were Sephardic, resented such exclusion and insensitivity.

During the late nineteenth century, many Jews had held the view that the millennia-old Jewish exile they continued to experience in the world had been caused by their sins and that only God, at his own choosing, could signal their return to Palestine and the rebuilding of the Temple.[150] Thus, as they learned of Herzl's ideas, Jews often perceived Zionism as the most abominable heresy in recent memory,[151] insisting that not only were its precepts incompatible with the teachings of Judaism, but that its vision of a Jewish state hardly even bore a Jewish mark.[152] The Rabbinical Council of Germany found Zionism so offensive, in fact, that it "formally and publicly condemned the 'efforts of the so-called Zionists to

149. Michel Warschawski, *On the Border* (2005:159).
150. M. Prior, *Zionism and the State of Israel* (1999:70).
151. Donald Harman Akenson, *God's People* (1992:159).
152. Theodor Herzl, *The Jewish State* (1988:96), quoted in Walter Laqueur, *A History of Zionism*, New York: MJF Books (1972:109).

create a Jewish national state in Palestine as contrary to Holy Writ.'"[153]
As Jakob Petuchowski explains, Jews had traditionally come to Jerusalem solely for religious purposes, never having even imagined a political landscape and they thus viewed Zionists as Jews meddling "with the Messianic time-table of Almighty God."[154] Moreover, many of the priests and the old Jewish settlements that comprised the traditional Sephardic communities of Jewish Palestine openly resented what they perceived as the arrogance of secular Jews who exhibited no respect whatsoever for the laws of the Torah.[155] Describing Israel's early years of statehood, Michel Warschawski observes:

> [T]he Orthodox communities lived just like oppressed
> communities, fighting to safeguard their existence in a
> state, which, in their eyes, was intending to liquidate the
> Jewish people, as they understood it. As for the believ-
> ers...they were made to feel ashamed as Jews who tried
> to assimilate an Israeli identity while maintaining their
> faith and their practice as discreetly as possible.[156]

Nevertheless, even early secular Zionists had slowly come to accept the emergence of religious Jews within the Zionist movement. Accordingly, Arthur Hertzberg, Herzl, Weizmann, and Ben-Gurion, among other secular Zionists, had sought to energize their agenda for nationhood by incorporating established Jewish sentiments regarding the Holy Land. Despite predominant threads of atheism and agnosticism with which they had woven their movement, "they refused to give up the notion that He—or his avatar, history—had given the Jews an unbreakable claim to the land of their ancestors."[157]

Thus, while secular Zionists exhibited little concern for Judaism as a religion, they nonetheless understood its potential utility for their political project. This is apparent in Herzl's statements regarding the choice of Palestine over other possible locations for a homeland: "Palestine is our ever-memorable historic home. The very name Palestine would attract

---

153. David Vital, *The Origins of Zionism*, Oxford: Clarendon Press (1975:336), cited in Michael Prior, *The Bible and Colonialism* (1997:109).
154. Jakob Petuchowski, *Zion Reconsidered*, New York: Twayne Press (1966:41), cited in Michael Prior, *Zionism and the State of Israel* (1999:70).
155. Michael Prior, *Zionism and the State of Israel* (1999:70).
156. Michel Warschawski, *On the Border* (2005:173).
157. Arthur Hertzberg, "Jerusalem and Zionism" (1996:152).

our people with a force of marvelous potency."[158] Herzl and his contemporaries hoped to attract the attention of both pious Jews as well as Protestant countries by appropriating ancient symbols of Promised Land and Covenant and by permitting a religious element within their nationalist discourse. As Michael Prior notes, "Zionism could be endowed with particular religious significance, if not immediately, at least *post factum*."[159] In this manner, Herzl, as would many that followed him, recognized that, despite his own antithetical beliefs, such notions as *Chosen People, return*, and *Promised Land* were potent vehicles with which to rally Jewish opinion.[160]

Chaim Weizmann held similar ideas and understood that in order for the Jewish nationalist movement to be successful, it was essential to bring religious Jews into the Zionist alliance by exploiting the biblical narrative of Palestine:

> The renaissance of the Jewish nation is bound up with Palestine. The choice made by destiny cannot be undone. Palestine is the Jewish people's birthplace and it gave birth to no other. It owes its place in history to the Jews and to no other people. The Jews as a people and Palestine as a country ceased to be truly creative when the bond between them was severed. But the hope of renewing that bond has kept the Jewish people alive, and meantime Palestine remained desolate.[161]

By including Scriptural texts that emphasized nationalist claims by means of violence and that defined the Promised Land as rightfully and exclusively Jewish, Weizmann found common ground between Zionism and Jewish Scripture.[162]

---

158. Theodor Herzl, *The Jewish State* (1988:96).
159. Michael Prior, *Zionism and the State of Israel* (1999:70).
160. Michael Prior, *The Bible and Colonialism* (1997:109).
161. Chaim Weizmann, "Memorandum on Palestine Policy" cited in Donald Harman Akenson, *God's People* (1992:159-60).
162. The Torah contains a number of appeals to uproot the inhabitants of the Promised Land in order to establish a nation. One such example is found in Deuteronomy (6:1-6): "When the Lord your God brings you into the land you are entering to possess and drives out before you many nations...and when the Lord your God has delivered them over to you and you have defeated them, then you must destroy them totally."

But it was David Ben-Gurion who most effectively joined the two discourses, insisting on numerous occasions that the land of Israel "always had been, and will remain, our country. We are here as of right."[163] With such statements, Ben-Gurion appropriated Scripture in much the same manner as have American Evangelists more recently, claiming Jewish right to a land inhabited by another population, thus rendering indigenous peoples alien to their own homeland: "The Bible is the Jews' sacrosanct title-deed to Palestine...with a genealogy of 3,500 years."[164] In using such a discourse, Evangelists and Zionists alike have qualified ancient accounts in order to eclipse actual facts on the ground. In a speech Ben-Gurion gave to a Zionist congress in Basle, he advocated that the Zionist movement should adopt "original sources" and the "Book of Books" as its guiding light:

> The stories of our forefathers 4,000 years ago; the acts and life of Abraham; the wanderings of Israel in the desert after the exodus from Egypt; the wars of Joshua and the judges that followed him; the lives and doings of Saul, David and Solomon; the deeds of Uziyahu, King of Judah, and Yeruboam II, King of Israel, all of these have more actuality, are closer, more edifying and meaningful for the younger generation maturing and living in the Land of Israel than all the speeches and debates of the Basle Congresses.[165]

Further, deepening this theme of commitment to historical Judaism, he employed a narrative describing the rebuilding of the Temple that would become a trademark of both Christian and Jewish fundamentalists: "The Temple will be visible from long distances, for it is only our ancient faith that has kept us together"; and he appealed for the support of religious Jews by claiming that "our community of race is peculiar and unique, for we are bound together only by the faith of our fathers."[166]

---

163. Donald Harman Akenson, *God's People* (1992:160).

164. David Ben-Gurion's address to the Basle Congresses of 1954, cited in Nur Masalha, *The Politics of Denial* (2003:42).

165. David Ben-Gurion cited in Mitchell Cohen, *Zion & State: Nation, Class and the Shaping of Modern Israel*, New York: Columbia University Press (1992:215).

166. Theodor Herzl, *The Jewish State* (1988:146), cited in Michael Prior, *Zionism and the State of Israel* (1999:5).

Thus, although the religious aspect of Zionism remained marginal to the overall nationalist movement and Orthodox as well as Reform Jews remained hostile to it until the state of Israel was established, it is evident that by the turn of the twentieth century, there had already existed a religious revision of traditional Messianic ideas with the intent of advancing the founding of a Jewish state; as had existed a sector of the religious Jewish community in which Zionists found support for their goal to establish such a state in Palestine.[167]

The first known religious nationalist figure to use Protestant Messianic ideas that posited the return of the Jews to Palestine as a prelude to the coming of the Messiah was Rabbi Yehuda Alkalai. He proposed that a human effort to establish Jewish colonies in the Holy Land would not contradict holy writ and that, on the contrary, it was a necessary preparation for the Redemption from exile itself. While this idea contradicted the mid-nineteenth-century Jewish notion that the Messiah would arrive only with a miraculous act of divine grace,[168] Alkalai

> invoked…that the days of the Messiah were to be ushered in by a forerunner of the true miraculous Redeemer. This first Messiah, the son of Joseph, would lead the Jews in the Wars of Gog and Magog; under him, they would conquer the Holy Land by the might of their sword.[169]

---

167. Eric Davis, "Religion against the State: A Political Economy of Religious Radicalism in Egypt and Israel," in Richard T. Antoun and Mary Elaine Hegland (eds.), *Religious Resurgence: Contemporary Cases in Islam, Christianity, and Judaism*, Syracuse, New York: Syracuse University Press (1987:151).

168. Arthur Hertzberg, *The Zionist Idea: A Historical Analysis and Reader*, Philadelphia and Jerusalem: Jewish Publication Society (1997:103).

169. Ibid. (1997:103). Yehuda Alkalai, in his 1843 essay, "The Third Redemption" ([1843]1997:105), explains: "It is written in the Bible: 'Return, O Lord, unto the tens and thousands of the families of Israel.' On this verse the rabbis commented in the Talmud as follows: it proves that the Divine Presence can be felt only if there are at least two thousands and two tens of thousands of Israelites together. Yet we pray every day: 'Let our eyes behold Thy return in mercy unto Zion.' Upon whom should the Divine Presence rest? On sticks and stones? Therefore, as the first step in the Redemption of our souls, we must cause at least twenty-two thousand to return to the Holy Land. This is the necessary preparation for a descent of the Divine Presence among us; afterward, He will grant us and all Israel further signs of His favor."

Rabbi Zvi Hirsch Kalischer was even more explicit in his insistence on the need to colonize Palestine with Jewish settlements in order to pave the way for the Messiah. In his 1862 essay, "Seeking Zion," he argues:

> [T]he Redemption of Israel, for which we long, is not to be imagined as a sudden miracle. The Almighty, blessed be his name, will not suddenly descend from on high and command His people to go forth. He will not send the Messiah from heaven in a twinkling of an eye, to sound the great trumpet for the scattered of Israel and gather them into Jerusalem. He will not surround the Holy City with a wall of fire or cause the Holy Temple to descend from the heavens. The bliss and the miracles that were promised by His servants, the prophets, will certainly come to pass—everything will be fulfilled—but...the Redemption of Israel will come by slow degrees and the ray of deliverance will shine forth gradually....For all this to come about there must first be Jewish settlement in the Land; without such settlement, how can the ingathering begin?[170]

The most significant spokesperson for this evangelized version of Judaism was Abraham Isaac Kook (1864-1935), the first Ashkenazi Chief Rabbi of Palestine (1921-1935). Stationed in British-ruled Jerusalem, Kook interpreted Kabbalist messianic traditions in novel ways in his efforts to resolve the deep divide between secular Zionists and Orthodox Jews, proposing, for example, that the performance of religiously inspired deeds would hasten the commencement of the Messianic era.[171] Most unique about Kook's theology was his insistence that even non-religious Zionist figures were preparing the grounds for the coming of the Messiah and that their lack of religious observance did not disqualify their efforts to produce a Jewish state from being an expression of Divine Will. In fact, Kook believed, Zionists were planting the seeds of a Jewish

---

170. Rabbi Zvi Hirsch Kalischer (1862), "Seeking Zion," in Hertzberg, *The Zionist Idea* (1997:111, 113).
171. Rosemary Ruether and Herman Ruether, *The Wrath of Jonah* (2002:56).

return from exile that would naturally bloom into a renewal of devout religious practice.[172] As Michael Prior further depicts:

> He was convinced that God was leading Jews, whether secular or religious, to return to the Holy Land, where ultimately the nation would return to its faith. The divine energy was at its strongest in the creative pioneers of the secular Zionist revolution who, unknowingly, were agents of God.[173]

Such contentions corresponded snugly with Evangelical aspirations of gathering Jews for the Second Coming, assuming in many ways a parallel narrative. One of the most striking and dangerous similarities between the two theological visions was a notion that the restoration of the ancient Temple in its original location would be the decisive event to usher in the Messianic era and that the reconstruction of the holy site itself represented the actualization of Redemption. This idea implied, of course, a foreseeable future with the Dome of the Rock absent from the Temple Mount.[174]

As the state of Israel was established in 1948 and followed in 1967 by a further expansion that engulfed East Jerusalem and other Palestinian territories, this uncompromising Evangelical/Zionist reading became evermore attractive to a growing sector of Israeli Jews, which resulted in the formation of a fanatical religious movement in 1974 known as Gush Enumim. Gush Enumim mobilized Kook's ideas regarding the essentiality of proactive construction on holy soil and added an element of ethnic cleansing to his discourse, spreading sentiment that Palestinians living in the Holy Land "were in the way: at best they were an annoyance to be controlled, at worst an enemy to be destroyed."[175]

The year 1967, in particular, had been a watershed year, signaling an era in which religious communities were not only demarginalized by the administration, but would come to be, within a generation's time, an es-

---

172. Ibid. (2002:57). Eric Davis similarly notes that "in [Kook's] view, Zionist settlers who rejected Judaism in religious terms were, in settling Palestine, regarded as unintentionally carrying out God's will by bringing the Jews back to the holy land of Eretz Israel." Eric Davis, "Religion against the State" (1987:151-52).
173. Michael Prior, *Zionism and the State of Israel* (1999:71).
174. Mark Juergensmeyer, *The New Cold War? Religious Nationalism Confronts the Secular State*, Berkeley: University of California Press (1993:67).
175. Mark Juergensmeyer, *The New Cold War?* (1993:65).

sential element of its policy-making.[176] During this time, Zionist officials from all parties courted prominent rabbis and formerly religious activities that typically took place by the Wailing Wall soon evolved into "massive nationalist and militarist parades, and degenerated finally, in the 1980s, into bloody racist pogroms, two or three times a year."[177] By this time, a great number of religious Jewish youth had begun to subscribe to Rabbi Kook's ideas and they no longer felt compelled to emulate secular standards. Warschawski further illustrates:

> In less than a generation, Messianic nationalism became an essential component of the new national discourse, even within labor-Zionist circles. From the right to the left, one spoke of the Holy Land, evoked the divine covenant and venerated the holy places. The Zionist movement and Israel were no longer a solution to the Jewish question, but elements in the redemption of the Jewish people and the liberation of the Holy Land.[178]

As Amos Elon vividly demonstrates, during this period, followers of Meir Kahane and other religious nationalist groups freely wore

> T-shirts saying "The People of Israel Lives" [and] painted Stars of David on the outside walls of mosques and yelled obscenities through the narrow lanes leading to the Haram…richly funded by American Christian fundamentalists, American Jewish donors, and secretly, on at least one occasion, by the Israeli government.[179]

The widespread shift in Israeli society toward embracing this brand of religious Zionism represented a change in behavior as well, in which the religious sector of "the Orthodox, Ashkenazi and Sephardi shed their humble, peaceful, indeed resigned Diaspora traits, the ones that Herzl had described as effeminate, to become more Israeli—macho, rough, aggressive and arrogant."[180] To this day, nowhere has this racist discourse been more evident than in East Jerusalem, where even the sight of prominent Muslim shrines in Old Jerusalem enrages militant Zionists and

---

176. Michel Warschawski, *On the Border* (2005:173).
177. Ibid. (2005:173).
178. Ibid. (2005:174).
179. Amos Elon, "The Deadlocked City" (October 18, 2001).
180. Michel Warschawski, *On the Border* (2005:178).

radical yeshiva (Jewish rabbinic academy) students, many of whom view the conquest of such sites for redemptive purposes as the single most important duty in their lives.[181]

Today, those who subscribe to Christian Messianic views and the large sector of Israeli Jews that has committed itself to militant political Messianism share a great affinity for one another.[182] The two movements have come to share a political-ideological framework which involves the idea that the conquest of land and religious sites from those who obstruct a pre-ordained narrative is a religious obligation. Both of these movements interpret the coming of a Messianic age not primarily as supernatural in character, but as a militarist conquest and deliverance of the Holy Land out of the hands of enemies, signifying Israel's long awaited vindication, in which the ancient calls for the obliteration of Canaanites and Amalekites have been revived to target Arabs in the contemporary world. Indeed, Israel's wars have widely been interpreted as holy and its defense forces have likewise been consecrated.[183] The rebuilding of the Jewish Temple, the gathering of the Jews, the removal of all gentiles, and all the prophecies awaiting fulfillment—only too recently the exclusive property of Christian Evangelists—now ironically form a central and seemingly original tenet of Jewish Zionism. As Donald Akenson concludes, "the literal belief that the biblical definition of 'the Land' was the proper one and that God had directly ordered Jews to take the land and to cleanse it"[184] is no longer just the idea of the Protestant colonizer, but an essential part of Israeli state ideology. Rewarded bountifully by a modern England of old and wholly disinterested in the lives of Arab men, women, and children, Israel has been a dutiful child.

---

181. Rosemary Ruether and Herman Ruether, *The Wrath of Jonah* (2002:181).
182. Ibid. (2002:179-80).
183. Ibid. (2002:180).
184. Donald Harman Akenson, *God's People* (1992:323).

IV
Jerusalem as Imagined by
Palestinian Nationalists

Why do we of all the peoples of the world,
have to invent our country every day so everything isn't lost and
we find we've fallen into eternal sleep?[185]

A nation which has long been in the depths of sleep only awakes if it
is rudely shaken by events, and only arises little by little....This was the
situation of Palestine, which for many centuries had been in the deepest
sleep, until it was shaken by the Great War, shocked by the Zionist
movement, and violated by the illegal policy of the British, and
it awoke, little by little.[186]

While Jewish nationalists constructed a new identity informed by European concepts of racial supremacy and in collusion with Christian Zionists, local Arab communities within Palestine, which were intent on safeguarding their interests, began to re-imagine themselves in opposition to European-Christian constructs of Palestine and, more fervently, against an aggressive Zionist campaign aiming at eclipsing their homeland with a new nation. Palestinian nationalism therefore emerged in the struggle with dominant social forces, as European and American Christians lavished special attention upon Palestine through colonial policies that were slanted in favor of an emerging Jewish nationalist movement.

Prior to the nineteenth century, the region of Palestine had been part of a much larger universalistic empire and had not emerged as *filastin* (Arabic word for Palestine), a designation that had long been extinct in the imperial lexicon, until Jerusalem and other major regional cities came under the provincial jurisdiction of *Sham* (Damascus) upon the complete destruction of the *umma*. While other regions, such as the developing nations of Egypt, Syria, and Lebanon spawned movements that were focused on breaking free from specific European colonial powers, the

---

185. Elias Khoury, *Gate of the Sun*, Brooklyn, New York: Archipelago Books (2006).
186. Khalil Sakakini, *Filastin ba'd al-Harb al-Kubra*, Jerusalem (1925:9), cited in Rashid Khalidi, "The Formation of Palestinian Identity," in James Jankowski and Israel Gershoni (eds.), *Rethinking Nationalism in the Arab Middle East*, New York: Columbia University Press (1997a:179).

struggle in Palestine was more complex in that Arab communities faced a colonial force that favored the introduction of an external nationalist movement. As a result, the indigenous population of Palestine encountered the unique situation of having an external nation imposed upon it, while its neighbors successfully overcame Western imperialism and developed modern nations of their own.

While many scholars impose a time-immemorialist understanding upon the Palestinian struggle, invoking an age-old conflict between Jews and Arabs, Palestinian nationalism, like Zionism, is more accurately understood as a product of the modern world, as its aspirations and struggles with the West and the new Jewish state are rooted in modern social realities, rather than in some primordial cultural or religious worldview. Its origins, for our purposes, can be understood to have been formed in the late nineteenth century with the incursion of aggressive European consular and missionary activities, and its maturity can already be seen in the 1920s, as the Zionist campaign began to represent a massive threat to the Palestinian community.

According to Rashid Khalidi, the construction of Palestinian identity has drawn upon many factors that existed prior to the Zionist threat, such as the increasingly aggressive European and American religious attachment to the "Holy Land" that was developing early in the nineteenth century and Istanbul's significant wholesale attempt, late in the Ottoman period, to restructure Palestine's Arab provinces.[187] The rise of Zionism, however, remains the most significant impetus for Palestinian nationalism, as it has represented the single most serious threat to the indigenous inhabitants of Palestine, simply because, throughout its history, it has explicitly called for the complete removal or destruction of Palestinian society.[188] Accordingly, to the extent that Palestine's recent history can be understood to have developed parallel nationalisms, the contemporary struggle over Jerusalem is most clearly understood as a political confrontation between two *modern* nationalist movements: one indigenous to the

---

187. As Rashid Khalidi recently argues in his essay, "The Formation of Palestinian Identity" (1997a:175-76): "Before going into details of this [Palestinian] reaction, it is worth stressing that these elements of attachment to Palestine all antedated the encounter with Zionism."

188. For a competent analysis of Zionist designs to expel Palestinians from the land of Palestine, see Nur Masalha, *Expulsion of the Palestinians: The Concept of 'Transfer' in Zionist Political Thought, 1882 to 1948*, Washington, D.C.: Institute of Palestine Studies (1992).

region and historically concerned with self-preservation, while the other has sought to establish itself ultimately as a mono-religious Jewish state.

Much of the current literature on this subject has either ignored or diminished the value of recent injustices suffered by the indigenous Arab population of Palestine. Moreover, politically motivated scholars frequently eclipse the modern and nationalist nature of this conflict by invoking grossly inaccurate and decontextualized readings of Islamic history in relation to Jews. An extreme example of this is found in Sam Harris's highly problematic accusation that Islam has, from its very beginnings, been anti-Semitic and violent toward Jews. In order to prove his point he presents a comprehensive list of dates that demonstrates the multi-regional frequency of what he purports to be pogroms by Muslims against the Jewish people:

> The truth is that life for Jews within the House of Islam has been characterized by ceaseless humiliation and regular pogroms. A state of apartheid has been the norm....In parts of the Arab world it has been the local custom for Muslim children to throw stones at Jews and spit upon them. These and other indignities have been regularly punctuated by organized massacres and pogroms: in Morocco (1728, 1790, 1875, 1884, 1890, 1903, 1912, 1948, 1952, and 1955), in Algeria (1805 and 1934), in Tunisia (1864, 1869, 1932, and 1967), in Persia (1839, 1867, and 1910), in Iraq (1828, 1936, 1937, 1941, 1946, 1948, 1967, and 1969), in Libya (1785, 1860, 1897, 1945, 1948, and 1967), in Egypt (1882, 1919, 1921, 1924, 1938-39, 1945, 1956, and 1967), in Palestine (1929 and 1936), in Syria (1840, 1945, 1947, 1948, 1949, and 1967), in Yemen (1947), etc.[189]

This long list of dates is arranged in such a manner as to convince the reader that Islam is by nature violent and particularly so toward Jews. It is not only historically inaccurate, but presents a context that is designed to veil the nationalist nature of modern-day conflicts between Jews and Arabs in favor of a hereditary portrayal, while shifting the association of victimhood from Palestinian Arabs to their Jewish neighbors.

---

189. Sam Harris, *The End of Faith: Religion, Terror, and the Future of Reason*, New York and London: W.W. Norton (2005:115).

In order to understand the violence that has occurred during the twentieth century between Jews and Arabs living in Palestine, it is essential to grasp the cataclysmic changes that indigenous inhabitants of Palestine have been forced to endure during the modern period. To that end, the present conflict, from the perspective of Palestinian nationalism, will be presented here as rooted within an indigenous population searching for a national identity that would permit it to forge "resistance to an other, who not only belonged to a different faith but was also an outsider and openly proclaimed that the realization of his aims involved emptying the country of its original inhabitants."[190]

THE EMERGENCE OF PALESTINIAN IDENTITY: WESTERN INFATUATION WITH THE HOLY LAND

As England and the United States produced Evangelical and Protestant religious innovations during the nineteenth century, packs of explorers and scholars produced literature about Palestine for Western consumption, extensively describing archeological excavations that brought ancient and biblical history to life. Tourists and pilgrims from Christian countries visited the Holy Land in greater numbers each year, as steamships allowed them to travel with ease.[191] The local inhabitants of Palestine had long referred to the region as *al-ard al-muqaddasa* (the holy land), acknowledging its status as an annual pilgrimage center for many neighboring populations,[192] and newfound interest among Westerners did not go unnoticed by local communities, particularly those in the vicinity of Jerusalem, as they further developed a sense of self-awareness in relation to the West that helped to shape an early formation of Palestinian identity.[193]

One of the first examples of this growing sense of local awareness takes place in 1701, when a French consul in Sidon had been permitted to settle in Jerusalem, causing a fear among the local Muslim population

---

190. Musa Budeiri, "The Palestinians: Tensions between Nationalist and Religious Identities," in James Jankowski and Israel Gershoni (eds.), *Rethinking Nationalism* (1997:196).
191. Butrus Abu-Manneh, "The Rise of the Sanjak of Jerusalem in the Late Nineteenth Century," in Ilan Pappe (ed.), *The Israel/Palestine Question: Rewriting Histories*, London and New York: Routledge (1999:42).
192. Rashid Khalidi, "The Formation of Palestinian Identity" (1997a:173-74).
193. Ibid. (1997a:175).

that this represented a formal imposition by foreign powers to colonize the Holy Land, "especially," in their words, "since our city [Jerusalem] is the focus of attention of the infidels."[194] In response, a group of Muslims sent a formal petition to local Ottoman authorities, professing, most likely as a reference to the Crusades: "we fear that we will be occupied as a result of this, as happened repeatedly in past times."[195] Some years later, in 1726, a prominent local, Shaykh Muhammad al-Khalil, complained in a formal letter that permitting European consuls to establish endowments in Jerusalem "constituted a danger to the future of the city, which must be built up and populated if Jerusalem were to be defended against the covetousness of these external enemies."[196]

Such fears were not just speculative, but grounded in a real shift in power that was occurring between the Arab population of the region and the West. In the late Ottoman period, Palestine became a new international reality, experienced through the lens of a renewed Christian interest. By the nineteenth century, Arab inhabitants began to see a significant increase in the presence of Western consular and missionary institutions in Jerusalem, beginning in 1860 with the highly visible Russian compound, with its "majestic viewpoint outside the walls," and quickly followed by a large entourage of new Western consulates, including those of the United States, Britain, France, and Germany.[197] Jerusalem had become a sort of new Paris, an essential visiting ground for European heads of state, including the future British Prime Minister Benjamin Disraeli and the German Kaiser Wilhelm II, who in 1898 entered Jerusalem through a specially constructed opening in the Jaffa Gate.[198]

Had the increased presence of European powers been limited to safeguarding the religious rights of Christians, the trend might not have had such a notable impact on local populations, but as ecclesiastical concerns were visibly mixed with those of extra-imperial ambitions, such intentions were difficult for locals to dismiss. Such a dynamic was clearly expressed in a memorandum with the arrival of the Russian foreign minister in early 1858:

---

194. Rashid Khalidi, *Palestinian Identity: The Construction of Modern National Consciousness*, New York: Columbia University Press (1997b:29).
195. Ibid. (1997b:30).
196. Ibid. (1997b:30).
197. Baruch Kimmerling and Joel Migdal, *The Palestinian People* (2003:72-73).
198. Bernard Wasserstein, *Divided Jerusalem: The Struggle for the Holy City*, New Haven and London: Yale University Press (2001:50-51).

We must establish our "presence" in the East not politically but through the church....While our influence was still strong we could afford to conceal our activities and thus avoid envy, but now that our influence in the East has weakened we, on the contrary, must try to display ourselves so that we do not sink in the estimation of the Orthodox population....Jerusalem is the centre of the world and our mission must be there.[199]

As the presence of Westerners increased in Jerusalem, a barrage of new construction of sites was launched throughout the city in an effort to establish "presence," including a large number of churches, convents, missionary schools, and hospitals—an initiative set forth by the combined majority of Europe.[200] Prior to the nineteenth century, the Ottomans had limited the permanent settlement of European consuls and Christian missions in Jerusalem, but as the empire had been pressured to accept contemporary stringent capitulations, it had little ability to continue its policy. Soon, Jerusalem natives, particularly notables who felt their influence slowly diminishing, would catch a whiff of the odorous smell that lay beyond benign foreign influence.

THE EMERGENCE OF PALESTINIAN IDENTITY: THE SANJAQ OF JERUSALEM

As Christian and Jewish European populations expanded in Jerusalem, indigenous Palestinian communities renewed their appraisal of the city, transforming it into a major symbol of resistance to emerging European and Zionist threats. In this sense, the Palestinian re-visioning of Jerusalem was intrinsically linked with the struggle that would take place within a modern colonial context. Meanwhile, Ottoman authorities had made internal changes within the administration of the Jerusalem district. While the Ottoman Empire had drastically declined in power, Istanbul had attempted to strengthen its hold over the Arab provinces through a number of measures known as the *Tanzimat*, in an effort to reverse the fragmentation of the Islamic *umma*. As a result of Istanbul's direct administration over the city, Jerusalem's old linkages to its surrounding

---

199. Ibid. (2001:59-60)
200. Butrus Abu-Manneh, "The Rise of the Sanjak of Jerusalem in the Late Nineteenth Century" (1999:42).

urban network had been broken. Ironically, this restructuring had increased the power of local notables, who assumed elite status in the larger region through their direct contact with Istanbul.[201] Such developments, which elevated the regional status of Jerusalem and enhanced the "local consciousness of Palestine as a discrete entity, based on religious tradition and long-standing administrative practice,"[202] had served to contribute a sense of context and reference for the transformations that were occurring in the native experience of identity.

By early twentieth century, the Ottoman Empire had totally collapsed, which signified for its Muslim subjects the end of "the Caliphate state, *Dawlat al-Khilafa*," and by the end of World War I, Jerusalem had been occupied by the British, "no longer administered according to the Islamic *shari'a*."[203] Suddenly, Jerusalem had been transformed from the third most important sacred city ruled by an ancient Islamic Empire into the symbolic center of an anti-colonialist movement in its infancy. This marks a pivotal moment in the emergence of a particularistic Arab identity in relation to the city of Jerusalem. As Rashid Khalidi notes, "in a period of a few years, Ottomanism as an ideology went from being one of the primary sources of identification for Palestinians and other Arabs to having no apparent impact at all."[204] The destruction of the Islamic *umma* was complete as European powers drew up new permanent boundaries and "now demanded passports and visas for previously uncontrolled routes," using "different currencies, customs regulations, and trade patterns" throughout the region.[205] As two post-Zionist historians have recently argued:

> The defeat of the Ottoman Empire and the imposition of British boundaries left Palestine's Muslims without the central religious institutions that had answered to the sultan in Istanbul. A significant amount of Palestinian political action during the mandate period took place within the framework of new institutions established to fill the void.[206]

---

201. Ibid. (1999:43).
202. Rashid Khalidi, "The Formation of Palestinian Identity" (1997a:174-75).
203. Musa Budeiri, "The Palestinians" (1997:191).
204. Rashid Khalidi, "The Formation of Palestinian Identity" (1997a:178).
205. Baruch Kimmerling and Joel S. Migdal, *The Palestinian* (2003:85).
206. Ibid. (2003:88).

The ideological and psychological impact of the Ottoman Empire's collapse upon Palestine's indigenous communities cannot be underestimated. Its incorporation of the Islamic *umma*, "within whose framework over twenty generations of Arabs had lived for four centuries in the countries of the Fertile Crescent," had represented the continuation of a universalistic tradition that infused many of its Muslim subjects with a great sense of pride and comfort. It is therefore not difficult to imagine that the rapidity with which this reality was shattered in exchange for a Western occupation that would soon recognize the national aspirations of a fledgling Zionist movement, while it negated those of the local inhabitants, created a political vacuum ripe for the emergence of Palestinian nationalism.[207] As Rashid Khalidi so lucidly argues:

> These upheavals in the world around them, upheavals that impinged directly on the structure of the lives of the entire population, made possible, and at the same time necessitated, extremely rapid changes in attitudes and consciousness on the part of the Palestinians.[208]

In a moment's time, Palestine's population, having known nothing but relative security for generations, was on its own, occupied by Britain and facing an emerging powerful Zionist movement. The perceived necessity for resistance that was a result of this experience would be the context within which Palestinian identity would inevitably find form.

THE CONSOLIDATION OF PALESTINIAN IDENTITY: ZIONISM AND THE ORIGINAL *INTIFADAS* OF 1929 AND 1936

Prior to the Israeli state's existence, the Zionist movement was a well-financed and highly motivated organization chiefly interested in creating new facts on the ground by appropriating as much Palestinian land as possible and turning it over to new Jewish settlers from Eastern Europe and elsewhere. Toward the end of the nineteenth century, Zionist land acquisitions had begun to occur on a small scale. By 1917, after the British conquest of Palestine had been successful, this trend had taken huge strides. Most frustrating for indigenous landholders of small properties was that not only were they forced off the land and made dependent

---

207. Rashid Khalidi, "The Formation of Palestinian Identity" (1997a:178).
208. Ibid. (1997a:179-80).

on wage work, but that subsequently they were denied employment by Jewish settlers who practiced an extreme form of segregationist ideology fueled by the Zionist quest for a mono-religious state.[209] Indeed, what Palestinians experienced was even more severe than the South African Apartheid, which at least held out the promise of some form of employment by white settlers toward those they dispossessed.[210] Many of these Palestinians emigrated to large metropolises such as Jerusalem and Haifa only to find that high-wage and permanent jobs were reserved for Jewish workers.

Predictably, Arab workers highly resented such new realities and began to regularly clash with these new sprawling Jewish settlements. Incidents of Palestinian resistance had taken place as early as the 1870s. As the crisis grew in scope, Jews and Arabs became more thin-skinned, using smaller and smaller scuffles to justify major conflicts. Increasingly, those who had been most directly affected by this double assault of dispossession and poor employment reacted with sporadic violence by "attacking, raiding, robbing, and generally harassing the new Jewish settlements."[211] Soon, Palestinians would begin to mobilize nationalist and religious symbols in resistance of the total marginalization of their communities. As we will see, during the major Arab revolts of 1929 and 1936, Jerusalem, with its al-Aqsa Mosque and its many other important religious markers, would become central to the emerging Palestinian movement. Indeed, it would not be until these pivotal rebellions—the so-called original *intifadas*—that the Palestinian movement would be able to transcend the many local and supra-identities of the transforming region.

The eruptions of violence in 1929 and again in 1936, which represent the first major violent clashes between Jews and Arabs, can only be properly understood primarily in light of developments contemporary to them. Such polemic scholarship as that of Sam Harris, which ascribes the emergence of conflict to an ingrained Muslim hatred of Jews, does little

---

209. For a detailed description of how this occurred, see Ted Swedenburg, "The Role of the Palestinian Peasantry in the Great Revolt (1936-9), in Ilan Pappe (ed.), *The Israel/Palestine Question* (1999:129-67).

210. For a comparative analysis of Apartheid in South Africa with that of Zionist policy in Palestine, see Gershon Shafir, *Land, Labor, and the Origins of the Israeli-Palestinian Conflict* (1996); Leila Farsakh, "What Future for Palestine: Independence or Bantustans," in *The Discourse of Sociology Practice*, University of Massachusetts, vol. 7, nos. 1&2, Spring/Fall (2005).

211. Ted Swedenburg, "Palestinian Peasantry in the Great Revolt" (1999:138).

to shed light on the effects of systemic inequality between contesting groups over issues of land and other material resources. Those who contend that religious influence over people is the primary motivating factor and who condemn a group under siege by a settler population as being anti-Semitic rarely consider such immediate concerns. Indeed, such studies are themselves ideological and intended to silence legitimate grievances.[212]

The horrific violence that occurred in 1929 was triggered by issues regarding the usage of sacred space at Jerusalem's Wailing Wall. Prior to these events, Jews had worshipped freely at the Wailing Wall, intermingling with Muslims who shared the understanding that it was a sacred space. Muslims had called the Wailing Wall *al-Buraq*, alluding to Muhammad's ascension to heaven following his night journey to Jerusalem, during which he pitched his horse at the Wall before taking flight. In the late nineteenth century, some Jews who were sympathetic to Jewish nationalism attempted to change the status quo in the usage of the Wall by taking up a greater area and insisting that it be looked after and repaired solely by Jewish groups—"measures inevitably interpreted [by the Palestinians] as an expression of rights of possession over the spot."[213]

In the context of the increasing number of Jewish settlements that received special protection from foreign consuls as well as from a British colonial administration that was itself calling for the creation of a Jewish homeland, Muslims began to fear that the changes that were taking place would be used to justify further adjustments.[214] According to the Israeli historian, Yehoshua Porath:

> [Palestinians] regarded Zionism from the beginning as a movement striving to change the national *status quo* in the country and to restore the glory of the ancient Israelite kingdom. Naturally, then, they began to develop fears lest the mosques of al-Aqsa and the Dome of the Rock also became objects for Jewish restorationism.[215]

---

212. On this issue see Alexander Cockburn and Jeffrey St. Clair (eds.), *The Politics of Anti-Semitism*, Oakland, California: AK Press (2003); Norman G. Finkelstein, *The Holocaust Industry: Reflection on the Exploitation of Jewish Suffering*, London and New York: Verso Press (2000).
213. Yehoshua Porath, *The Emergence of the Palestinian-Arab National Movement, 1918-1929*, London: Frank Cass (1974:258).
214. Charles Smith, *Palestine and the Arab-Israeli Conflict* (1996:88).
215. Yehoshua Porath, *The Emergence of the Palestinian* (1974:258).

As Muslims witnessed Zionist Jews acquiring legal possession of the Wailing Wall under British colonial rule, they began to suspect further intentions to encompass the whole area, given that recent Zionist maneuvers in Palestine "had taught the Muslims that any deviation from the customary habits created a new rule, and any change in the *status quo* inevitably became a new *status quo*."[216] The argument coming from the representatives of the Muslim population, for instance, claimed "that the Jews' tears and kisses at the Wall were not a product of their love for the Wall itself but of their fond desire to take over *al-Haram al-Sharif*, as everyone knows."[217]

Such fears of a Zionist conspiracy to take over the entire al-Aqsa compound were further aggravated by the discovery atop the Dome of the Rock of a painting depicting the Star of David that was produced by Zionist authorities in the late nineteenth century.[218] Upon its detection in 1929, the Jewish painting was heavily circulated by Muslim authorities in Jerusalem who were intent on demonstrating the intentions of the Zionists.[219]

The subsequent violent clash unfolded when the Mufti of Jerusalem began to pressure British authorities to protect Muslim rights over the property of the Wailing Wall in July of 1929. In response, a Zionist paper urged the Jews of Jerusalem to rebuild the Temple and Rabbi Kook suggested to the young Jewish settlers that they ought to be "willing to sacrifice their lives in the cause of their Holy Place," after which, he raised "the Zionist flag, and sang the Zionist anthem."[220] As Muslims witnessed such displays, many gave sermons calling for a defense of the area and thousands stormed the wall, setting afire notes containing prayers that Jews had placed within it.[221] Violent clashes ensued with hundreds of casualties on both sides.

Immediately afterward, the British appointed a commission to investigate the 1929 Wailing Wall riots. The commission, known as the Shaw Report of 1930, concluded emphatically that Zionist-nationalist aspirations at the expense of Arabs, as well as land policies that forced Arabs off their land had caused the riots:

---

216. Ibid. (1974:261).
217. Ibid. (1974:262).
218. Charles Smith, *Palestine and the Arab-Israeli Conflict* (1996:88).
219. Yehoshua Porath, *The Emergence of the Palestinian* (1974:262-63).
220. Charles Smith, *Palestine and the Arab-Israeli Conflict* (1996:89).
221. Ibid. (1996:89).

> The fundamental cause [of the outbreak] is the Arab
> feeling of animosity and hostility towards the Jews con-
> sequent on the disappointment of their political and na-
> tional aspirations and fear for their economic future....
> The feeling as it exists today is based on the two-fold
> fear of the Arabs that by Jewish immigration and land
> purchases they may be deprived of their livelihood and
> placed under the economic domination of the Jews.[222]

Indeed, it was the displaced Palestinian *fellahin* (peasants) who would
form the largest base of the movement during the next great revolt of
1936.[223]

From the Palestinian perspective, the commission had only stated the
obvious, as the following account by a Palestinian witness illustrates so
vividly:

> That day was a day of honor, splendour and glory in the
> annals of Palestinian-Arab history. We attacked Western
> conquest and the Mandate and the Zionists upon our
> land. The Jews had coveted our endowments and
> yearned to take over our holy places. Silence they had
> seen as weakness. Therefore, there was no more room in
> our hearts for patience and peace....The Arabs stood up,
> checked the oppression, and sacrificed their pure and
> noble souls on the sacred altar of nationalism.[224]

As Ilan Pappe explains, it seemed self-evident that a clear relationship existed between Zionist pursuits within Jerusalem and the combination of land acquisitions with isolationist policies regarding the availabil-
ity of labor.[225] But even after several clear warnings had been officially
issued that highlighted the social roots of unrest among the local population, Zionist land purchases in the 1930s continued to increase at an even
greater scale, resulting in a major land crisis for the Palestinians. A mid-
1930s report from Haifa, for example, revealed that "11,160 Arab work-

---

222. Quoted in Ibid. (1996:90).
223. Rashid Khalidi, "The Formation of Palestinian Identity" (1997a:176).
224. Baruch Kimmerling and Joel Migdal, *The Palestinian* (2003:105).
225. Ilan Pappe, *A History of Modern Palestine: One Land, Two Peoples*, Cambridge, U.K.: Cambridge University Press (2004:92).

ers were living in 2,500 gasoline can huts."[226] On a larger scale, roughly
a third of the Palestinian village dwelling population had been rendered
landless by 1930, while a large majority of those who had managed to
retain some degree of ownership had lost the capacity to be self-
subsisting.[227]

Given such dire circumstances, it is not difficult to imagine the des-
perate need that local Palestinian communities must have felt to forge a
unified nationalist response. The Arab Revolt of 1936 was the first initiative that would embody such a response—a momentous event that many
Palestinians still discuss to this day and call the first *intifada*.[228] The revolt mobilized a large sector of the Palestinian population, including
"Arabs from every stratum of society, all over the country, heralding the
emergence of a national movement."[229] Following the assassination at the
hands of the British of the highly popular peasant guerrilla fighter,
Shaykh 'Iz al-Din al-Qassam, a spontaneous strike was called by the Arabs in 1936, which would soon erupt into an all-out rebellion. During the
revolt, "the British briefly lost control of much of the country, including
cities like Jerusalem and Nablus, before a massive campaign of repression by tens of thousands of troops and numerous squadrons of aircraft in
1938-39 was able to restore 'order.'"[230]

After the outbreak of the Arab Revolt in April of 1936, David Ben-
Gurion openly acknowledged that the Arabs of Palestine had a national
character, and he admitted in front of the Jewish agency executive in
May of 1936 that "We and they want the same thing: We both want Palestine. And that is the fundamental conflict."[231] But rather than evoking
sympathy for the Palestinians, Zionists remained unmoved and the British reacted brutally, pouring in thousands of troops to crush the Palestinian resistance.[232]

In October of 1938, the British imposed military rule over Jerusalem
and throughout the country, proceeding to use methods that would later
become familiar to Palestinians under Israeli rule, such as collective

---

226. Charles Smith, *Palestine and the Arab-Israeli Conflict* (1996:94-95).
227. Ted Swedenburg, "Palestinian Peasantry in the Great Revolt" (1999:143).
228. On Palestinian memory of the Great Revolt, see the fine work of Ted Swedenburg, *Memories of Revolt: The 1936-1939 Rebellion and the Palestinian
National Past*, Fayetteville, Arkansas: University of Arkansas Press (2003).
229. Baruch Kimmerling and Joel Migdal, *The Palestinian* (2003:102).
230. Rashid Khalidi, *Palestinian Identity* (1997b:189-90).
231. David Ben-Gurion cited in Avi Shlaim, *Iron Wall* (2001:18).
232. Baruch Kimmerling and Joel Migdal, *The Palestinian* (2003:102-3).

fines, demolition of homes, and punishment of villages suspected of collaborating with the rebels. The British also built a massive "barbed wire barrier between Palestine and Syria"[233] known as the Tegart Wall—another innovation that the future Israeli administration would use on a much more extensive scale.

This extremely brutal use of collective punishment by the British would not only weaken the Palestinian resistance to imperial rule, but would break the back of the movement, weakening the Palestinian capacity to form a viable response to the Zionist call for the establishment of the state of Israel in 1948, which Palestinians would come to call *al-nakba*, or "the catastrophe." In this sense, British rule would pave the way for the eventual Zionist conquest over the Palestinians. As Kimmerling and Migdal persuasively argue:

> The Arab population found itself worn down at the revolt's end, and disarmed by British forces. When the Zionists began their own rebellion against the British following World War II, "the Palestinian Arabs," notes W. F. Abboushi, "proved too exhausted by the effort of rebellion between 1936 and 1939 to be in any condition to match it."[234]

It would not be until many years later that the Palestinians would be able to recover and begin mounting a movement with some capacity to resist the very powerful and well-financed state of Israel. Faced with a double assault by both the British and the Zionist movement, Palestinians saw their nationalist aspirations crushed and, unlike other Third World anti-colonialist movements, they were unable to successfully enter the transition from colonial rule to independence. Far from it, they instead would have to live through six decades of brutal occupation by the new Israeli state, culminating "in a process of expulsion, dispersal, and dissolution."[235]

After 1948, and especially with the Israeli occupation of 1967, Israeli control over the lives of Palestinians would continue to grow, with many thousands of Palestinian homes either confiscated or demolished and much of the land usurped by the Israelis would eventually be used to house the hundreds of thousands of Jewish settlers. In East Jerusalem

---

233. Ibid. (2003:129).
234. Ibid. (2003:103).
235. Musa Budeiri, "The Palestinians" (1997:198).

alone, there are now over 200,000 Jewish settlers. But the most excruciating part of the occupation is its impact on the daily life of the Palestinians. As Mourid Barghouti recounts his experience of living under occupation:

> Occupation prevents you from managing your affairs in your own way. It interferes in every aspect of life and death; it interferes with longing and anger and desire and walking in the street. It interferes with going anywhere and coming back, with going to market, the emergency hospital, the beach, the bedroom, or distant capital.[236]

As Jewish settlers crisscrossed the entire Occupied Territories after 1967, Palestinians found their capacity for travel limited by checkpoints, delays, searches, and other intrusions. Further, they were forced into ghetto-like camps, with every detail of their lives regulated by Israeli policy, from visits to relatives in nearby villages and emergency trips to local hospitals, to the use of water or the ability to pray at the al-Aqsa Mosque in Jerusalem. Indeed, the Israeli administration, far from "uniting" Jerusalem, had imposed a divisive atmosphere the likes of which had not been seen since the days of the Crusades.

Such a constricted reality has continued to this day for Palestinians. The recent *intifadas* of 1987 and 2000 cannot be properly understood outside of the context of nationalist identity development, both of Zionist and of Palestinian initiative. In September of 2000, Ariel Sharon, the future Israeli Prime Minister "visited" the Temple Mount, guarded by nearly a thousand Israeli troops, a calculated incident that could only have been interpreted as a declaration of sovereignty over the sacred site that contains the Dome of the Rock and the al-Aqsa Mosque. The fact is that contemporary Palestinians are all too conscious, as were their predecessors in the 1929 and 1936 Arab Revolts, that every Israeli initiative, regardless how minute, seems always to represent another step toward changing the facts on the ground at their expense. It continues to be clear, as it was to the British in 1930, that what has given the most energy and momentum to Palestinian resistance has not been fanatical religious influence, as many contend and as is particularly evident in the depictions of most U.S. media, but rather the insistently aggressive nature of the Israeli occupation.

---

236. Mourid Barghouti, *I Saw Ramallah* (2000:48).

The Oslo Peace Process, begun in 1993, has proven little more than a humiliating experience for Palestinian leadership, as the PLO has been unable to bring much concrete success to the Palestinian people, resulting in a complete loss of credibility in the minds of Palestinians. Meanwhile, under the pretense of a peace process, Israeli authorities have continued to employ strategies of expulsion, home demolition, and appropriation of Palestinian land, while tightening their hold over the Occupied Territories. As a result of this combination of diplomatic failures with the continuation of aggressive policies over a long period of time, radical sentiments of resistance have been revived. In this sense, Israeli intransigence over the status of Jerusalem, the refusal to negotiate the rights of refugees to return, and the hundreds of thousands of Jewish settlers who remain securely anchored in East Jerusalem and the West Bank have all directly contributed to the victory of the more militant sector of the Palestinian political movements: Hamas.

V
Conclusion

In summation, what was once a symbiotic city, encapsulating many intertwined identities, has been thoroughly shattered with the coming of modern nationalism, specifically as a result of the incipient nature of British rule over Jerusalem and the aggressive nationalist aspect of Jewish Zionism. Responding to intentions of transforming the facts on the ground, Palestinians have been forced into defensive postures, sometimes violent in nature, but always as a result of the dire circumstances in which they have found themselves.

The limits of time-immemorialist scholarship, with its focus on an inherent religious bias toward violence, are evident. In presenting an alternative to this perspective, our hope is to illuminate that much of what appears on the surface to be religious in character is actually a product of very recent developments that are based upon issues of humanitarian concern: the history of Zionist settlements, the mass demolition of Palestinian homes, the massive creation of Palestinian refugee camps, and the production of an apartheid system of Bantustans under Israeli occupation. While Qur'anic passages and the preaching of Jihad have been used to fan flames among sectors of the Arab world, such developments cannot be understood as occurring in a vacuum, as many scholars and media sources try to do, but must be analyzed within the context of a massive

ethnic cleansing campaign that has threatened to extinguish the livelihood that Palestinians have historically known in the land of Palestine.
Such an analysis is rooted here around the issues of power, land, and resources, as opposed to those of religious fanaticism that are designed to
demonize Palestinians and Arab Muslims in general. The notion that
Muslims and Arabs, owing to their traditional and religious beliefs, are
inherently violent toward Jews does not hold weight in light of a historical analysis that takes into account the cataclysmic effect that colonial
rule coupled with Zionist ideology has had on the Palestinian people.
Indeed, as we hope to have illustrated, this lengthy conflict has been far
from religious in nature, but rather has been the direct product of two
nationalist movements seeking the same real estate: one, having amassed
the power to dislocate an indigenous people, while the other has found its
form out of a forced sense of desperation.

5

BEYOND NATIONALISM: JERUSALEM AND THE NEGATION OF PEOPLEHOOD

I want you to be a Ka'aba for the people of the earth,
A spacious house
Without guards;
I love you . . . a voice from a minaret,
The sound of horns
Mingled with church bells.
I love you, a jasmine in the open air.[1]

The fundamental characteristic of nationalism in the modern age with which we have been concerned has been its capacity to provide a meaningful language with which to reformulate identity through the re-definition of populations under a nation's jurisdiction in such a way as to construct a purified notion of subjecthood. This social construct, within a short span of time, assumed enough power to force apart communities that had long lived within varying degrees of symbiosis. Muslims, Christians, and Jews, for example, living within overlapping communities and districts were forced to identify with one nation or another that dictated its "own" natural sense of cultural space in an ethnically purified and territorial manner, completely externalizing all "others" that did not fit such national classifications. During this period, we have argued, violent confrontations between different groups, particularly surrounding sacred world cities, which have often been attributed to the residues of ancient

---

1. Yusuf Hamdan quoted in Abdel Wahab M. El-Messiri, "The Palestinian Wedding, Major Themes of Contemporary Palestinian Resistance Poetry," *Journal of Palestine Studies*, vol. 10, no. 39, Spring (1981:89).

tribal or religious antagonisms, are more accurately understood as rooted within the very act of nation production. This has engendered divisions and notions of otherness far more extreme and conclusive than any to be found in the ancient religious texts of the Qur'an, the Torah, or the New Testament.

During its early years, the Jewish-Christian movement, most specifically led by Paul, forged a diasporic element within Judaism, intending to create a sense of compatibility with the universalistic Greco-Roman Empire. As Christianity eventually became *the* imperial religion, the hybrid form of this movement was replaced with an extremely oppressive form of universalism in which all forms of difference were violently eradicated. This was especially the case for the Jews of Jerusalem who were either completely repressed or removed by the new Christian Empire.

With the seventh-century rise of Islam, under the direction of the Prophet Muhammad, a more pluralistic form of universalism emerged in which the "People of the Book," namely Jews and Christians, were integrated into the Arab-Islamic civilization and permitted to live relatively comfortably within a largely Muslim populated Empire. Muslims, Jews, and Christians interacted relatively freely with one another thus creating a symbiotic space, especially in Jerusalem, where the sacred spaces of all three communities formed a complicated mosaic that took synergistic form. Not only was the coexistence of differing sacred spaces tolerated, but as a unified expression of monotheistic devotion, they formed a space that undermined any attempt to naturalize difference, or to reify one religious community as separate from and in contrast with the other, as Jewish and Christian sites were protected under Islamic law. Indeed, Christian and Jewish sites were rarely understood as forms exterior to Islam, but formed instead an essential component of Muslim identity. As Muslims recognized most sites as part of their own history, any sense of clear separation between the sacred spaces of each faith was blurry. The notion, therefore, of removing Jewish and Christian sacred spaces made little sense in this context, as such an act would negate the very Muslim identity itself. However, the Islamic pluralistic version of universalism only extended to the "People of the Book," allowing for the repression of any group that fell outside the category, particularly any of the multiple polytheistic tribes that were scattered throughout the territory who were either brutally oppressed or forced to convert.

In recounting a history filled with periods of symbiotic existence, the current study aims to offer an alternative view from the dominant trend, which posits such conflicts as that of the Palestinian-Israeli as intractable, consisting of peoples with incompatible cultures, religions, or nationalities, as though they were composed of two chemical compounds destined to combust if mixed together. Historic examples of relative tolerance and symbiosis offer the possibility of aspiring toward greater forms of inter-communal reality. If Scriptural or Qur'anic formulations of identity are to be questioned, then the very ontology of modernity itself must be equally scrutinized; and as it is perhaps the most visited example in contemporary times, violence between Jews and Arabs/ Palestinians must be understood as a product of absolutist and nationalist constructs in which the notion of peoplehood has been so thoroughly and deeply fixed that it confuses an essential part of its Self as its Other.

This book is thus intended with the hope that by uncovering the ideological underpinnings of the modern nation-state we can more effectively deconstruct the highly problematic national identity and begin the process of constructing more sustainable forms of community. As Walid Khalidi recently suggests, we are "on the threshold of the second century of the Zionist Arab conflict," and he asks us to take "a moment of introspection" by which we can re-evaluate a century of vulgarity in which "the contemporary engineers of nationalism" have created havoc for the inhabitants of Palestine.[2] Rooting the cause of contemporary conflicts within ancient soil as represented by religious texts, be they occurring in Jerusalem or anywhere else, renders the expression of violence unintelligible and beyond the reach of change, and further foments greater violent sentiment as it postulates inherent and irresolvable differences that are racist in form. Religion of any variety does not exist exterior to humanity, acting mysteriously upon it, and its reification in the manner that has become so common only translates into a denial of responsibility.

I
Time to Say Goodbye to the People

As the nation-state essentially produces a purified notion of a people encapsulated within a territorial space of its own, we must find a new discourse that not only tolerates the "Other," but in fact disarms the assumption of power that produces peoplehood in the first place. National-

---

2. Walid Khalidi, *All That Remains: The Palestinian Villages Occupied and Depopulated by Israel in 1948*, Washington, D.C.: Institute for Palestinian Studies (1992:xxxiv).

ism and any other concept of the people, be it Jewish, Arab, American, French, or any other, will constantly shift its internal borders and find new binaries to reproduce its Self. Such a state of tolerance is always an event away from genocide and only a short distance from identifying as a citizen to a more chauvinistic attitude of fighting to secure its implicit identification of rights from a foreign enemy. In this reality, borders are the site of security as well as exclusion.

In the Israeli and Palestinian case, even when the Other is tolerated, there is a constant discourse of demography and numbers, with the assumption that too many Arab or Jewish births is a danger to the purity of the nation. Positing this type of racist discourse as natural and unproblematic takes an incredibly powerful ideology of absolutist claims to identity and land. What makes this possible is the commonsensical assumption that one cannot be both Jewish and Palestinian at once; that one's identity is self-contained and self-evident, and that any other identification is inconceivable.

Nationalism posits that humanity is composed of a number of cultures, with each having a singular essence. It reifies the nation in the most rigid way, by making it into a *thing* and, in the process, naturalizing it. It produces an identity that inspires a sense of naturally belonging to "a territory embedded with cultural meanings, a shared history, and a linguistic community," and it continuously produces an ideological structure that creates and reproduces "the purity of the people" at the expense of those Others on the outside, working like "a machine that produces Others, creates racial difference, and raises boundaries that delimit and support the modern subject of sovereignty."[3] The Arab, the Muslim, and the Palestinian as a unified identity produces its own Other in response to the Israeli Jew, negating the external identity in the perceived need for its very own state. The Jewish state is produced in the same fashion, but its power can render the Arab invisible, at times in a crude and brutal fashion. The identity of the nation rests heavily not only on the negation of the Other, but on the fixity of the constructed border. In this sense, the Jewish or Arab Self needs the continuous clash and confrontation with its Other in order for it to maintain its power, a process understood by both Zionist and Jihadist groups, who literally need each other for their own reproduction.

---

3. Michael Hardt and Antonio Negri, *Empire*, Cambridge, Massachusetts: Harvard University Press (2000:114).

By understanding that nationalism *invents* nations where they do not exist, it is possible to understand that the collective "we" unit is a *product* of the nation-state itself, and not something naturally preceding it.[4] The Wall that runs through Jerusalem is not simply erected on naturally marked borders, but is itself politically constructed in order to naturalize an otherwise artificial division. As Edward Said eloquently argues, difference is not something given in nature, an inert fact waiting to be mapped by the geographer or named by the anthropologist, but is created by the power to narrate an Other as its most distant point.[5] This creates the illusion of an extremely lengthy distance, often beyond the horizon—or, in the current example, behind the Wall—toward making real contact with the Other in a manner that reflects the Self. In this way, the Jew and the Arab, each experiencing itself as naturally belonging to a people that is diametrically opposed to the other, form an ideological and artificial construct which can never produce genuine security with regard to one another. Ultimately, the Wall produces not security and well-being, as is its supposed intention, but rather encourages the exact opposite: mistrust, bitterness, resentment, and ultimately insecurity—on both sides.

II
"Tolerant" Nationalists: Blurring the Binaries?

A nationalist identity is a reductionist and one-dimensional reality, in which we "define ourselves solely in relation to a flag, as belonging to a unique identity, and thus divide the world between an ethnic or national 'us' and all others."[6] In the case of the "Israeli" and the "Palestinian," reduced to a simplistic bi-national classification scheme, the quest for security and basic rights has instead created a century of deep trauma. The notion of finding some measure of mutual affirmation through a two-state settlement, although seeming a reasonable solution to the degree of antagonism and violence that each group experiences, nonetheless remains problematic as it fails to confront the naturalized ontology of Self and Other implicit in the national schema. Such a project con-

---

4. Benedict Anderson, *Imagined Communities: Reflections on the Origin and Spread of Nationalism*, London: Verso Press (1995).
5. Edward Said, *Orientalism*, New York: Vintage Books (1979).
6. Michel Warschawski, *On the Border*, Cambridge, Massachusetts: South End Press (2005:xvii).

notes a consolidated Self that, while it affirms the existence of the Other, nonetheless accepts those very same binaries present in more chauvinistic nationalist projects. In this sense, affirming the Other, while admittedly better than the present *status quo*, leaves the Jew and the Arab with no common ground and does not address or resolve the deep complexity of the multitude's identity.

An example of this complexity can be found in the figure of Ella Shohat, for whom this either/or reduction is especially problematic, as she is a *Mizrahi* Jew born in Israel, whose Jewish-Arab parents migrated from Baghdad. As a Jew who identifies as both Jewish and Arab, it becomes literally impossible "to hide our Middle Easterness under one Jewish 'we'." In her words:

> Our history simply cannot be discussed in European Jewish terminology. As Iraqi Jews, while retaining a communal identity, we were generally well integrated and indigenous to the country, forming an inseparable part of its social and cultural life. Thoroughly Arabized, we used Arabic even in hymns and religious ceremonies....Prominent Jewish writers, poets and scholars played a vital role in Arab culture, distinguishing themselves in Arabic-speaking theater, in music, as singers, composers, and players of traditional instruments.[7]

Shohat's identity is more complicated than nationalist categories permit, yet Shohat herself, even after taking into account her serious charges against present Israeli nationalist classifications, reaffirms and reclaims those very same classifications by positing an "Arab" past, thus continuing to naturalize the notion of peoplehood. The limits of this can best be evaluated in the work of less radical, liberal Jews like Ahad Ha'am and Martin Buber. Ha'am, for example, a highly spiritual and tolerant Jew who, although utterly committed to the Zionist nationalist cause, is nonetheless highly critical of the self-righteous wing of the Zionist movement, engages in an honest and critical assessment of their policies to uproot the Palestinians. In prophetic fashion, he warns that their efforts to restore Israel through the trampling of Palestinian Arabs

---

7. Ella Shohat, "Dislocated Identities: Reflections of an Arab-Jew," in Tony Kushner and Alis Solomon (eds.), *Wrestling with Zion: Progressive Jewish American Responses to the Israeli-Palestinian Conflict*, New York: Grove Press (2003:196).

have not only obscured the humanity of the Other, but may have as well irretrievably damaged the moral consciousness of the Jewish movement:

> We must surely learn, from both our past and present history, how careful we must be not to provoke the anger of the native people by doing them wrong, how we should be cautious in our dealings with a foreign people among whom we returned to live, to handle these people with love and respect and, needless to say, with justice and good judgment. And what do our brothers do? Exactly the opposite!...This...has planted despotic tendencies in their hearts....They deal with the Arabs with hostility and cruelty, trespass unjustly, beat them shamefully for no sufficient reason, and even boast about their actions. There is no one to stop the flood and put an end to this despicable and dangerous tendency....Even if [the Arabs] are silent and endlessly reserved, they keep their anger in their hearts. And these people will be revengeful like no other....[But as long as things continue the way they are,] the society that I envision, if my dream is not just a false notion, this society will have to begin to create itself in the midst of fuss, noisiness and panic, and will have to face the prospects of both internal and external war.[8]

Given the current circumstances, Ha'am's words some seven decades past is reassuring. Similarly, Buber's deep and just desire to teach other Zionists the skill of putting themselves "in the place of the other individual, the stranger, and to make his soul ours"[9] is highly inspiring. Yet, even in Buber's view, the Jew and Arab remain two self-contained people in search of dignity. While Buber is able to make the stranger's suffering visible to the Jew, the Arab remains exterior to his Jewish identity.

The discourse of "two peoples" needing to respect and tolerate each other's existence remains within the nationalist paradigm, in which Is-

---

8. Ahad Ha'am, "A Truth from Eretz Yisrael," in Tony Kushner and Alisa Solomon, *Wrestling with Zion: Progressive Jewish-American Responses to the Israeli-Palestinian Conflict*, New York: Grove Press (2003:15-16).

9. Martin Buber, "No More Declarations," reprinted in his collection, *A Land of Two Peoples*, New York: Oxford University Press ([1929] 1983:79-80).

raeli and Palestinian continue to be naturalized and thus fundamentally unbridgeable. The Jew and Arab still stand as two separate people, with their own heritage, traditions, and languages that function in the same way museums ornamentalize difference. Indeed, as Ammiel Alcalay has recently argued:

> The very assumption that Arabic [Muslim, and Jewish] culture are so distant they must somehow be bridged— even by scholars trying to prove connections—is itself an entirely ideological construct that would have made little sense to a twelfth-century Parisian, a seventeenth-century Venetian, or even an early-twentieth-century Syrian.[10]

III
The Other Is inside the Self

The particularistic model of national identity, even when interpreted liberally and with good will toward the Other, cannot go beyond a reified construct of reality, in which insider and outsider are each understood as having a singular will to act culturally, politically, creatively, destructively. In this model, certain kinds of behaviors and customs can always be attributed to a group in taxonomical form. Such universalistic projects as Christianity and Islam have attempted to provide an alternative model that idealizes the dissolution of divisions that are based on particularistic structures, but they have fallen short in that they have failed to escape a binary understanding of the social world. However, perhaps the monotheistic religions—Judaism included, as it espouses, for example, a notion of welcoming the stranger as one would welcome a cherished guest—have planted the seeds of a pluralistic multiplicity in which Self and Other cease to exist in binary or dialectical fashion, but exist instead in constant dialogue. Perhaps it is possible to envision the formation of open social relations that have historically been so thoroughly constitutive one of the other that to think of them as two interacting peoples with utterly different sets of identity would be a contradiction in terms.

---

10. Ammiel Alcalay, *After Jews and Arabs: Remaking Levantine Culture*, Minneapolis: University of Minnesota Press (1993:7).

A good example of this can be found in the writings of the famous Palestinian poet Mahmud Darwish, who constantly complicates nationalist categories:

> There will be a time when the Jew will not be ashamed to find the Arab part inside of himself, and the Arab will not be ashamed to declare that he is constituted also by Jewish elements. Especially when talking about Eretz Yisrael in Hebrew and Falestin in Arabic. I am a product of all the cultures that have passed through this land— Greek, Roman, Persian, Jewish, and Ottoman. A presence that exists even in my language. Each culture fortified itself, passed on, and left something. I am a son to all those fathers, but I belong to one mother. Does that mean my mother is a whore? My mother is this land that absorbed us all, was a witness and was a victim. I am also born of the Jewish culture that was in Palestine.[11]

What is most inspiring about Darwish's intervention is that he directly and unequivocally challenges the binary logic of nationalism and provides a clear example for those who are struggling to produce a new ontology of Self and Other that undermines the nationalist narrative. The affirmation of the Other inside the Self as a means of contesting the notion of peoplehood is extremely important to such an aim, because it provides the hope of a break with the classic view of the nation.

A more contemporary figure is the Jewish American Daniel Boyarin, who has written extensively on the question of identity and is himself in search of an alternative to the binaries that nationalism and other institutional forms of power force on us. Although he is not a scholar of the Palestinian-Israeli conflict, his scattered comments are highly suggestive. In a forward to his recent book, *Border Lines*, for instance, he reflects on this very issue:

> As I write, in occupied Palestine literal physical boundaries of barbed wired and electrified fencing are being raised to separate violently one "people" from another. In the process of maintaining our own identities...can

---

11. The Palestinian poet Mahmud Darwish cited in Baruch Kimmerling and Joel Migdal, *The Palestinian People: A History*, Cambridge, Massachusetts: Harvard University Press (2003:416).

we learn the lessons of the past and prevent ourselves at
the eleventh hour from the path of new and even more
violent heresiologies? Jews and Christians are called
upon at this moment to learn from our own difficult histories, without in any way rendering those histories
equivalent phenomenologically or morally, and do
something different now. The prophet teaches: Zion will
be redeemed only though justice.[12]

Darwish and Boyarin, each in his own unique way, share the notion
that what appears at first distant and strange becomes very close when
understood in terms of dialogue—so close indeed that the Other can be
felt inside the Self. Thus, rather than describing cultures capable only of
superficial interaction through some externalized scheme of contact, both
of these writers attempt to blur the division by positing the Other as intimate to the Self. Their examples not only blur the division between two
identities in struggle, but also render those very boundaries, with all their
notions of purity, difficult if not impossible to police.

So how does Jerusalem fit into this project of blurring Self and
Other? Where nationalism posits the Self as an enclosed, bound cultural
space, premised on maintaining a border to differentiate its Self from an
external Other, Jerusalem serves as a powerful symbol for those interested in re-ontologizing notions of both Arab and Jew. It is a symbolic
sacred space that provides the ultimate site in which to negate and remove the antinomies themselves. An unbound terrain can integrate its
diversity into networks across open space, rendering old dualisms, divisions, negations, and borders of the modern state indecipherable. In such
a vision, the al-Aqsa Mosque, the Wailing Wall, and the Holy Sepulcher
can stand as symbols not of purified sacred spaces, but of intertwined
identities.

Moreover, adopting the usurpation of the Other into the Self makes it
difficult for the state not only to police difference, but to actually reproduce and fashion further nationalist projects. Jerusalem's intricate system
of sacred space is so intertwined as understood from this perspective, that
it becomes impossible for a state to appropriate the city for itself, as the
insider/outsider model is torn asunder and replaced by that of hybridism.

Those who occupy privileged positions regarding the construction of
meaning (namely, the archeologists, the poets, the historians, the soci-

---

12. Daniel Boyarin, *Border Lines: The Partition of Judeo-Christianity*, Philadelphia: University of Pennsylvania Press (2004:xv).

ologists, the art historians, the Middle Eastern and Islamic scholars, etc.) form a powerful social force armed with the skill to denaturalize people-hood. Rather than operating from the perspective of a national binary system, as has most often been the case until recently, we must offer an alternative which takes seriously the notion of fuzzy spaces; thus, in our efforts to negate a typical modern atlas with its clear lines dividing up the nations of the world, we must offer paintings of the world composed as "diverse points of colors such that no clear pattern can be discerned in any detail."[13]

Jerusalem, as a sacred space, must be transformed by the artist, the writer, the priest, the Mufti, the Sheikh, the *Ulama*, and the Rabbi to become a place at once unified and diffused in such a way that it is impossible to distinguish any inside from outside. We must all shed as dead skin the model of straight lines and binaries and recognize the fuzzy space of symbioses and complexities. We must not only revise our modern nationalized constructs of the Other, but engage with full and open heart in the production of art and historical analyses and sociological analyses that fracture the Self and Other to the point where the Other can no longer be bound and made to stand distinct from the Self. In this way, Jerusalem is a grand symbol for all who are interested in a new ontology; it can become an authentically global sacred city, a genuinely universalistic symbol that safely allows the multitude to mutate their imagined bodies, their sacred spaces, their nations, their religions, their trade relations, their al-Aqsa Mosque, their Wailing Wall into true visions of universal unity.

---

13. Ernest Gellner, *Nations and Nationalism*, Ithaca, New York: Cornell University Press (1983:139).

BIBLIOGRAPHY

Abou-El Haj, Barbara, *The Medieval Cult of Saints: Formations and Transformations*, Cambridge, United Kingdom: Cambridge University Press (1997).

Abu el-Hajj, Nadia, "Translating Truths: Nationalism, the Practice of Archeology, and the Remaking of Past and Present in Contemporary Jerusalem," in *American Ethnologist*, vol. 25, no. 2 (May 1998).

Abu-Manneh, Butrus, "The Rise of the Sanjak of Jerusalem in the Late Nineteenth Century," in Ilan Pappe (ed.), *The Israel/Palestine Question: Rewriting Histories*, London and New York: Routledge (1999).

Adams, Charles C., *Islam and Modernism in Egypt: A Study of the Modern Reform Movement Inaugurated by Muhammad 'Abduh*, London: Oxford University Press (1933).

Akash, Munir (ed.), *The Open Veins of Jerusalem*, Syracuse, New York: Jusoor Book distributed by Syracuse University (2005).

Akenson, Donald Harman, *God's People: Covenant and Land in South Africa, Israel, and Ulster*, Ithaca, New York: Cornell University Press (1992).

Albrecht-Carrie, Rene, *A Diplomatic History of Europe: Since the Congress of Vienna*, New York: Harper and Row (1973).

Alcalay, Ammiel, *After Jews and Arabs: Remaking Levantine Culture*, Minneapolis: University of Minnesota Press (1993).

Alcock, Susan E., *Graecia Capta: The Landscapes of Roman Greece*, Cambridge and New York: Cambridge University Press (1993).

Alexander, Loveday (ed.), *Images of Empire*, Sheffield, England: JSOT Press (1991).

Algar, Hamid, *Wahhabism: A Critical Essay*, Oneonta, New York: Islamic Publications International (2002).

Ali,Tariq, *The Book of Saladin*, London: Verso Press (1998).

Anderson, Benedict, *Imagined Communities: Reflections on the Origin and Spread of Nationalism,* London: Verso Press (1995).

Anderson, Lisa, *The State and Social Transformation in Tunisia and Libya, 1830-1980*, Princeton, New Jersey: Princeton University Press (1986).

Andrae, Tor, *Mohammed: The Man and His Faith*, New York: Harper and Brothers (1960).

Antoun, Richard T., and Mary Elaine Hegland (eds.), *Religious Resurgence: Contemporary Cases in Islam, Christianity, and Judaism*, Syracuse, New York: Syracuse University Press (1987).

Appadurai, Arjun, *Modernity at Large: Cultural Dimensions of Globalization*, Minneapolis: University of Minnesota Press (1997).

Armstrong, Karen, *Jerusalem: One City, Three Faiths*, New York: A.A. Knopf (1996).

Arrighi, Giovanni, *The Long Twentieth Century: Money, Power, and the Origins of Our Times*, London and New York: Verso Press (1994).

221

Aruri, Naseer H., *The Obstruction of Peace: The United States, Israel, and the Palestinians*, Monroe, Maine: Common Courage Press (1995).

———, "Misrepresenting Jerusalem," in Munir Akash (ed.), *The Open Veins of Jerusalem*, Syracuse, New York: Jusoor Book distributed by Syracuse University (2005).

Asad, Talal, *Genealogies of Religion: Discipline and Reasons of Power in Islam and Christianity*, Baltimore, Maryland: Johns Hopkins University Press (1993).

Asali, Kamil J. (ed.), *Jerusalem in History: 3000 BC to the Present Day*, London and New York: Kegan Paul International (1997).

Avalos, Hector, *Fighting Words: The Origins of Religious Violence*, Amherst, New York: Prometheus Books (2005).

Bainton, Roland, *Reformation of the Sixteenth Century*, Boston: Beacon Press (1985).

———, *Here I Stand: A Life of Martin Luther*, New York: Meridian Press (1995).

Barber, Benjamin, *Jihad vs. McWorld*, New York: Ballantine Books (2001).

Barber, Richard, *Pilgrimages,* Woodbridge, Suffolk: Boydell Press (1991).

Barefoot, Brian, *The English Road to Rome*, Upton-upon-Severn, U.K.: Images Publishing (1993).

Barghouti, Mourid, *I Saw Ramallah*, New York: Anchor Books (2000).

Barraclough, Geoffrey, *The Medieval Papacy*, New York and London: W.W. Norton (1979).

Barsamian, David, and Edward W. Said, *Culture and Resistance: Conversations with Edward W. Said*, Cambridge, Massachusetts: South End Press (2003).

Benjamin, Walter, "Paris, Capital of the Nineteenth Century," in his *Reflections: Essays, Aphorism, Autobiographical Writings*, New York: Schocken Books (1986:146-62).

———, *Reflections: Essays, Aphorisms, Autobiographical Writings*, New York: Schocken Books (1986).

Benvenisti, Meron, *City of Stone: The Hidden History of Jerusalem*, Berkeley: University of California Press (1998).

———, *Sacred Landscape: The Buried History of the Holy Land since 1948*, Berkeley: University of California Press (2000).

Berkowitz, Michael, *Zionist Culture and West European Jewry before the First World War*, Chapel Hill: University of North Carolina Press (1996).

Bowersock, G.W., "Palestine: Ancient History and Modern Politics," in Edward W. Said and Christopher Hitchens (eds.), *Blaming the Victim: Spurious Scholarship and the Palestinian Question*, London: Verso Press (1989).

Boyarin, Daniel, *A Radical Jew: Paul and the Politics of Identity*, Berkeley: University of California Press (1994).

———, *Border Lines: The Partition of Judeo-Christianity*, Philadelphia: University of Pennsylvania Press (2004).

Braudel, Fernand, "History and the Social Sciences: The *Longue Durée*," in his *On History*, Chicago: University of Chicago Press (1982).

————, *On History*, Chicago: University of Chicago Press (1982).

Brown, Peter, *The Making of Late Antiquity*, Cambridge: Harvard University Press (1978).

Brown, R. Allen, *The Origins of Feudalism*, London: Allen & Unwin (1973).

Buber, Martin, "No More Declarations," reprinted in his collection, *A Land of Two Peoples*, New York: Oxford University Press ([1929] 1983).

Budde, Michael L., *The Two Churches: Catholicism and Capitalism in the World-System*, Durham, North Carolina: Duke University Press (1992).

Budeiri, Musa, "The Palestinians: Tensions between Nationalist and Religious Identities," in James Jankowski and Israel Gershoni (eds.), *Rethinking Nationalism in the Arab Midde East*, New York: Columbia University Press (1997).

Burgess, Anthony, *Man of Nazereth: A Novel*, New York: McGraw Hill, (1979).

Burns, Gene, *The Frontiers of Catholicism: The Politics of Ideology in a Liberal World*, Berkeley: University of California Press (1992).

Cameron, Averil, *Christianity and the Rhetoric of Empire: The Development of Christian Discourse*, Berkeley: University of California Press (1991).

Chadwick, Henry, *The Early Church,* Baltimore, Maryland: Penguin (1967).

Chadwick, Owen, *The Popes and European Revolution*, New York: Oxford University Press (1981).

————, *A History of the Popes: 1830-1914*, New York: Oxford University Press (1998).

Chase-Dunn, Christopher, and Thomas D. Hall, "Cross World-System Comparisons: Similarities and Differences," in Stephen K. Sanderson, *Civilizations and World Systems: Studying World Historical Change*, Walnut Creek, California: AltaMira Press (1995:109-35).

Chastel, Andre, *The Sack of Rome, 1527*, Princeton, New Jersey: Princeton University Press (1983).

Chatterjee, Partha, *Nationalist Thought and the Colonial World: A Derivative Discourse*, Minneapolis: University of Minnesota Press (1986).

Chidester, David, *Christianity: A Global History*, San Francisco: Harper Press (2000).

Cleveland, William, "The Role of Islam as Political Ideology in the First World War," in Edward Ingram (ed.), *National and International Politics in the Middle East: Essays in Honor of Elie Kedourie*, London, Eng.: Frank Cass Press (1986).

Cline, Eric, *Jerusalem Besieged: From Ancient Canaan to Modern Israel*, Ann Arbor: University of Michigan Press (2004).

Cockburn, Alexander, and Jeffrey St. Clair (eds.), *The Politics of Anti-Semitism*, Oakland, California: AK Press (2003).

Cohen, Mark, *Under Crescent and Cross: The Jews in the Middle Ages*, Princeton, New Jersey: Princeton University Press (1994).

Cohen, Mitchell, *Zion & State: Nation, Class and the Shaping of Modern Israel*, New York: Columbia University Press (1992).

Cohen, Shaye J.D. *From the Maccabees to the Mishnah*, Philadelphia: Westminster Press (1988).

Coleman, Simon, and John Elsner, *Pilgrimage: Past and Present in the World Religions*, Cambridge, Massachusetts: Harvard University Press (1995).

Cooley, Charles Horton, *Human Nature and the Social Order,* New York: Schocken Books (1964).

Cornwell, John, *Hitler's Pope: The Secret History of Pius XII*, New York: Viking Press (1999).

Coppa, Frank, *The Modern Papacy since 1789*, London and New York: Longman (1998).

Crone, Patricia, *Meccan Trade and the Rise of Islam*, Princeton, New Jersey: Princeton University Press (1987).

Dabashi, Hamid, *Authority in Islam: From the Rise of Muhammad to the Establishment of the Umayyads*, New Brunswick, New Jersey: Transaction Publication (1989).

Davies, W.D., *The Gospel and the Land: Early Christianity and Jewish Territorial Doctrine*, Berkeley: University of California Press (1974).

Davis, Eric, "Religion against the State: A Political Economy of Religious Radicalism in Egypt and Israel," in Richard T. Antoun and Mary Elaine Hegland (eds.), *Religious Resurgence: Contemporary Cases in Islam, Christianity, and Judaism*, Syracuse, New York: Syracuse University Press (1987).

Dawisha, Adeed, *Arab Nationalism in the Twentieth Century*, Princeton and Oxford: Princeton University Press (2003).

Dawson, Christopher H., "The Christian West and the Fall of the Empire," in his *Medieval Essays*, New York: Ayer Co. Pub. (1954:28-52).

———, *Medieval Essays*, New York: Ayer Co. Pub. (1954).

de Gaury, Gerald, *Rulers of Mecca*, London: George G. Harrap & Co. (1951).

Dehio, Ludwig, *The Precarious Balance: Four Centuries of the European Power Struggle*, New York: Vintage Books (1965).

Dillenberger, John, *Martin Luther: Selections from His Writings*, New York: Anchor Books (1962).

Dodds, E.R., *Pagan and Christian in an Age of Anxiety*, Cambridge, United Kingdom: Cambridge University Press (1965).

Duffy, Eamon, *Saints and Sinners: A History of the Popes*, New Haven, Connecticut: Yale University Press (1997).

Eaton, Richard, *The Rise of Islam and the Bengal Frontier,* Berkeley: University of California Press (1993).

Eck, Diana, "Introduction," in Bardwell Smith and Holly Baker (eds.), *The City as a Sacred Center: Essays on Six Asian Contexts*, Leiden and New York: Brill (1987).

Edwards, Douglas R., *Religion and Power: Pagans, Jews, and Christians in the Greek East*, New York: Oxford University Press (1996).

Eire, Carlos M.N., *War against the Idols: The Reformation of Worship from Erasmus to Calvin*, Cambridge and London: Cambridge University Press (1986).

Ekelund, Robert B., et al., *Sacred Trust: The Medieval Church as an Economic Firm*, New York: Oxford University Press (1996).

Eliade, Mircea, *The Sacred and the Profane: The Nature of Religion*, San Diego, California: Harcourt Brace Jovanovich ([1957] 1987).

Elon, Amos, "The Deadlocked City," *The New York Review of Books* (October 18, 2001).

Esman, Milton J., and Itamar Rabinovich, *Ethnicity, Pluralism, and the State in the Middle East*, Ithaca and London: Cornell University Press (1988).

Eytan, Walter, *The First Ten Years, a Diplomatic History of Israel*, New York: Simon and Schuster (1958).

Faroghi, Suraiya, *Pilgrims and Sultans: The Hajj under the Ottomans, 1517-1683*, London: I.B. Taurus & Co. (1994).

Farsakh, Leila, "What Future for Palestine: Independence or Bantustans," in *The Discourse of Sociological Practice*, vol. 7, nos. 1&2, Spring/Fall (2005).

Farsoun, Samih, *Palestine and the Palestinians*, Boulder Colorado: Westview Press (1997).

Feuerlicht, Roberta, *The Fate of the Jews: A People Torn between Israeli Power and Jewish Ethics*, New York: New York Times Book Co. (1983).

Finkelstein, Norman G., *The Holocaust Industry: Reflection on the Exploitation of Jewish Suffering*, London and New York: Verso Press (2000).

———, *Beyond Chutzpah: On the Misuse of Anti-Semitism and the Abuse of History*, Berkeley: University of California Press (2005).

Foss, Michael, *People of the First Crusade*, New York: Arcade Publishing (1997).

Fowden, Garth, *Empire to Commonwealth: Consequences of Monotheism in Late Antiquity*, Princeton, New Jersey: Princeton University Press (1993).

Fredriksen, Paula, *From Jesus to Christ: The Origins of the New Testament Images of Jesus*, New Haven and London: Yale University Press (1988).

Frend, W.H.C., *The Rise of Christianity*, Philadelphia: Fortress Press (1984).

Friedman, Richard Elliott, *Who Wrote the Bible?* Englewood Cliffs, New Jersey: Prentice Hall (1987).

Friedmann, John, "The World City Hypothesis," in Paul Knox and Peter Taylor, *World Cities in a World-System*, Cambridge, New York: Cambridge University Press (1995).

Friedmann, John, and Goetz Wolf, "World City Formation," in Paul Knox and Peter Taylor (eds.), *World Cities in a World-System*, Cambridge, New York: Cambridge University Press (1995).

Fromkin, David, *A Peace to End All Peace: The Fall of the Ottoman Empire and the Creation of the Modern Middle East*, New York: Avon Books (1990).

Gabrieli, Francesco, *Arab Historians of the Crusades*, Berkeley: University of California Press (1969).

Geertz, Clifford, *The Interpretation of Culture*, New York: Basic Books (1973).

Gellner, Ernest, *Nations and Nationalism*, Ithaca, New York: Cornell University Press (1983).

Gerges, Fawaz A., *America and Political Islam: Clash of Cultures or Clash of Interests?* New York: Cambridge University Press (1999).

Gershoni, Israel, and James Jankowski, *Redefining the Egyptian Nation, 1930-1945*, Cambridge, U. K.: Cambridge University Press (1995).

Ghayasuddin, M., *The Impact of Nationalism on the Muslim World*, London: Open Press (1986).

Gibb, H.A.R., *Mohemmedanism: A Historical Survey*, London and New York: Oxford University Press (1969).

Goitein, S.D., "The Historical Background of the Erection of the Dome of the Rock," in *Journal of the American Oriental Society* (1950:104-8).

———, "Jerusalem in the Arab Period," *Jerusalem Cathedra*, vol. 2 (1982:168-96).

Golan-Agnon, Daphna, *Next Year in Jerusalem*, New York and London: New Press (2005).

Goldberg, David Theo, *The Racial State*, Malden, Massachusetts: Blackwell Publishers (2002).

Goodman, Martin, *The Ruling Class of Judaea: The Origins of the Jewish Revolt against Rome AD 66-70*, Cambridge, U.K. and New York: Cambridge University Press (1987).

———, "Opponents of Rome: Jews and Others," in Alexander Loveday (ed.), *Images of Empire*, Sheffield, England: JSOT Press (1991:222-38).

Gordon, Cyrus H., and Gary A. Rendsburg, *The Bible and the Ancient Near East*, New York: W.W. Norton & Company (1998).

Gorenberg, Gershom, *The End of Days: Fundamentalism and the Struggle for the Temple Mount*, New York: Oxford University Press (2000).

Gray, John, *Al-Qaeda and What It Means to Be Modern*, New York and London: The New Press (2003:20).

Greenspoon, L., "Mission to Alexandria: Truth and Legend about the Creation of the Septuagint," *Bible Review*, vol. 5, August (1989:34-41).

Griffiths, J. Gwyn, "Hellenistic Religions," in Robert M. Seltzer, *Religions of Antiquity*, New York: MacMillan Press (1989:237-58).

Grosfoguel, Ramon, "World Cities in the Caribbean: The Rise of Miami and San Juan," in *Review,* vol. 17, no. 3, Summer (1994).

Ha'am, Ahad, "A Truth from Eretz Yisrael," in Tony Kushner and Alisa Solomon, *Wrestling with Zion: Progressive Jewish-American Responses to the Israeli-Palestinian Conflict*, New York: Grove Press (2003).

Hadawi, Sami, *Bitter Harvest: A Modern History of Palestine*, New York: Olive Branch Press (1991).

Haim, Sylvia G., *Arab Nationalism: An Anthology*, Berkeley: University of California Press (1974).

Hales, E.E.Y., *The Catholic Church in the Modern World: A Survey from the French Revolution to the Present*, Garden City, New York: Doubleday Image Books (1960).

Hardt, Michael, and Antonio Negri, *Empire*, Cambridge, Massachusetts: Harvard University Press (2000).

Harris, Sam, *The End of Faith: Religion, Terror, and the Future of Reason*, New York: W.W. Norton & Company (2005).

Harnack, Adolph, *The Mission and Expansion of Christianity in the First Three Centuries*, 2 vols., New York: G.P. Putnam's Sons (1908).

Harris, Ruth, *Lourdes: Body and Spirit in the Secular Age*, New York: Penguin Press (2000).

Heer, Friedrich, *The Medieval World: Europe from 1100 to 1350*, London: Sphere (1967).

Hengel, M., *Judaism and Hellinism: Studies in Their Encounters in Palestine*, 2 vols., Philadelphia: Fortress Press (1974).

Herrin, Judith, *The Formation of Christendom*, Princeton, New Jersey: Princeton University Press (1987).

Hertzberg, Arthur, "Jerusalem and Zionism," in Nitza Rosovsky (ed.), *City of the Great King: Jerusalem from David to the Present*, Cambridge and London: Harvard University Press (1996).

————, (ed.), *The Zionist Idea: A Historical Analysis and Reader*, Philadelphia and Jerusalem: Jewish Publication Society (1997).

Herzl, Theodor, *Old New Land*, translated from German by Lotte Levensohn, Princeton, New Jersey: Markus Wiener ([1902] 1997).

————, *The Jewish State,* New York: Dover Publications (1988).

Hiyari, Mustafa, "Crusader Jerusalem: 1099-1187 AD," in Kamil J. Asali (ed.), *Jerusalem in History: 3000 BC to the Present Day*, London and New York: Kegan Paul International (1997).

Hodgson, Marshall G.S., *The Ventures of Islam: Conscience and History in a World Civilization*, 3 vols., Chicago and London: University of Chicago (1974).

Hourani, Albert, *Arabic Thought in the Liberal Age: 1798-1939*, London and New York: Oxford University Press (1967).

————, *A History of the Arab Peoples*, New York: Warner Books (1992).

Huntington, Samuel, "The Clash of Civilizations?" in *Foreign Affairs*, vol. 72, no. 3, Summer (1993).

————, *The Clash of Civilizations: Remaking of World Order*, New York: Simon & Schuster (1996).

ibn Ishaq, "*Sirat Rasul Allah,"* in F.E. Peters, *Muhammad and the Origins of Islam*, Albany, New York: SUNY Press (1994).

Ibrahim, Mahmood, *Merchant Capital and Islam*, Austin: University of Texas Press (1990).

Ignatiev, Noel, *How the Irish Became White*, New York: Routledge (1995).

Ingram, Edward (ed.), *National and International Politics in the Middle East: Essays in Honor of Elie Kedourie*, London, Eng.: Frank Cass Press (1986).

Jankowski, James, and Israel Gershoni, (eds.), *Rethinking Nationalism in the Arab Middle East*, New York: Columbia University Press (1997).

Jansen, G.H., *Zionism, Israel, and Asian Nationalism*, Beirut: Institute for Palestine Studies (1971).

Janz, Denis R., *A Reformation Reader*, Minneapolis: Fortress Press (1990).

Johnson, Paul, *A History of the Jews*, New York: Harper Collins (1988).

Juergensmeyer, Mark, *The New Cold War? Religious Nationalism Confronts the Secular State*, Berkeley: University of California Press (1993).

Kanaaneh, Rhoda, *Birthing the Nation: Strategies of Palestinian Women in Israel*, Berkeley: University of California Press (2002).

Karpat, Kemal, *An Inquiry into the Social Foundations of Nationalism in the Ottoman State: From Social Estates to Classes, from Millets to Nations*, Princeton, New Jersey: Princeton University Center of International Studies, Research Monograph no. 39 (1973).

————, "The Ottoman Ethnic and Confessional Legacy in the Middle East," in Milton J. Esman and Itamar Rabinovich, *Ethnicity, Pluralism, and the State in the Middle East*, Ithaca and London: Cornell University Press (1988).

Kedouri, Elie, *Islam in the Modern World and Other Studies*, London: Mansell Publishing (1980).

————, "Religion and Nationalism in the Arab World," in his *Islam in the Modern World and Other Studies*, London: Mansell Publishing (1980).

Kerr, Malcolm H., *Islamic Reform: The Political and Legal Theories of Muhammad 'Abduh and Rashid Rida*, Berkeley: University of California Press (1966).

Keyder, Caglar, *State and Class in Turkey: A Study in Capitalist Development*, London and New York: Verso Press (1987).

Khalidi, Rashid, "The Formation of Palestinian Identity," in James Jankowski and Israel Gershoni (eds.), *Rethinking Nationalism in the Arab Middle East*, New York: Columbia University Press (1997a).

————, *Palestinian Identity: The Construction of Modern National Consciousness*, New York: Columbia University Press (1997b).

Khalidi, Tarif, "Palestinian Historiography: 1900-1948," *Journal of Palestine Studies*, vol. 10, no.3, Spring (1981:59-76).

Khalidi, Walid, *All That Remains: The Palestinian Villages Occupied and Depopulated by Israel in 1948*, Washington, D.C.: Institute of Palestine Studies (1992).

Khoury, Elias, *Gate of the Sun*, Brooklyn, New York: Archipelago Books (2006).

Khoury, Philip S., and Joseph Kostiner (eds.), *Tribes and State Formation in the Middle East*, Berkeley: University of California Press (1990).

Kimmerling, Baruch, and Joel Migdal, *The Palestinian People: A History*, Cambridge, Massachusetts: Harvard University Press (2003).

King, Anthony, "Re-presenting World Cities: Cultural Theory/Social Practice," in Paul Knox and Peter Taylor, *World Cities in a World-System*, London and New York: Cambridge University Press (1995).

————, (ed.), *Re-presenting the World City: Ethnicity, Capital and Culture in the 21st Century Metropolis*, New York: NYU Press (1995).

Kister, M.J., "*Labbayka, Allahumma, Labbayka:* On a Monotheistic Aspect of a Jahiliyya Practice," in her *Society and Religion from Jahiliyya to Islam*, Aldershot, Hampshire, Great Britain: Variorum Gower Publishing (1990a).

————, "Mecca and the Tribes of Arabia," in her *Society and Religion from Jahiliyya to Islam*, Aldershot, Hampshire, Great Britain: Variorum Gower Publishing (1990b).

————, *Society and Religion from Jahiliyya to Islam*, Aldershot, Hampshire, Great Britain: Variorum Gower Publishing (1990).

Knox, Paul, and Peter Taylor, *World Cities in a World-System*, London and New York: Cambridge University Press (1995).

Kornberg, Jacques, *Theodor Herzl: From Assimilation to Zionism*, Bloomington and Indianapolis: Indiana University Press (1993).

Kostiner, Joseph, "Transforming Dualities: Tribe and State Formation in Saudi Arabia," in Philip S. Khoury and Joseph Kostiner (eds.), *Tribes and State Formation in the Middle East*, Berkeley: University of California Press (1990).

Kramer, Lloyd, *Threshold of a New World: Intellectuals and the Exile Experience in Paris, 1830-1848*, Ithaca, New York: Cornell University Press (1988).

Kramer, Martin, *Islam Assembled: The Advent of the Muslim Congress*, New York: Columbia University Press (1986).

Krautheimer, Richard, *Rome, Profile of a City, 312-1308,* Princeton, New Jersey: Princeton University Press (1980).

————, *Three Christian Capitals: Topography and Politics*, Berkeley: University of California Press (1983).

Kushner, Tony, and Alis Solomon (eds.), *Wrestling with Zion: Progressive Jewish American Responses to the Israeli-Palestinian Conflict*, New York: Grove Press (2003).

Ladner, Gerhart B., *God, Cosmos, and Humankind: The World of Early Christian Symbolism*, Berkeley: University of California Press (1992).

Lapidus, Ira M., "Tribes and State Formation in Islamic History," in Philip Khouri and Joseph Kostiner (eds.), *Tribe and State Formation in the Middle East*, Berkeley: University of California Press (1990).

————, *A History of Islamic Societies*, New York: Cambridge University Press (1990b).

Laqueur, Walter, *A History of Zionism*, New York: MJF Books (1972).

Levine, Lee I., *Judaism and Hellinism in Antiquity: Conflict or Confluence?* Washington: University of Washington Press (1998).

————, "Second Temple Jerusalem: A Jewish City in the Greco-Roman Orbit," in his (ed.), *Jerusalem: Its Sanctity and Centrality to Judaism, Christianity, and Islam*, New York: Continuum Pub. (1999).

————, (ed.), *Jerusalem: Its Sanctity and Centrality to Judaism, Christianity, and Islam*, New York: Continuum Pub. Group (1999).

LeVine, Mark, *Overthrowing Geography: Jaffa, Tel Aviv, and the Struggle for Palestine, 1880-1948*, Berkeley: University of California Press (2005).

Lewis, Bernard, "The Roots of Muslim Rage," *The Atlantic Monthly* 266, September (1990).

————, *Islam and the West,* New York: Oxford University Press (1993).

Lie, John, *Modern Peoplehood*, Cambridge, Massachusetts: Harvard University Press (2004).

Lieven, Anatol, *America Right or Wrong: An Anatomy of American Nationalism*, New York: Oxford University Press (2004).

Lindsey, Hal, *The Late Great Planet Earth*, Grand Rapids, Michigan: Zondervan (1970).

Logan, Jon, and Harvey Molotch, *Urban Fortunes: The Political Economy of Place*, Berkeley: University of California (1995).

Long, Theodore E., "Two Aspects of the Development of Universalism in Christianity: The First to the Fourth Centuries," in Roland Robertson et al. (eds.), *Religion and Global Order,* New York: Paragon House (1991).

Lustick, Ian, "Reinventing Jerusalem," *Foreign Policy*, no. 93, Winter (1994).

MacMullen, Ramsay, *Paganism in the Roman Empire*, New Haven, Connecticut: Yale University Press (1981).

———, *Christianizing the Roman Empire*, New Haven, Connecticut: Yale University Press (1984).

Malcolm X, *The Autobiography of Malcolm X: As Told to Alex Haley*, New York: Ballantine Press (1973).

Malkki, Lissa, "National Geographic: The Rooting of Peoples and the Territorialization of National Identity among Scholars and Refugees," *Cultural Anthropology*, vol. 7, no. 1 (February 1992).

Margalit, Avishai, "The Myth of Jerusalem," in *The New York Review of Books* (Dec. 19, 1991).

Markus, R.A., "How on Earth Could Places Become Holy? Origins of the Christian Idea of Holy Places," in *Journal of Early Christian Studies*, vol. 2, no. 3 (1994:257-71).

Masalha, Nur, *Expulsion of the Palestinians: The Concept of 'Transfer' in Zionist Political Thought, 1882 to 1948*, Washington, D.C.: Institute of Palestine Studies (1992).

———, The Politics of Denial: Israel and the Palestinian Refugee Problem, London: Pluto Press (2003).

Mauner, George, et al., *Paris: Center of Artistic Enlightenment*, Philadelphia: Pennsylvania State University (1988).

McAlister, Melani, *Epic Encounters: Culture, Media, and U.S. Interest in the Middle East, 1945-2000*, Berkeley: University of California Press (2001).

McNeill, William, *The Rise of the West: A History of the Human Community*, Chicago: University of Chicago Press (1991).

Meeks, Wayne, *The First Urban Christians: The Social World of the Apostle Paul*, New Haven, Connecticut: Yale University Press (1983).

Mendels, Doron. *The Rise and Fall of Jewish Nationalism: Jewish and Christian Ethnicity in Ancient Palestine*, New York: Edermans Publishing (1992).

———, "The Temple in the Hellenistic Period and in Judaism," in Benjamin Kader and R.J. Werblowsky, *Sacred Space: Shrine, City, Land*, New York: New York University Press (1996).

Mendenhall, George E., *The Tenth Generation: The Origins of the Biblical Traditions,* Baltimore, Maryland: Johns Hopkins University (1974).

———, "Jerusalem from 1000 to 63 BC," in Kamil J. Asali (ed.), *Jerusalem in History: 3000 BC to the Present Day,* London and New York: Kegan Paul International (1997:42-74).

Menocal, Maria Rosa, *The Arabic Role in Medieval Literary History: A Forgotten Heritage,* Philadelphia: University of Pennsylvania Press (2004).

Messiri, Abdel Wahab M., "The Palestinian Wedding, Major Themes of Contemporary Palestinian Resistance Poetry," *Journal of Palestine Studies,* vol. 10, no. 39, Spring (1981:89).

Mirsepassi, Ali, *Intellectual Discourse and the Politics of Modernization: Negotiating Modernity in Iran,* Cambridge, UK: University of Cambridge Press (2000).

Momigliano, Arnaldo, "Roman Religion of the Imperial Period," in Robert M. Seltzer (ed.), *Religions of Antiquity,* New York: MacMillan (1989:218-33).

Moody, Joseph, "The New Forces and the Papacy," in his (ed.), *Church and Society; Catholic Social and Political Thought and Movements, 1789-1950,* New York: Arts, Inc. (1953).

———, (ed.), *Church and Society; Catholic Social and Political Thought and Movements, 1789-1950,* New York: Arts, Inc. (1953).

Mullet, Michael, *Radical Religious Movements in Early Modern Europe,* London: George Allen & Unwin (1980).

Mumford, Lewis, *The Cultures of Cities,* New York: Harcourt, Brace and Company (1938).

———, *The City in History,* New York: Harcourt, Brace and Company (1961).

Nelson-Pallmeyer, Jack, *Is Religion Killing Us? Violence in the Bible and the Qur'an,* Harrisburg, Pennsylvania: Trinity Press International (2005).

Nevo, Joseph, "Religion and National Identity in Saudi Arabia," in *Middle Eastern Studies,* vol. 34, no. 3, July (1998).

Nock, Arthur D., *The Old and the New in Religion from Alexander the Great to Augustine of Hippo,* Oxford: Clarendon Press (1933).

Oberman, Heiko A., *Luther: Man between God and the Devil,* New York: Doubleday Anchor Books (1989).

O'Brien, Conor Cruise, *God Land: Reflections on Religion and Nationalism,* Cambridge and London: Harvard University Press (1988).

Ozment, Steven, *The Reformation in the Cities: The Appeal of Protestantism to Sixteenth-Century Germany and Switzerland,* New Haven and London: Yale University Press (1975).

———, *The Age of Reform (1250-1550): An Intellectual and Religious History of Late Medieval and Reformation Europe,* Westford, Massachusetts: Yale University Press (1980).

———, *Protestant: The Birth of a Revolution,* New York: Doubleday Image Books (1993).

Pagels, Elaine, *The Gnostic Gospels,* New York: Vintage Books (1989).

Painter, Borden W., Jr., *Mussolini's Rome: Rebuilding the Eternal City*, New York: Palgrave Macmillan (2005).

Pappe, Ilan (ed.), *The Israel/Palestine Question: Rewriting Histories*, London and New York: Routledge (1999).

————, *A History of Modern Palestine: One Land, Two Peoples*, Cambridge, U.K.: Cambridge University Press (2004).

Pearson, M.N., *The Pilgrimage to Mecca: The Indian Experience 1500-1800*, New York: Markus Weiner Publication (1996).

Peters, F.E., *Jerusalem and Mecca: The Typology of the Holy City in the Near East*, Cambridge, New York: New York University Press (1986).

————, *Muhammad and the Origins of Islam*, Albany, New York: SUNY Press (1994).

————, *Jerusalem: The Holy City in the Eyes of Chroniclers, Visitors, Pilgrims, and Prophets from the Days of Abraham to the Beginnings of Modern Times*, Princeton, New Jersey: Princeton University Press (1995).

————, "The Holy Places," in Nitza Rosovsky (ed.), *City of the Great King: Jerusalem from David to the Present*, Cambridge and London: Harvard University Press (1996).

Petuchowski, Jakob, *Zion Reconsidered*, New York: Twayne Press (1966).

Pieterse, Jan, *Empires and Emancipation*, Cambridge, Massachusetts: Cambridge University Press (1989).

Pirenne, Henri, *A History of Europe: From the Thirteenth Century to the Renaissance and Reformation*, vols. 1 and 2, Garden City, New York: Doubleday Anchor Books (1958a).

————, *Muhammad and Charlemagne*, New York: Barnes and Noble Books (1958b).

————, *The Medieval Cities: Their Origins and the Revival of Trade*, Princeton, New Jersey: Princeton University Press (1974).

Polanyi, Karl, *The Livelihood of Man*, New York: Academic Press (1977).

————, *The Great Transformation*, Boston: Beacon Press (1980).

Porath, Yehoshua, *The Emergence of the Palestinian-Arab National Movement, 1918-1929*, London: Frank Cass (1974).

Price, S.R.F., *Rituals and Power: The Roman Imperial Cult in Asia Minor*, Cambridge, Massachusetts: Cambridge University Press (1984).

Prior, Michael, *The Bible and Colonialism: A Moral Critique*, Sheffield, Eng.: Sheffield Academic Press (1997).

————, *Zionism and the State of Israel*, London and New York: Routledge (1999).

Rahman, Fazlur, *Islam*, Chicago: University of Chicago Press (1979).

Ravitsky, Aviezer, *Messianism, Zionism, and Jewish Religious Radicalism*, Chicago: University of Chicago Press (1996).

Redfield, Robert, and Milton Singer, "The Cultural Role of Cities," in *Man in India*, vol. 36, no. 3 (1966:161-94).

Rejwan, Nissim, *Israel's Place in the Middle East: A Pluralist Perspective*, Gainesville & Tallahassee: University Press of Florida (1999).

————, *Israel in Search of Identity*, Gainesville and Tallahassee: University Press of Florida (1999).

Roberts, J.M., *The Triumph of the West: The Origin, Rise, and Legacy of Western Civilization*, New York: Barnes & Noble Book (1998).

Robertson, Ritchie, *The "Jewish Question" in German Literature, 1749-1939*, New York: Oxford University Press (1999).

Robertson, Roland, et al. (eds.), *Religion and Global Order,* New York: Paragon House (1991).

Rodinson, Maxine, *Muhammad,* New York: Pantheon Books (1980).

Roediger, David, *The Wages of Whiteness*, London: Verso Press (1991).

Rogan, Eugene, and Avi Shlaim (eds.), *The War for Palestine: Rewriting the History of 1948*, Cambridge, U. K.: University of Cambridge Press (2001).

Romann, Michael, and Alex Weingrod, *Living Together Separately: Arabs and Jews in Contemporary Jerusalem*, Princeton, New Jersey: Princeton University Press (1991).

Rose, John, *The Myths of Zionism*, London: Pluto Press (2004).

Roseberry, William, *Anthropologies and Histories: Essays in Culture, History, and Political Economy,* New Brunswick, New Jersey: Rutgers University Press (1991).

Rosovsky, Nitza (ed.), *City of the Great King: Jerusalem from David to the Present*, Cambridge and London: Harvard University Press (1996).

Rossing, Barbara R., *The Rapture Exposed: The Message of Hope in the Book of Revelation*, New York: Basic Books (2004).

Ruether, Rosemary, and Herman Ruether, *The Wrath of Jonah: The Crisis of Religious Nationalism in the Israeli-Palestinian Conflict*, Minneapolis: Fortress Press (2002).

Ruggie, John, "Continuity and Transformation in the World Polity," *World Politics*, vol. 35, no. 2 (1983:261-85).

————, "Territoriality and Beyond: Problematizing Modernity in International Relations," in *International Organizations*, vol. 47, no. 1, Winter (1993).

Ruthven, Malise, *Islam in the World*, New York: Oxford University Press (1984).

Sabini, John, *Armies in the Sand: The Struggle for Mecca and Medina*, New York: Thames and Hudson (1981).

Said, Edward, *Orientalism*, New York: Vintage Books (1979).

————, "On Michael Walzer," in Edward Said and Christopher Hitchens, *Blaming the Victim: Spurious Scholarship and the Palestinian Question*, London: Verso Press (1989).

————, et al., "A Profile of the Palestinian People," in Edward Said and Christopher Hitchens, *Blaming the Victim: Spurious Scholarship and the Palestinian Question*, London: Verso Press (1989).

————, *Cultures and Imperialism*, New York: Vintage Books (1993).

————, "Keynote Essay," in Ghada Karmi, *Jerusalem Today,* Ithaca, New York: Cornell University Press (1996).

Said, Edward W., and Christopher Hitchens (eds.), *Blaming the Victim: Spurious Scholarship and the Palestinian Question*, London: Verso Press (1989).

Sanderson, Stephen K., *Civilizations and World Systems: Studying World Historical Change*, Walnut Creek, California: AltaMira Press (1995).

Sardar, Ziauddin, and M.A. Zaki Badawi. *Hajj Studies*, London: Croom Hill for Hajj Research Centre, King Abdul Aziz University, Jeddah (1978).

Sassen, Saskia, *The Global City: New York, London, Tokyo*, Princeton, New Jersey: Princeton University Press (1991).

———, *Cities in a World Economy*, Thousand Oaks, California: Pine Forge Press (2000).

Sauerlander, Willibald, "Medieval Paris, Center of European Taste, Fame, and Realities," in George Mauner et al., *Paris: Center of Artistic Enlightenment*, Philadelphia: Pennsylvania State University (1988).

Schafer, Peter, *Judeophobia: Attitudes toward the Jews in the Ancient World*, Cambridge and London: Harvard University Press (1998).

Schlor, Joachim, *Tel Aviv: From Dream to City*, London: Reaktion Books (1999).

Schneidau, Herbert, "The Hebrews against the High Cultures," in his *Sacred Discontent: The Bible and Western Tradition*, Baton Rouge: Louisiana State University Press (1976).

Schwartz, Regina, *The Curse of Cain: The Violent Legacy of Monotheism*, Chicago: University of Chicago Press (1997).

Scruton, Roger, *The West and the Rest*, Wilmington, Delaware: ISI Books (2002).

Sears, John, *Sacred Places: American Tourist Attractions in the Nineteenth Century*, New York: Oxford University Press (1989).

Segal, Alan F., *Paul the Convert: The Apostolate and Apostasy of Saul the Pharisee*, New Haven, Connecticut: Yale University Press (1990).

Segev, Tom, *One Palestine Complete: Jews and Arabs under the British Mandate*, New York: Metropolitan Books (2000).

Seltzer, Robert M., (ed.), *Religions of Antiquity*, New York: MacMillan (1989).

Shafir, Gershon, *Land, Labor, and the Origins of the Israeli-Palestinian Conflict, 1882-1914*, Berkeley: University of California Press (1996).

Shariati, Ali, *Hajj*, Houston, Texas: FILINC: Book Distribution Center (1980).

Sharif, Regina, *Non-Jewish Zionism: Its Roots in Western History*, London: Zed Press (1983).

Shlaim, Avi, *The Iron Wall: Israel and the Arab World*, New York: W.W. Norton & Company (2001).

Shohat, Ella, "Dislocated Identities: Reflections of an Arab-Jew," in Tony Kushner and Alis Solomon (eds.), *Wrestling with Zion: Progressive Jewish American Responses to the Israeli-Palestinian Conflict*, New York: Grove Press (2003).

Siddiqui, Kalim, "Nation-States as Obstacles to the Total Transformation of the *Ummah*," in M. Ghayasuddin, *The Impact of Nationalism on the Muslim World*, London: Open Press (1986).

Simon, Marcel, *Verus Israel: A Study of the Relations between Christians and Jews in the Roman Empire, 135-425*, New York: Oxford University Press (1996).

Smith, Anthony, *The Ethnic Origins of Nationalism*, New York: Oxford University Press (1986).

————, *Chosen Peoples*, New York: Oxford University Press (2003).

Smith, Bardwell, and Holly Baker, *The City as a Sacred Center: Essays on Six Asian Contexts,* Leiden and New York: Brill Academic Publishers (1987).

Smith, Charles D., *Palestine and the Arab-Israeli Conflict*, New York: St. Martin's Press (1996).

Smith, Dennis Mack, *Modern Italy: A Political History,* Ann Arbor: University of Michigan Press (1997).

Smith, J.Z., *To Take Place: Toward Theory in Ritual*, Chicago: University of Chicago Press (1987).

Snyder, Greyden, *Ante Pacem: Archeological Evidence of Church Life before Constantine*, Macon, Georgia: Mercer University Press (1985).

Sokolow, Nahum, *The History of Zionism*, vol. 1, New York: KTAV Pub. House (1919).

Southern, R.W., *Western Society and the Church in the Middle Ages*, London: Penguin Books (1990).

Spencer, Robert, *Islam Unveiled*, San Francisco: Encounter Books (2002).

Stanislawski, Michael, *Zionism: Cosmopolitanism and Nationalism from Nordau to Jabotinsky*, Berkeley: University of California Press (2001).

Stark, Rodney, *The Rise of Christianity*, San Francisco: Harper Press (1997).

Stavrianos, L.S., *Global Rift: The Third World Comes of Age*, New York: William Morrow and Company (1981).

Steinberg, Stephen, "Reform Judaism: The Origins and Evolution of a Church Movement," *Review of Religious Research*, vol. 7 (1965).

Sugree, Francis, *Popes in the Modern World*, New York: Thomas Y. Crowell Company (1961).

Sullivan, Andrew, "This *Is* a Religious War," in *New York Times Magazine* (2001).

Sutcliffe, Anthony (ed.), *Metropolis: 1890-1940*, Chicago: University of Chicago Press (1984).

Swedenburg, Ted, "The Role of the Palestinian Peasantry in the Great Revolt (1936-9)," in Ilan Pappe (ed.), *The Israel/Palestine Question: Rewriting Histories*, London and New York: Routledge (1999:129-67).

————, *Memories of Revolt: The 1936-1939 Rebellion and the Palestinian National Past*, Fayetteville: University of Arkansas Press (2003).

Tabari, *Annals*, Albany: State University of New York Press, multiple volumes (1988-1999).

Tierney, Brian, *The Crisis of Church and State: 1050-1300*, Englewood Cliffs, New Jersey: Prentice-Hall (1964).

Tilley, Virginia, "The One-State Solution," *London Review of Books*, vol. 25, no. 21 (Nov. 6, 2003).

Trimingham, J.S., *Christianity among the Arabs in Pre-Islamic Times*, London: Longman (1979).

Trouillot, Michel-Rolph, *Silencing the Past: Power and the Production of History*, Boston: Beacon Press (1995).

Turner, Victor, "The Center Out There: Pilgrims Goal," *History of Religions* 12 (1973:191-230).

———, *The Ritual Process: Structure and Anti-Structure*, Chicago: Aldine de Gruyter (1995).

Turner, Victor, and Edith Turner, *Image and Pilgrimage in Christian Culture*, New York: Columbia University Press (1978).

Van der Veer, Peter, *Religious Nationalism: Hindus and Muslims in India*, Berkeley: University of California Press (1994).

Van der Veer, Peter, and Hartmut Lehmann (eds.), *Nation and Religion: Perspectives on Europe and Asia*, Princeton, New Jersey: Princeton University Press (1999).

Vital, David, *The Origins of Zionism*, Oxford: Clarendon Press (1975).

Wagner, Don, "Beyond Armegeddon," in *The Link*, vol. 25, no. 4 (1992).

Walker, P.W.L., *Jesus and the Holy Land: New Testament Perspectives on Jerusalem*, London and New York: Ederman Press (1996).

Wallace, Lillian Parker, "The Occupation of Rome," in her *The Papacy and European Diplomacy: 1869-78*, Chapel Hill: University of North Carolina Press (1948).

———, *The Papacy and European Diplomacy: 1869-78*, Chapel Hill: University of North Carolina Press (1948).

Wallerstein, Immanuel, *The Modern World-System I: Capitalist Agriculture and the Origins of the European World-Economy in the Sixteenth Century*, New York: Academic Press (1974a).

———, "The Rise and Future Demise of the World Capitalist System: Concepts for Comparative Analysis," *Comparative Studies in Society and History*, vol. 16, no. 4 (1974b:387-415).

———, "Civilizations and Modes of Production: Conflicts and Convergence," in his *The Politics of the World-Economy: The States, the Movements and the Civilizations*, New York: Cambridge University Press (1984:159-68).

———, *The Politics of the World-Economy: The States, the Movements and the Civilizations*, New York: Cambridge University Press (1984).

———, *Unthinking Social Science: The Limits of the Nineteenth Century Paradigm*, Cambridge, Massachusetts: Polity Press (1991).

———, "The Invention of TimeSpace Realities: Towards an Understanding of Our Historical Systems," in his *Unthinking The Social Sciences*, Cambridge, Massachusetts: Polity Press (1991:135-48).

———, *Utopistics: Or, Historical Choices of the Twenty-first Century*, New York: New Press (1998).

Warschawski, Michel, *On the Border*, Cambridge, Massachusetts: South End Press (2005).

Wasserstein, Bernard, "The Politics of Holiness in Jerusalem," in *The Chronicle of Higher Education* (September 21, 2001).

———, *Divided Jerusalem: The Struggle for the Holy City*, New Haven and London: Yale University Press (2001).

Watt, Montgomery, *Muhammad: Prophet and Statesman*, London: Oxford University Press (1974).

Weber, Max, *Ancient Judaism*, Glencoe, Illinois: Free Press (1967).

Wheatcroft, Geoffrey, *The Controversy of Zion: Jewish Nationalism, the Jewish State, and the Unresolved Jewish Dilemma*, Reading, Massachusetts: Addison-Wesley Publishing (1996).

Wheatley, Paul, *The Pivot of the Four Quarters: A Preliminary Enquiry into the Origins and Character of the Ancient Chinese City*, Chicago: Aldine Pub. (1981).

White, L. Michael, *The Social Origins of Christian Architecture: Building God's House in the Roman World: Architectural Adaptations among Pagans, Jews and Christian*, Cambridge, Massachusetts: Harvard University Press (1990).

Whitelam, Keith W., *The Invention of Ancient Israel: The Silencing of Palestinian History*, London and New York: Routledge (2001).

Wilken, Robert, *The Land Called Holy: Palestine in Christian History and Thought*, New Haven and London: Yale University Press (1992).

Wilkinson, John, *Jerusalem Pilgrims before the Crusades*, Warminster, Eng.: Aris & Phillips (1977).

———, *Jerusalem Pilgrimage, 1099-1185*, London: Hakluyt Society (1998).

Wittkower, Rudolph, *Art and Architecture in Italy: 1600 to 1750*, Baltimore, Maryland: Johns Hopkins University Press (1964).

Wolf, Eric, "The Social Organization of Mecca and the Origins of Islam," in *The Southwestern Journal of Anthropology*, vol. 7, no. 4 (1951).

Woolf, Martin, *Financial Times,* September 4, 2002.

Zukin, Sharon, *The Culture of Cities*, Cambridge, Massachusetts: Blackwell Publishers, Oxford (1995).

———, *Landscapes of Power: From Detroit to Disney World*, Berkeley: University of California Press (1991).

INDEX

ABOUT THE AUTHOR

Khaldoun Samman was born in Zarqa, Jordan. He moved to New Jersey at a young age and, years later, began his academic training at the Community College of Morris in New Jersey. He received his B.A. from George Washington University in Washington, D.C., and completed his Ph.D. at Binghamton University in New York. He is currently writing a second book entitled *The Modern Orientalist World-System and the Clash of Identities in the Middle East*, which will expand upon the line of reasoning advanced in the current book, analyzing nationalist discourses of Kemalists, Zionists, Arab nationalists and contemporary Islamists. It is a comparative study of states that attempt to remove the "Orient" from their societies with the effort to produce an Occidentalized population (Israel, Turkey, and pre-revolutionary Iran) with those of Islamist movements that desire to remove the "Occident" in order to produce an imagined authentic Islamic culture. Khaldoun Samman has taught at a number of colleges and universities. He is now an assistant professor of sociology at Macalester College in Saint Paul, Minnesota, where he teaches a wide variety of courses that range from "Social Theory" to "Islam and the West." His special fields of interest include world-systems analysis, sociology of religion, historical/comparative sociology, and social theory.